Create Your First Mac® Web Page

In a Weekend®

Steve Callihan

PRIMA TECH

A Division of Prima Publishing

To Deborah and Laura

A Division of Prima Publishing

Prima Publishing, colophon, and In a Weekend are registered trademarks and PRIMA TECH is a trademark of Prima Communications, Inc., Rocklin, California 95765.

Publisher: Stacy L. Hiquet
Associate Publisher: Nancy Stevenson
Marketing Manager: Judi Taylor
Managing Editor: Dan J. Foster
Senior Acquisitions Editor: Deborah F. Abshier
Project Editor: Kevin W. Ferns
Technical Editor: Jan L. Harrington
Copy Editor: Chuck Brandstater
Interior Layout: ExecuStaff Composition Services
Cover Design: Prima Design Team
Indexer: Sherry Massey

ISBN: 0-7615-2135-6
Library of Congress Catalog Card Number: 99-64746
Printed in the United States of America

99 00 01 02 03 II 10 9 8 7 6 5 4 3 2 1

CONTENTS AT A GLANCE

CONTENTS

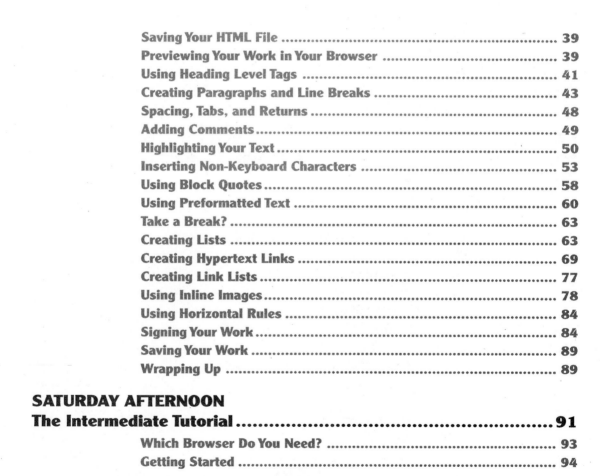

SATURDAY AFTERNOON
The Intermediate Tutorial 91

SATURDAY EVENING
Introduction to Adobe PageMill 3.0 (Bonus Session) 161

SUNDAY MORNING
Planning Your First Web Page 199

SUNDAY AFTERNOON
Creating Your First Web Page 229

ACKNOWLEDGMENTS

Many thanks to Kevin Ferns, Jan Harrington, Chuck Brandstater, Debbie Abshier, and the folks behind the scenes at PRIMA TECH for their invaluable contributions to this book.

ABOUT THE AUTHOR

Steve Callihan is a freelance and technical writer from Seattle. He has authored several other books with PRIMA TECH, including *Create Your First Web Page In a Weekend* (two editions for Windows), *Learn HTML In a Weekend* (two editions), and *Create Web Animations with Microsoft Liquid Motion In a Weekend*, and he co-authored (with Lisa D. Wagner) *Create Microsoft FrontPage 2000 Web Pages In a Weekend*. Steve has also written for various computer publications (including *Internet World*) and has extensive experience producing, designing, and writing software and hardware user manuals. He is a Microsoft MVP (Most Valuable Professional).

INTRODUCTION

You live in a busy world in which time is at a premium. You've surfed the Web and wondered what it would take to start creating your own Web pages. It seemed as if you had to become an expert on HTML (*Hypertext Markup Language*), and somehow you just never managed to find the time. But you don't have to wait anymore! Even if you know absolutely nothing about HTML, you can create your first Web page in just one weekend! You also don't have to become an HTML expert—the HTML tutorials scheduled for Saturday tell you everything you need to know about HTML to create a wide variety of Web pages.

 NOTE

This book was written using an iMac, but anybody with a fairly recent Mac OS computer can use this book. It is not necessary to purchase any extra software tools to create your first Web page. Adobe PageMill and AppleWorks, both bundled with the iMac, are used in two out of the seven work sessions—Mac OS users can download trial versions of both programs from the Web if they don't already own them.

Who Should Read This Book

The Web is so liberating because you don't have to be a computer expert to take advantage of its benefits. Everyone has interests besides computers. The good news is that you don't have to become an expert to take advantage of the benefits of HTML. One assumption this book makes is that you have interests that complement your computer skills. The computer is a tool that enables people to do stuff, not an end in itself. So, also, should be the Web and HTML. The Web, via HTML, should serve as an extension of your interests and purposes. What tends to get in the way is that many people think they need to know more than is really necessary. Don't make the mistake of thinking HTML and Web publishing are only for computer professionals and programmers. HTML is for everyone! Consequently, this book, like the Web, is also for everybody—or at least for anybody who wants to learn how to get a Web site up and running right away, without having to become an expert first.

Web publishing isn't something you learn first and do later. It's more like riding a bicycle, because you'll learn by doing. Don't worry about making mistakes. Mistakes are just experimental results by another name. Play around with it, experiment, and try new and different things. That's the only way you're going to truly learn.

What You Can Do in a Weekend

I'm not going to promise that you'll be able to learn HTML and develop a full-blown multi-page Web site in a single weekend. That would be selling snake oil! The Saturday Morning session, "The Basic HTML Tutorial," covers everything you need to know to create a pretty credible Web page, including creating headings, inline images, number and bullet lists, hypertext links, link lists, and much more. Whatever more you can manage to do this weekend is frosting on the cake.

The point of this book is to get the learning of HTML out of the way so you can move on to what you really want to do. You might want, for instance, to create your own personal page so you can tell the world about yourself. You might want to create a page for your family, your fraternity or sorority, or your church or club. If you're looking for a job or want to advance your career, you might want to create an online version of your résumé. You might want to put up a page featuring a hobby, interest, or area of expertise

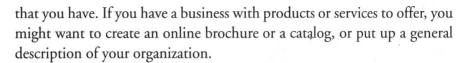

that you have. If you have a business with products or services to offer, you might want to create an online brochure or a catalog, or put up a general description of your organization.

If you have information or expertise you want to share with others, you might want to create a glossary or a FAQs (*Frequently Asked Questions*) page. If you are helping to run a civic organization or a social club, you might want to create a calendar of upcoming events, or publish the agenda for your next meeting. If you're creative, you could put up a page of your poetry, a short story, or a gallery of your drawings, paintings, or photographs. If you're a student, you might want to publish an online version of an abstract, book review, or thesis. Professors might publish course outlines, required reading lists, and assignment descriptions. You could publish your own page of movie reviews, or your own newsletter or journal. The list goes on and on—your options are unlimited!

You don't have to do all of the work sessions included in this book in one weekend. The evening sessions are "bonus sessions," which you can leave for another weekend if you wish. The Saturday Afternoon session is also an optional session. And nothing says that you *have to* do the sessions over a weekend—they can be done over a period of seven evenings, if you wish.

What You Need to Begin

If you have an Apple iMac, you already have everything that you need to get started learning HTML and creating your first Web page right now; if you have a different Mac OS computer, you may need to do a few extra things before you can get started. Apart from a computer, of course, you really only need a connection to the Internet, a graphical Web browser, a text editor, and an image editor (if you plan to create your own custom Web images).

Connecting to the Internet

You can create and edit your Web pages in a local folder without having to be connected to the Internet, so you don't actually need a connection until you are ready to upload to the Web. The iMac comes all set up and ready to connect to the Internet—you just need to decide what online service you want to subscribe to. In the Friday Evening session, "Getting Started," I cover in more detail exactly what you'll need to get up and running on the Internet.

Choosing a Web Browser

You'll need to set up a graphical Web browser so you can see what your page is going to look like as you go along. The Apple iMac comes with both Microsoft Internet Explorer and Netscape Navigator bundled and installed. In the Friday Evening session, I cover in more detail what some of your options are if you don't already have a graphical Web browser installed.

Choosing a Text Editor

You don't need anything fancy to create your own HTML files; any text editor will do. For the illustrations included in this book, I used the SimpleText editor included with the Mac OS. There are a number of other text editors available for the Mac that you can download from the Web and use for free. In the Friday Evening session, I cover in more detail what your different options are for creating your own "raw" HTML files.

Choosing an Image Editor

If you want to create your own custom Web art images, banners, logos, buttons, and so on, you'll need to have an image editor capable of creating GIF and JPEG images. The Apple iMac comes bundled with AppleWorks, which includes Painting and Drawing modules that are very capable tools for creating Web images. The Sunday Evening session, "Creating Your Own Web Images," covers using AppleWorks to create your own Web art special effects. Other users can download a "try out" version of AppleWorks from the Web, if they want to do that session.

You don't need to learn how to create your own custom Web art images before creating your first Web page. In the Sunday Morning and Afternoon sessions, where you plan and create your first Web page, I provide some sample images you can use as placeholders until you get around to creating your own custom images.

There are many shareware and commercial photo-paint programs available for the Mac that can be used to create professional-looking Web art images. In the Friday Evening session, I cover in detail what your options are for selecting and getting an image editor.

How This Book Is Organized

The book is divided into seven sessions, beginning on Friday evening and continuing into Sunday evening. Each session should take from two to four hours to complete. The following overview details each session's highlights:

- **Friday Evening: Getting Started.** Covers essential background information and the minimum requirements necessary to do the two Saturday HTML tutorials. This session also teaches you how to run your browser offline and includes an optional section on tools and resources that can help you apply HTML in the creation of Web pages.

- **Saturday Morning: The Basic HTML Tutorial.** This is a step-by-step tutorial that covers the basic HTML codes most commonly used to create Web pages. It's organized according to function, to teach you what each code does and to give you an overall view of HTML and how it works. Although this tutorial is slated for Saturday morning, feel free to take all day to do this tutorial. It covers everything you need to know to create your first Web page on Sunday.

- **Saturday Afternoon: The Intermediate HTML Tutorial.** This optional tutorial covers intermediate HTML, which is largely composed of codes originally introduced as "Netscape extensions" that have since been incorporated into HTML 3.2 and HTML 4.0. You don't need to know these codes to create your first Web pages. This session will teach you how to create more appealing, attractive, and effective Web pages.

- **Saturday Evening (Bonus Session): Introduction to Adobe PageMill 3.0.** The evening sessions are bonus sessions, so feel free to leave this session for another weekend. This session shows you how to use Adobe PageMill to implement many of the HTML codes covered in the Saturday Morning and Afternoon sessions.

- **Sunday Morning: Planning Your First Web Page.** This is a hands-on session that walks you through planning your first Web page, including defining an objective, making an outline, and assembling or creating the different materials that will make up your page. Example Web pages are provided that you can follow in organizing the materials to include in your own Web page. Your end-result will be a mock-up text file that includes the base text for your Web page, along with pointers to where you'll include a banner or logo image, any other inline images you want to include, and any Web addresses you want to link to.

- **Sunday Afternoon: Creating Your First Web Page.** Here you create your first Web page, using the mock-up text file you created in the morning session. You'll follow a decision tree that'll help you choose what HTML features you want to include in each section of your page (top, middle, and bottom).

- **Sunday Evening (Bonus Session): Creating Your Own Web Images.** This optional session shows you how to use the AppleWorks Painting and Drawing modules to create your own custom Web art images. You don't need to be a graphics pro to create your own professional-looking Web art—you just need to know how to use the right tools.

I've included lots of extra goodies in the appendixes, including:

- Pointers to where on the Web you can find lots of additional Web publishing resources, including HTML references, guides, tutorials, and software tools.

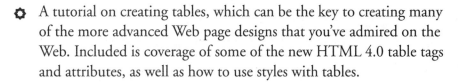

A tutorial on creating tables, which can be the key to creating many of the more advanced Web page designs that you've admired on the Web. Included is coverage of some of the new HTML 4.0 table tags and attributes, as well as how to use styles with tables.

A chart of all of the HTML codes for special characters (characters not on your keyboard) that can be included in a Web page.

Guidance in finding a Web presence provider to host your pages, as well as guidance in using an FTP program, PageMill, or AOL to transfer your Web page or pages up to your Web space folders on the Web.

A rundown on the past and future of HTML, including how HTML got to be what it is today and where it's headed in the future.

You'll also find much more on this book's CD-ROM, including an assortment of Web art images you can use (icons, buttons, rules, background images), a selection of HTML templates you can adapt to your own purposes, and a wide variety of shareware and evaluation software. For more details on what's included on the CD-ROM, see Appendix F, "What's on the CD-ROM."

Special Features of This Book

This book uses a number of icons and typographical conventions to make your job easier as you work through the sessions. They're used to call your attention to notes, tips, cautions, buzzwords, additional resources located on the Web, and programs or other resources included on the CD-ROM. Here are some examples of what you'll see:

● ●　 ，● ● ● ● ● ● ● ● ● ● ● ● ● ● ● ● ●

Notes are food for thought as you work through the tutorials. They'll bring up points of interest and other relevant information you might find useful as you develop your abilities with Web publishing and HTML.

● ●

Tips offer helpful hints, tricks, and ideas to apply as you progress in the creation process.

Cautions warn you of possible hazards and point out pitfalls that typically plague beginners.

Buzzwords are terms and acronyms that you should keep in mind as you develop and expand your Web publishing skills.

FIND IT ▶
ONLINE

This icon marks resources or tools located on the Web that may be helpful to you in your Web publishing endeavors.

FIND IT ON ▶
THE CD

This icon marks resources or tools located on the CD-ROM that you may find useful.

Visit This Book's Web Site

Check out this book's Web site at **www.callihan.com/create_imac/**, where you can download all the example graphics and files used in the tutorials. You'll also find information on finding a Web host for your Web pages, additional software tools and utilities to assist you in Web publishing, and resources on just about everything you might want to know about HTML and Web publishing. And in case you have any questions that this book doesn't answer, you can contact me at **create_imac@callihan.com**.

Getting Started

- ○ Getting the tools you'll need
- ○ The scoop on the Internet and the World Wide Web
- ○ Thinking about your first web site

It's Friday evening—at least if you're following the schedule. For the purposes of this book, Friday evening constitutes part of the weekend. If you're going to learn some HTML and then plan and create your first Web page this weekend, it doesn't hurt to get a bit of a head start. The first part of this session provides a quick rundown on the tools you'll be using to complete the tutorials, and to plan and create your first Web page. These include a text editor, a Web browser, and an image editor (optional for this weekend).

The rest of the session includes general background information on the Internet, the World Wide Web, HTML, and Web pages. You really should have some grounding in the medium before you start the HTML tutorials on Saturday or begin to create your first Web page on Sunday. Of course, if you're already familiar with something covered in these sections, feel free to skip or merely skim it.

What Tools Do You Need?

You don't need any special software tools to create and edit your own HTML files. All you really need are:

- A simple text editor
- A graphical Web browser so you can preview your HTML files
- An image editor that can save GIF and JPEG files (if you want to create your own personalized Web art images)

Using a Text Editor to Create and Edit HTML Files

As HTML files are just ordinary text files, all you need is a simple text editor. SimpleText, part of Mac OS 8.x, for example, works just fine for creating and editing HTML files, as does TeachText, part of Mac OS 7.x.

FIND IT ON ▶ THE CD

Look on the CD-ROM for additional text editors, such as BBEdit Lite, Text-Edit Plus, and Scribbling Works, that you can try out.

You could also use a word processor such as the one included in AppleWorks. Other word processors may also work well to create and edit HTML files, but some may not let you resave an HTML file if it is open in your Web browser at the same time. Another concern with using a word processor is that you have to go out of your way to save your HTML file as a text file—if you save it in the word processor's native format, viewers won't be able to see your page in their browsers. A text editor, on the other hand, will automatically save your file in a format (as a straight text file) that can be read by any Web browser.

Another option is to use an HTML editor, such as Adobe PageMill 3.0, which you'll cover in the Saturday Evening bonus session. (It is on the CD-ROM for the iMac. You can also download a "tryout" version of Adobe PageMill from Adobe's Web site at **www.adobe.com/prodindex/pagemill/demodnld.html**; the Macintosh tryout version will expire 30 days after you install it, so you should wait to install it until you're ready to use it.)

FIND IT ON ▶ THE WEB

My recommendation is that you learn first by typing in the actual HTML codes in a text editor, rather than using the toolbars, pull-down menus, or assistants that an HTML editor might provide. You'll gain a much more intimate understanding of HTML by typing in the codes yourself. Don't worry—it's not hard. Later, after you've done at least the Basic HTML Tutorial, scheduled for tomorrow morning, feel free to go ahead and try using an HTML editor.

NOTE One good reason to stick to using a simple text editor for creating and editing HTML files is that it takes up very little memory. Word processors and full-feature WYSIWYG HTML editors, on the other hand, can be real memory hogs. By using a simple text editor, you'll have much more memory available for other programs that you may want to have open while creating and editing your HTML files. For instance, you might want to have an image editor open so that you can easily create on-the-fly images. Or you might want to have both Microsoft Internet Explorer and Netscape Navigator open, so you can easily check out how your pages will look in the two major browsers. Other types of programs you might want to have open, depending on what you're adding to your Web pages, are a GIF animator, a sound editor, a 3-D modeler, and a Java applet compiler.

Using a Web Browser to Preview Your HTML Files

While creating and editing your HTML files in your text editor, you'll want to be able to dynamically preview your Web pages in a Web browser. Both Internet Explorer 4.0+ and Netscape Navigator 4.0+ are included with the Mac OS 8.x. If your Mac is running an operating system prior to Mac OS 8.x, you should check to see if you have a Web browser installed. Any graphical Web browser can be used to create a basic Web page, but before trying out advanced features (which you'll cover on Saturday afternoon), you'll want to have one of the more recent graphical Web browsers installed.

Do You Need a Connection to the Internet?

It is not required that you have a connection to the Internet to create and preview HTML files on your local computer. You'll need to have a connection to the Internet if you actually want to publish your Web pages to a Web server, however. For more information on getting Web space and transferring your Web pages onto the Web, see Appendix D, "Putting It Up on the Web."

iMac users have the option of subscribing to EarthLink Total Access or AOL to get access to the Internet. You'll need to have your iMac's modem plugged into a phone jack and have your credit card handy—that's all. Just click the Browse the Internet icon on your desktop. iMac users get one month free on EarthLink and 100 hours free on AOL. Both EarthLink and AOL provide free Web space that you can use for publishing your Web pages up onto the Web. Figure 1-1 shows the personal start page that I set up through EarthLink.

Using an Image Editor to Create Your Own Web Art

Creating your own personalized Web art images for your Web pages can add a lot of excitement and satisfaction to your Web publishing endeavors. If you don't get around to it this weekend, before too long you'll want to get an image editor capable of creating GIF and JPEG images.

If you're an iMac user, a number of different image editing tools are already included with your system. The AppleWorks application suite (formerly

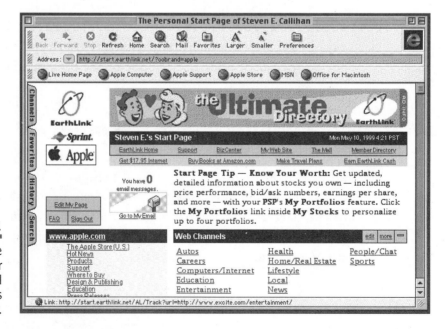

Figure 1-1

Before you'll be able to publish your Web pages, you'll need to get access to the Internet.

ClarisWorks) includes both painting and drawing programs that can create GIF and JPEG images. In the Sunday Afternoon session, you'll learn how to use the AppleWorks Painting and Drawing modules to create your own Web images. If you're not using the iMac, you can download a trial version of AppleWorks from Apple's Web site at **www.apple.com/appleworks/** (you only have 30 days to try out the program, so wait until you're ready to use it before you install it). Also included with the iMac is Kai's PhotoSoap SE, which allows you to enhance and add special effects to your photographs and other images.

For now, you don't need to worry about installing an image editor if you don't have one yet. All of the example images used in the tutorials are included on the CD-ROM, as well as a selection of other Web art images, including background images, icons, buttons, rules, and so on; you can use these when creating your first Web page on Sunday. I've also included some sample Web page banners and logos that you can use as placeholders until you get around to creating your own.

What Is the Internet?

It could be said that the Internet is the most valuable legacy left over from the Cold War. It originally came into being as the *ARPANet,* which was founded by the U.S. Defense Department's Advanced Research Projects Agency (ARPA) to link academic research centers involved in military research.

Today's Internet has grown far beyond its original concept. Originally linking just four university research centers, the Internet has become a global system consisting of hundreds of thousands of *nodes* (servers). In many ways, it has become what Marshall McLuhan called "the global village," in that every node is functionally right next door. You can communicate just as easily with someone in Australia as with someone just two blocks down the street—and if the person down the street isn't on the Internet, it's actually easier to communicate with the bloke in Australia. The founders may not have anticipated this, but it has become an increasingly pervasive reality.

◄ ◄

A *client* is a computer that requests something from another computer. A *server* is a computer that responds to requests for service from clients.

◄ ◄

◄ ◄

An *internet* is a network of networks—a kind of *meta-network*. Simply put, the Internet is a set of protocols (rules) for transmitting and exchanging data among networks. In a broader sense, however, it's a worldwide community, a global village, and a repository of global information resources.

◄ ◄

◄ ◄

TCP/IP *(Transmission Control Protocol/Internet Protocol)* is the standard rule set for Internet communication. The essence of the Internet is not the wire, but the means for sending and receiving information across the wire. It doesn't matter what types of systems are connected to the Internet, be they mainframes, minicomputers, or microcomputers. All that matters is that they all use the same protocol, TCP/IP, to communicate with each other.

◄ ◄

What Is the Web?

The World Wide Web (also called the *Web*) dates back to 1989, when the concept was first proposed by Tim Berners-Lee (often called the inventor of the Web). Many others have been critically involved, but Berners-Lee gets the credit for originally proposing and evangelizing the idea as a way to facilitate collaboration between scientists and other academics over the Internet.

On the original Web page for the World Wide Web Project, posted on the CERN (the European Laboratory of Particle Physics, birthplace of the Web) server in 1992, Tim Berners-Lee described the Web as "a wide-area hypermedia information retrieval initiative aiming to give universal access to a large universe of documents." Today he'd be more likely to describe the Web as the "universal space of all network-accessible information." Ted Nelson, inventor of the concept of hypertext, wrapped all this up in a wonderfully apt term, describing the Word Wide Web as a "docuverse."

Like the Internet, the Web is defined by a set of protocols:

- **HTTP (HyperText Transfer Protocol).** Used to exchange Web documents across the Internet. When you request a Web document from a server, the protocol used for the request is HTTP.

- **HTML (HyperText Markup Language).** Enables users to present information over the Web in a structured and uniform fashion. HTML is used to mark up documents so that a Web browser can interpret and then display them. See "What Is HTML?" later in this session for more information.

- **URLs (Uniform Resource Locators).** Addresses that identify a server, a directory, or a specific file. HTTP URLs, or *Web addresses*, are only one type of address on the Web. FTP, Gopher, and WAIS are other types of addresses you'll find fairly often on the Web as well. See "What Is a URL?" later in this session for additional information.

- **CGI (Common Gateway Interface).** Serves as an interface to execute local programs through a gateway between the HTTP server software and the host computer. Therefore, you can include a hypertext link in a Web document that will run a server program or script, for example, to process input from a customer request form.

While the Internet comprises a variety of different server types, of which Web servers are only one, the Web has come to represent the whole. That's because most Web browsers can access not only Web servers using the HTTP protocol, but the entirety of the Internet, including Gopher, FTP, Archie, Telnet, and WAIS, as well as mail and news servers. The Web's tendency to embrace and incorporate all other media, thus operating as a universal medium, is its most revolutionary characteristic.

A Little History

The beginnings of the Internet go back at least as far as 1957, to the founding of the Defense Department's Advanced Research Projects Agency (ARPA) in response to the Soviet Union's launching *Sputnik*. In 1963, ARPA asked the Rand Corporation to ponder how to form a command-and-control network capable of surviving attack by atomic bombs. The Rand Corporation's response (made public in 1964) was that the network would "have no central authority" and would be "designed from the beginning to operate while in tatters." These two basic concepts became the defining characteristics of what would eventually become the Internet. The Internet was conceptualized as having no central authority and as being able to operate in a condition of assumed unreliability (bombed-out cities, downed telephone lines). In other words, it would have maximum redundancy. All nodes would be coequal in status, each with authority to originate, relay, and receive messages.

What happened between this first military initiative and the Internet we know today? Here are some of the highlights:

1965: Ted Nelson invents the concept of and coins the term *hypertext*.

1969: ARPANet, the forerunner of the Internet, is commissioned by the Department of Defense. Nodes at UCLA, Stanford, UC Santa Barbara, and the University of Utah are linked.

1971: The number of nodes on the Internet increases to 15 (23 hosts). New nodes include MIT, RAND, Harvard, and NASA/Ames, among others.

1972: Telnet is introduced.

1973: The first international connections to the ARPANet occur from England and Norway. FTP (File Transfer Protocol) is introduced.

1977: E-mail is introduced.

1979: Usenet newsgroups are introduced.

1982: The ARPANet adopts TCP/IP (Transmission Control Protocol/Internet Protocol), the real beginning of the Internet.

1984: DNS (*Domain Name Server*) is implemented, allocating addresses among six basic domain types: gov, mil, edu, net, com, and org (for government, military, educational, network, commercial, and noncommercial hosts, respectively). One thousand hosts (computer systems each identified by a unique IP address) are present on the Internet.

1985: First registered domain name is assigned.

1986: NSFNet is formed by the NSF (*National Science Foundation*) using five supercomputing centers. Unlike ARPANet, which is focused on military and government research, NSFNet is available for all forms of academic research.

1989: Tim Berners-Lee proposes the creation of the World Wide Web. Australia (AU), Germany (DE), Israel (IL), Italy (IT), Japan (JP), Mexico (MX), Netherlands (NL), New Zealand (NZ), Puerto Rico (PR), and the United Kingdom (UK) join the Internet. One hundred thousand hosts are on the Internet.

1990: ARPANet closes down. The first commercial provider of dial-up access to the Internet opens shop. Eleven more countries from Europe, South America, and Asia join the Internet.

1992: The Internet Society (ISOC) is formed. Viola, the first English-language graphical Web browser, is released. "Surfing the Internet" is coined by Jean Amour Polly. One million hosts are on the Internet.

1993: Marc Andreesen's Mosaic browser is released by NCSA. The White House goes online.

1994: NCSA Mosaic 1.03 is the first Web browser released for the Macintosh. Mosaic Communications, later to become Netscape Communications, is formed by Marc Andreesen and James Clark, ex-president of Silicon Graphics. The first meeting of the World Wide Web Consortium (or *W3C*) is held at MIT. The first cybermalls form.

1995: Netscape goes public. Web traffic on the Internet outstrips FTP, with the Web becoming the most popular form of accessing the Internet. RealAudio is introduced. InterNIC starts charging for registering domain names.

1996: Bill Gates and Microsoft jump into the game with the Internet Explorer browser. Ten million hosts are on the Internet.

1997: HTML 3.2 and 4.0 are released. The Justice Department files an antitrust complaint against Microsoft.

1998: Two million domain names are registered. XML 1.0 (Extensible Markup Language) is released by the W3C. Netscape is purchased by AOL. The total number of users on the Web is estimated at between 35 and 50 million.

1999: The draft specification for XHTML 1.0 (Extensible HTML), a reformulation of HTML 4.0 in XML, is announced by W3C. Web Content Accessibility Guidelines, which improve access to Web sites for people with disabilities, are published. Over 40 million hosts are on the Internet.

Take a Break?

You might want to use this opportunity to take a break. Relax and stretch a bit. Fix a cup of tea or get yourself a glass of juice. I'll see you back in five minutes or so for the remainder of this session.

What Is Hypertext?

You could say the Web is a graphical, platform-independent, distributed, decentralized, multiformatted, interactive, dynamic, nonlinear, immediate, two-way communication medium. The basic mechanism that enables all this is actually quite simple—the *hypertext link*. It's a kind of "jump point" that allows a visitor to jump from a place in a Web page to any other Web page, document, or data object, such as a graphic, audio, video, or any other type of file, located on the Web. Not only can you jump to another Web page, but you can jump to another place, in either the same Web page or another Web page. If you've ever clicked on a link and then jumped to a place in the middle of either the same or another Web page, you've seen this capability in action. A link can connect you to anything that has an address (or URL) anywhere on the Internet. See Figure 1-2 for a general representation of how hypertext links work.

Figure 1-3 illustrates some of the different kinds of data objects to which you can link from a Web page. Note the difference between an inline image, which appears as part of the Web page, and other graphics, which your browser or viewer can link to and display separately.

A hypertext link actually works much like a cross-reference in a book, except that you can immediately go to it simply by clicking the link, whether it's a link within the same document or one to a page or document half-way around the world. You don't have to thumb through the book or go to the local library to find the reference. Anything that has an address on the Web can be linked, including Gopher documents, FTP files, and newsgroup articles.

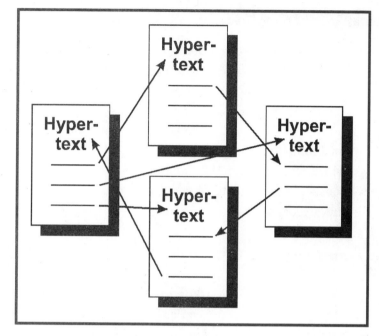

Figure 1-2

Using hypertext links, you can jump from one Web page to another Web page.

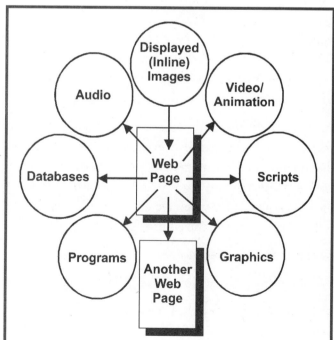

Figure 1-3

A Web page can link to many other kinds of data objects besides other Web pages.

What Is Hypermedia?

Given that hypertext linking occurs within and between documents, it makes sense that *hypermedia* (a term coined by Ted Nelson) would refer to connecting with and between other non-text media such as graphics, audio, animation, video, and software. Over time, the Web may evolve from a system predominantly composed of static hypertext Web pages to one predominantly composed of dynamically interlinked hypermedia, within which text is just another medium; for now, though, the Web still mainly consists of documents, or *pages*, and you can still think of hypermedia as a subcategory of hypertext.

What Is HTML?

HTML (HyperText Markup Language) was originally intended as a subset of SGML (*Standard Generalized Markup Language*). SGML was developed to standardize the *markup*, or preparation for typesetting, of computer-generated documents. HTML, on the other hand, was specifically developed to mark up, or *encode*, hypertext documents for display on the World Wide Web. Due to the many ad hoc extensions that have been added to it, HTML can no longer be said to be merely a subset of SGML, and has taken on a life of its own.

An HTML document is a plain text file (or what is often called an *ASCII file*) with codes (called *tags*) inserted in the text to define elements in the document. HTML tags generally have two parts—an on-code and an off-code—which contain the text to be defined. A few tags don't require off-codes (I'll note these when we cover them). You can represent a tag in the following way, where the ellipsis (. . .) represents the text you want to tag:

```
<Tagname>...</Tagname>
```

The following is the tag for a Level 1 heading in a Web document:

```
<H1>This is a Level 1 heading</H1>
```

HTML's purpose isn't to specify the exact formatting or layout of a Web page, but to define and specify the specific elements that make up a page—the body of the text, headings, paragraphs, line breaks, text elements, and so on. You use HTML to define the composition of a Web page, not its appearance. The particular Web browser you use to view the page controls the display of the Web page. For instance, you can define a line using the `<H1>...</H1>` tag, but the browser defines the appearance of a first-level heading. One browser might show an H1 element in 18-point Times Roman text, whereas another might show it in a totally different font and size.

To understand why this is the way it is, you need to understand how HTML-coded Web pages and Web browsers work together. To display a Web page on your computer, a Web browser must first download it and any graphics displayed on the page to your computer. If the Web page were to specify all the formatting and display details, it would increase the amount of data to be transmitted, the size of the file, and the amount of time it takes to transfer. Leaving all the formatting and display details to the Web browser means that the size of HTML documents sent over the Web can remain relatively small, because they're just regular ASCII text files. It's rare to have an HTML file that exceeds 30KB (not counting any graphics it may contain).

However, this means that every Web browser may have its own idea about how to best display a particular Web page. Your Web page may look different in Netscape Navigator than it does in Microsoft Internet Explorer, and different still in NCSA Mosaic, CyberDog, or iCab; that's why you'll want to test your completed page in more than just one browser. Your page may even look different in the Macintosh and the Windows versions of the same browser!

The latest versions of HTML, 3.2 and 4.0, do give you much more control over how your page will appear in supporting browsers. The more you try to do this, the more likely it is that a different browser may not display your page like how you want it to be displayed.

In the Basic HTML Tutorial, scheduled for Saturday morning, you'll learn how to work with HTML 2.0 elements to specify the structure, but not necessarily the appearance, of your Web page. In the Intermediate HTML Tutorial, scheduled for Saturday afternoon, you'll learn how to effectively incorporate HTML 3.2 and HTML 4.0 features in order to have more control over the look and feel of your Web pages.

The advent of the new HTML 4.0 specification adds more complications to the mix: The current versions of Netscape Navigator and Internet Explorer support only portions of what's included in HTML 4.0.

If you're concerned about compatibility with the vast majority of current graphical Web browsers, it may be wise for the time being to stick with HTML 3.2 elements and attributes, at least until HTML 4.0 is more fully supported. If you want to incorporate any of the new HTML 4.0 features, you should thoroughly check your pages out in both of the main Web browsers. Although other Web browsers, or earlier versions of Navigator and Internet Explorer, simply ignore unrecognized tags, you should be aware that a Web page that looks fantastic in a Web browser that supports HTML 4.0 may look terrible in one that doesn't. It's probably not a bad idea to keep an older Web browser installed on your system, so you can check and make sure your pages display acceptably in browsers that don't support HTML 4.0. And if your page has any major display problems in older browsers, you might want to clearly label it as an "HTML 4.0 only" page, or create a front page that has links to HTML 4.0 and non-HTML 4.0 versions of your page.

What Is a URL?

A URL identifies the address, or location, of a resource on the Internet. Every Web page has its own unique URL. If you know the URL of a Web page and access is not restricted, you can connect to it and view it in your browser. A URL can connect to resources other than just Web pages—it can also connect to FTP, Telnet, WAIS, Gopher, CGI, or Usenet resources on the Web. A URL may consist of the following parts:

- **Service.** This designator specifies the service being accessed: http (for the Web), ftp, gopher, wais, telnet, or news.

- **Host.** The host designator specifies the domain name of the server being accessed. For instance: `www.myserver.com`.

- **Port number.** The port number only needs to be specified if it's a nonstandard port number for the service being accessed. In the vast majority of cases, this is not included in a URL, since the default port number for HTTP servers (80) or FTP servers (21) is used. If you see a port number in a URL, however, you'll have some idea of what it is.

- **Resource path.** This specifies where the resource being accessed is located on a host. The "path" is the chain of folders that needs to be traversed, starting with a server's or host's root folder, in order to reach the resource (a Web page file, for example). On a Web server, the forward slash ("/") marks each step along the folder path. For instance, `http://www.mydomain.com/myfile.html` would specify that the resource (myfile.html) is located in the host's root folder. On the other hand, `http://www.mydomain.com/myfolder/myproject/myfile.html` would indicate that the resource (myfile.html) is located in the myproject folder in the myfolder folder in the host's root folder.

NOTE

• •

Above, I use the word *host* instead of *server*. That's because a server can actually host multiple domains (or domain names), in what is sometimes referred to as a *virtual host* arrangement. A server is a host, in other words, but a host isn't necessarily a server. My URL, www.callihan.com, is hosted virtually on my Web space provider's server. You can host a domain without owning your own server.

• •

Figure 1-4 shows a diagram of a URL. Because most Web addresses don't use port numbers, this illustration leaves out the port number.

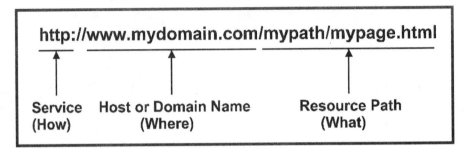

Figure 1-4

A Uniform Resource Locator (URL) is the address of a resource on the Internet.

A URL is actually an instruction or request from an agent (such as a Web browser) to a server on the Internet that specifies the following three things:

- **How?** This is the protocol for the transaction. For Web pages, this is HTTP. Essentially, the protocol tells the server what software it needs to run to manage the transaction. More than one server can reside on the same computer—for instance, a single computer can function both as an FTP server and as an HTTP (or Web) server.

- **Where?** This is the address where the transaction is to take place. For instance, www.mydomain.com/mypath/ specifies the domain name and the location within that domain of what is to be transacted.

- **What?** This is the name of what is to be transacted. For instance, mypage.html specifies the actual HTML document, or Web page, as the subject of the transaction.

What Is a Domain Name?

Every Internet server has a numerical IP (Internet Protocol) address, which usually consists of four numbers between 0 and 255, separated by periods (something like 185.35.117.0, for instance). Computers prefer numeric addresses of this type because they're precise. Unfortunately, humans have trouble remembering numbers—we prefer meaningful text addresses such as www.mysite.com. That's what a domain name is: a text alternative to an

IP address. You can usually use the two interchangeably. The point is that if you know the domain name, you don't have to know anything about the IP address. You will, however, sometimes run into an odd URL on the Web that specifies the IP address rather than the domain name (and nothing forbids a server from having an IP address but no domain address).

The registration of domain names has in the past been handled exclusively by InterNIC (the *Internet Network Information Center*), which was run by Network Solutions, Inc. If you wanted a domain name, you had to register it with InterNIC. A new, non-profit, international organization, ICANN (*Internet Corporation for Assigned Names and Numbers*), has been formed to take over the U.S. government's responsibility for "coordinating domain name system management, IP address space allocation, protocol parameter assignment coordination, and root server system management." These responsibilities had previously been handled by IANA (*Internet Assigned Numbers Authority*) under the auspices of the U.S. government. Part of ICANN's responsibilities is the accreditation of domain registrars that will handle the registration of domain names for the .com, .net, and .org domains. ICANN initially accredited five domain registrars to participate in their test-bed program—once the test bed program has been completed (provisionally slated for July, 1999), you'll be able to register a domain name through any accredited domain registrar of your choice. Due to the introduction of competition in this process, the price of registering and renewing a domain name is expected to come down (from the current $70 to register and $35 to renew).

Most servers have applied for and received a domain name. As long as your Web pages are located on a server that has a domain name, you can use that domain name in the addresses, or URLs, for those Web pages. You don't have to have your own server to have your own domain name. You can also set up a Web site on someone else's server and use your own domain name in what is often referred to as a *virtual host* arrangement: to the outside world, you appear to have your own server (www.yourname.com, for instance).

NOTE Registering domain names used to be free, but this led to a free-for-all somewhat similar to the Oklahoma Land Rush, as companies and individuals scrambled to grab up domain names before anyone else could claim them. Because an organization or individual could claim an unlimited number of domain names, speculative trading (in other words, scalping) in domain names evolved. For these reasons, as well as to help fund the costs of registering rapidly increasing domain name requests, as of September, 1995, InterNIC started charging a fee for registering and maintaining a domain name—initially $100 for the first two years, and $50 a year thereafter, although the cost has since been reduced to $70 to register and $35 to renew. Even so, one company still forked out the $70 to grab up as many last names (smith.com, jones.com, etc.) as they could, so they could resell them for Web-based e-mail addresses (luckily, I got mine, callihan.com, before they started doing this).

A domain name represents a hierarchy, starting with the most general word on the right and moving to the most specific word on the left. It can include a country code, an organization code, and a site name. For instance, myname.com.au, reading from right to left, specifies the name of a site in Australia (au) in the commercial (com) subcategory, called "myname." Every country connected to the Internet has its own code: "uk" (United Kingdom), "ca" (Canada), "fr" (France), "nz" (New Zealand), and so forth. The country code for the United States is "us"; most sites in the United States don't include the country code, however, because the Internet began in the United States and the country codes were created later, after the Internet went international. Here's a list of the organization codes (see Figure 1-5):

○ **EDU for *education.*** Schools and universities, for instance, use this organization code.

○ **GOV for *government.*** Various governmental departments and agencies use this organization code.

○ **MIL for *military.*** The Internet was, after all, originally a U.S. Defense Department initiative (the ARPANet).

Figure 1-5

Internet domains can be organized in general categories, such as COM or EDU, or they can be organized in "international" categories, such as CA (for Canada) or UK (for the United Kingdom).

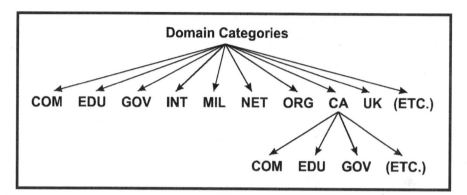

- **NET for *network*.** Refers to a network connected to the Internet. In practice, you usually run into this organization code with ISPs (Internet Service Providers) offering public access to the Internet.

- **COM for *commercial*.** This code was created to accommodate commercial usage of the Internet by business enterprises.

- **ORG for *organization*.** This code is for noncommercial, nonprofit organizations.

What Is a Web Page?

A *Web page* is a hypertext (HTML) document contained in a single file. To have more than one Web page, you must have more than one file. Despite the connotation of the word *page*, a Web page can be any length, although display of most Web pages extends to no more than two or three screens.

A Web page is simply a plain text document. All codes are entered into the document as ordinary text, with none of the binary-level formatting a word processor would embed in it. When you mark some text as italic in a word processing document, you don't see the actual computer code that causes the text to appear or print in italics. In HTML, you have to do it all yourself; there's no underlying program code to translate what you type as you go. You type in <I> where you want the browser to turn on italics and </I>

where you want it to turn them off. This cuts down on the computer overhead, allowing Web pages to remain small but still pack quite a punch.

When a browser displays a Web page, the page may appear to contain special graphical elements such as logos or buttons. These graphics don't reside in the HTML file itself; they're separate files that the HTML file references. For instance, you might see a line like this in the HTML file:

```
<IMG SRC="mylogo.gif">
```

When a browser reads this line, it displays the image that is referenced, also known as an *inline image*, rather than displaying the code. You can include a banner or logo, buttons, icons, separator bars, navigational icons, and more. See Figure 1-6 for a graphical representation of a Web page that contains these different kinds of elements.

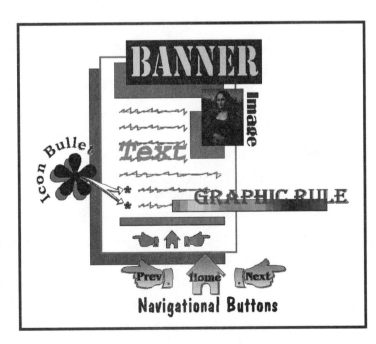

Figure 1-6

Graphic elements are actually separate files linked to and displayed as part of your Web page.

What Is a Web Site?

The term *Web site* has a couple of different (although analogous) meanings. Servers are often called Web sites (sites on the Web), but any grouping of related and linked Web pages sharing a common theme or subject matter may also be called a Web site. To avoid confusion, in this book, I'll always refer to a collection of related Web pages as a *Web site*. I'll refer to a Web server as simply that: a *Web server*. I'll refer to a domain hosted on a Web server (www.callihan.com, for instance) as a *Web host* (a server can host multiple domains).

Your access provider (the company or organization that provides access to the Internet) may give you space for a personal, noncommercial Web site at little or no cost. If you're a student, you may be able to have your pages hosted by your school's server. Online services such as America Online also may also provide free or inexpensive Web space. If you want to create a commercial Web site that offers a product or service, or if you want to create a more sophisticated Web site that requires more space, higher traffic allowances, more technical support, and a wider range of features than your access provider will give you, you may need to rent your Web space from what is commonly called a *presence provider*. A presence provider focuses on or specializes in providing Web space, and can offer a fuller menu of services aimed specifically at Web publishers; it can also register and maintain a domain name for you, usually at a reasonable cost, making it look to the outside world as if you own your own server.

A Web site is simply a collection of allied Web pages, similar to the chapters in a book, tied and linked together, usually through a home page (sometimes also called an *index page*) that serves as the directory to the rest of the Web site. The different Web pages that compose the site are interlinked and related to each other as parts of a whole. Dissimilar Web pages that are unrelated and therefore unlinked don't form a Web site, even if they're stored in the same directory on the same server. A Web site could also be composed of Web pages residing on more than one server.

What Is a Home Page?

The term *home page* can have a number of different meanings. When you start your browser, it loads whatever Web page you designate as its home page (which can be a Web page up on the Internet or even a page on your own hard drive). Most browsers have a Home button or command that takes you back to the page designated as the browser's home page. This page may vary according to the browser or access provider you're using—it could be Netscape's Netcenter Web site or Microsoft's Web site if you're using either of their browsers, or it could be the home page of your access provider. You can, however, usually specify whichever page you want as your browser's home page. This is also sometimes referred to as a *start page*.

The term *home page* can also refer to an entry point (or *front door*) to a Web site or a group of linked and related Web pages. It can also designate any Web page that stands on its own (in keeping with the front door comparison, you could think of a standalone Web page as a one-room shack). The diagram in Figure 1-7 shows the relationship between home and Web pages.

Most servers let you create a default home page (most often named index.html), which loads automatically without the file name having to be specified in the URL. This allows you, for example, to have `http://`

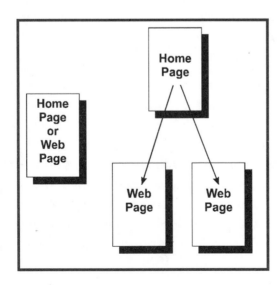

Figure 1-7

A home page can be either a standalone Web page or an entry point to a Web site.

www.myserver.com/mydirectory/ as your URL rather than http://
www.myserver.com/mydirectory/index.html. This is often also
referred to as an *index page*.

Home pages used as entryways are generally kept small, often serving simply
as menus or directories to the Web pages that make up the rest of the Web
site. The idea here is that a viewer needs only to display the home page,
which is relatively small, and then decide what else to view in the remainder
of the Web site.

Having a Web site go deeper than three or four levels is rare, but the number
of levels of Web pages you can have appended as subpages to your home
page is technically unlimited. The deeper a Web page is (a subpage of a
subpage of a subpage of a subpage of your home page), the less accessible it
will be to visitors of your site. Pages you want to be the most readily accessible
to visitors of your site should be prominently linked from its home page or
from a subpage of its home page, and not buried five levels deep. See Figure
1-8 for an illustration of a multilevel Web site.

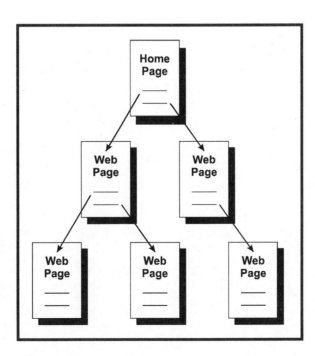

Figure 1-8

A Web site can
have several
levels, although
you should keep
it to three or
fewer levels.

You can also create a home page that links together multiple home pages. You might have a series of Web sites that are relatively autonomous, share a common theme, are produced by the same department, or are part of a larger project.

Wrapping Up

If you finished reading all the material included in this session, you should have an idea of what tools you'll need to do the tutorials and work sessions (at minimum, just a text editor and a graphical Web browser), as well as a good grounding in the basics of the Internet and the World Wide Web. You should have a basic grasp, of URLs, hypertext, HTML, and Web pages. I've included additional background information about HTML in Appendix E, "HTML— Past and Future." If you want to learn more about the development of HTML and what's slated for it in the future, feel free to check it out when you have the time. Get a good night's sleep and I'll see you back here first thing tomorrow, when you'll learn some basic HTML!

The Basic HTML Tutorial

- ⚙ Anatomy of an HTML tag
- ⚙ Headings, paragraphs, and line breaks
- ⚙ Text highlighting (bold, italic, and monospace)
- ⚙ Lists, hypertext links, and link lists
- ⚙ Inline images and image links

Last night you learned about the tools you'll need to create, edit, and preview your HTML files. You also read up on the Internet, the Web, hypertext, and Web pages. You should now have a pretty good idea of what Web publishing is all about.

If you haven't yet decided which tools you'll be using for working with HTML files, you should go back and read the "What Tools Do You Need?" section at the start of the Friday Evening session. To do the Basic HTML Tutorial this morning, you only need a program for editing text files, and a graphical Web browser for previewing your HTML files. A simple text editor, such as SimpleText, is recommended. If you're running Mac OS 7.x, go ahead and use the TeachText text editor. If you don't have one of the more current Web browsers installed, don't worry—for this tutorial, any graphical Web browser you have installed should do.

This morning's tutorial walks you through a top-down approach to learning HTML, organized according to function. By the end of this morning, you'll know enough HTML to create a wide range of Web pages.

HTML contains many more tags and attributes for defining document elements than most people could learn in an entire week, let alone in a weekend. Fear not; this book cuts it down to size. This tutorial covers basic HTML, which includes the most useful of the HTML 2.0 tags. Most graphical Web browsers should fully support HTML 2.0.

HTML 2.0, with a few minor exceptions, is almost entirely included in and forms the core of the later versions of HTML (HTML 3.2 and 4.0). You don't need to be concerned that it will ever go out of style or become outmoded; as long as HTML exists, what counts for basic HTML will remain largely unchanged. (The optional Intermediate HTML Tutorial that's scheduled for this afternoon covers many of the HTML 3.2 tags, along with a few of the new HTML 4.0 tags.)

Everyone has their own learning style and speed. Although the Basic HTML Tutorial is designed to be done in a single morning, you may want to take more or less time to do it. The most important thing is to work at your own speed without feeling rushed. If you want to take the whole day to do just this one tutorial, do so. So relax, sit back, and have some fun.

Copying the Example Files

On the CD-ROM are example graphics and other files for you to use in this tutorial and the other tutorials in this book. To copy these files to your Desktop, just do the following:

1. Insert the CD-ROM in your CD-ROM drive. When the disc has been mounted on your Desktop, double-click it to open it in the Finder.

2. Double-click the Book Examples folder. Drag and drop the HTML Tutorials folder onto your Desktop.

FIND IT ON ▶
THE WEB

If you don't have a CD-ROM drive or can't access this book's CD, you'll be glad to know that all the example files are available for download from this book's Web site at **www.callihan.com/create_imac/**. Just download the .sit file and use an unstuffing utility to unstuff the HTML Tutorials folder, then just use that folder as your working folder for doing the tutorials. If you don't have an unstuffing utility, I've included a link at this book's site to where you can download Stuffit Expander, a freeware unstuffing utility from Aladdin Systems.

● ●

I instructed you to drag and drop the HTML Tutorials folder to your desktop. Feel free to drag and drop it to any folder on your hard drive, if you want. Make sure that the example files are located in the same folder where you'll save the HTML files you'll create in the HTML tutorials (and not in a folder in that folder!). If they aren't in the same folder as your tutorial HTML files, the example graphics won't show up when you preview your work in your browser.

● ●

A Quick Word About HTML

Before you begin to do the exercises in the tutorial, a quick reminder about the nature of HTML might save you some confusion. The philosophy behind HTML is to specify the framework of a page, not its actual appearance or display. In principle, how a Web page is displayed is determined by the browser used to view it. You do have a fair amount of control over how most browsers present your page; today's graphical Web browsers allow you to include inline graphics, interlaced and transparent graphics, background images and colors, animation, streaming audio, and more.

Although most current graphical Web browsers now support most of these enhancements, HTML 2.0 specifies only some of them. Many facilities for more complete control over how your Web page will be displayed have been incorporated into HTML 3.2 and HTML 4.0.

The Basic HTML Tutorial covers everything you need to know to start creating Web pages. It sticks to HTML 2.0, which should be compatible with all Web browsers. In the Intermediate HTML Tutorial, you'll learn how to use some stuff from the newer standards—HTML 3.2 and 4.0—to give your Web pages more of a designer look.

Anatomy of a Tag

The term *tag* or *tag element* refers to the HTML code that defines the elements in an HTML file—the headings, images, paragraphs, lists, and so on. There are two kinds of tags: *containers* (which bracket or contain text or other tag elements), and *empty tags* (which stand alone). A container tag actually consists of two tags, a start tag and an end tag, which bracket the text or other elements they affect. An empty tag functions as a standalone element within an HTML document and therefore doesn't bracket or contain anything else.

NOTE Whenever I use the word "element" in this tutorial, remember that I'm referring not just to the tag codes, but to everything that is included between the start tag and the end tag, as well.

HTML tags are inserted into a document between less than (<) and greater than (>) symbols (also referred to as *left* and *right angle brackets*). For example, a start tag of a container tag or an empty tag element looks like this:

`<tagname>`

You always precede an end tag of a container tag element with a forward slash (/) to distinguish it from a start tag:

`</tagname>`

To tag a section of text, you place it between the start and end tags of a tag element. For example, text contained in a Level 1 heading tag would look like this, where `<H1>` is the start tag and `</H1>` is the end tag:

`<H1>This is a Level-One Heading</H1>`

A level-one heading tag is both the start and end tags. When I want to refer specifically to a start tag or an end tag, I'll say "the start tag" or "the end tag;" note that a few tags look like empty tags, but actually are container tags that have implied end tags. Typing tag names in all capital letters is somewhat conventional, although by no means required; this helps distinguish HTML tags from the remainder of the text being tagged. As a rule, this book presents tag names in all caps.

Tag Attributes

Attributes allow you to specify how Web browsers should treat a particular tag. An attribute is included within the actual tag (between the left and right angle brackets), either within a start tag or a standalone tag.

End tags can't contain attributes. Most of the tags covered in this tutorial don't use attributes, but toward the end of the tutorial, you'll use some attributes to include inline images or hypertext links in a Web page. Most attributes are combined with a value, to allow you to specify different options for how a Web browser should treat the attribute. Here's the format for including an attribute value in a tag:

```
ATTRIBUTE="value"
```

For instance, to specify that the middle of an image should be aligned with the line of text it appears on, you would include the following attribute value inside the IMG tag:

```
ALIGN="middle"
```

Tag attributes are, by convention, usually typed in all caps, with any values assigned to them typed in lowercase. You don't have to do it this way, but this convention does make it easier to pick these attributes out. In many cases, you can get away with not placing values inside quotation marks; however, enough instances exist in which this won't work that it's a good idea to stick to adding the quotes.

Nesting HTML Tags

You should always *nest* HTML tags and never overlap them. For example, always do this:

```
<B><I>Always nest tags inside each other.</I></B>
```

Notice that the `<I>...</I>` pair is nested within the `<B>...</B>` pair. Never overlap tags so that the outer tag ends before the inner tag:

```
<B><I>Don't overlap tags, like this.</B></I>
```

HTML operates in a hierarchical, top-down manner. A tag element may have other tag elements nested in it, or it can be nested within other tag elements. If you overlap two tags, a browser can't tell what should fall inside what, and it may not be able to display your file at all. Be kind to your browser as well as your potential readers: Don't overlap tag elements.

The Scratch Pad Model

The model that this tutorial employs resembles a "scratch pad" approach. Think of your text editor as a scratch pad. As you do the Basic HTML Tutorial, enter the suggested tags and text as though you were jotting them down on a scratch pad; in other words, you don't have to clean the slate each time you move on to a new section. Just move down the page, leaving everything you've already done in place. When you're done, you'll have a sample file that you can return to and refer to later.

 NOTE Any instructional steps included in this book assume that you're using Mac OS 8.0 or higher. If you're using an earlier version of the Mac OS, the steps required may be slightly different from those described here.

Starting Your HTML File

Run the text editor you want to use. I recommend that you use either the SimpleText text editor that comes with Mac OS 8.x or the TeachText text editor that is built into Mac OS 7.x, but any text editor you have available on your system will do.

NOTE

File names on the Macintosh generally don't use file extensions to identify the file type. To make sure your files are readable on other systems, such as UNIX or Windows, you need to add the file extension. This is necessary not only for HTML files, but also for JPEG and GIF files that you may want to include in your Web pages. When you save these file types, be sure to type the following at the end of their file names: **.html** at the end of the file name of an HTML file, **.jpg** at the end of the file name of a JPEG file, and **.gif** at the end of the file name of a GIF file.

Starting Your Page: Document Tags

All HTML files should include at least these tags:

- The HTML tag
- The HEAD tag
- The TITLE tag
- The BODY tag

The following sections discuss each of these tags.

TYPOGRAPHY LEGEND

In the tutorials in this book, words and code that you should type are formatted as `bolded and monospaced` text.

Text that shouldn't be typed in by you (that is, text that's shown for the purpose of an example) or text that you've already typed is formatted as `monospaced` text.

Italicized text in the input examples does not represent actual typed text. Instead, it indicates what should be typed. *Your Name*, for instance, would indicate that your actual name should be typed.

The HTML Tag

Recall that a tag defines a structural element within an HTML document. The HTML tag should always be the topmost element in an HTML file, within which all other tags and text should be nested. Here's an example:

```
<HTML>
```

Your HTML document's contents and all other tags . . .

```
</HTML>
```

In your scratch pad file, type the start and end tags for the HTML element, putting a single hard return between them, like this:

<HTML>

</HTML>

 NOTE Remember that the HTML start tag (<HTML>) must remain at the very top of your file, whereas the HTML end tag (</HTML>) must remain at the very bottom of your file. Everything else must fall between these two tags.

The HEAD Tag

The HEAD tag serves as a container for other tags that can provide information about your HTML file and identify it to the outside world. The HEAD tag is nested within the HTML tag. Type the HEAD tag inside the HTML tag now, like this:

```
<HTML>
```

<HEAD>

</HEAD>

```
</HTML>
```

Usually, the only tag contained within the HEAD tag is the TITLE tag. There are other tags that can be included here, but you don't need to bother about them just starting out.

The TITLE Tag

The TITLE tag is nested inside the HEAD tag. It serves as a welcome mat to the rest of the world; for instance, a search engine such as Yahoo! or WebCrawler might display the text included in your TITLE tag as a link to your page. The tag also displays on your browser window's title bar, but it doesn't appear as part of the page. Make the title descriptive, but keep it under 50 characters, if possible. Try to use a short title followed by a brief description; someone else should be able to tell what your page is about simply by looking at the title. Now, type the TITLE tag inside the HEAD tag. (Feel free to substitute a title here of your own choosing; this is just for practice, however, so don't spend all day trying to think up a good one.)

```
<HTML>

<HEAD>

<TITLE>Your Title: Describe Your Title</TITLE>

</HEAD>

</HTML>
```

Officially, the TITLE tag is a required element that you should include in each HTML document. In practice, however, most Web browsers let you get away with not including a TITLE tag. Still, you should include a TITLE tag in your HTML document. If you don't include a title, the title of your page appears in some browsers as "Untitled." In others, the URL for the page appears on the browser's title bar. Also, if your page doesn't have a title, anybody who bookmarks your page in Navigator, for instance, will end up with a blank bookmark entry in their bookmark list. If you want the page to show up without a title, nothing stops you from including a TITLE tag and leaving it blank. However, that defeats the whole purpose of including the tag in the first place.

The BODY Tag

The BODY tag is the complement of the HEAD tag; it contains all the tags, or elements, that a browser actually displays as the body of your HTML document.

Both the HEAD tag and the BODY tag are nested inside the HTML tag, and the BODY tag comes after the HEAD tag; they denote separate parts of the HTML document.

NOTE The HEAD and BODY tags are the only tags that are nested directly inside the HTML tag. Other than the TITLE tag, which you inserted within the HEAD tag for this example, you should nest all text and tags you enter in this tutorial inside the BODY tag. Be sure to keep both the </BODY> and </HTML> end tags at the bottom of your HTML file.

Type the BODY tag after the HEAD tag but inside the HTML tag, like this:

```
<HTML>
<HEAD>
<TITLE>Your Title: Describe Your Title</TITLE>
</HEAD>
<BODY>
</BODY>
</HTML>
```

You've officially started your HTML file. All HTML files begin the same way—only the titles are different. What you've typed so far should look like this:

```
<HTML>
<HEAD>
<TITLE>Your Title: Describe Your Title</TITLE>
</HEAD>
<BODY>
</BODY>
</HTML>
```

Saving a Starting Template

Every HTML file should include the tags you've added so far. If you want, you can save what you've done so that you can re-use it as a template for starting your HTML files in the future. That way, you won't have to retype the same stuff all over again each time you want to start an HTML file. Select File and Save As, and then save it in the HTML Tutorials folder on the Desktop (or anywhere else you want to save it). Type **startpage.html** as the name of this file—I'll be referring to it later in the other HTML tutorials by that name. Then, whenever you want to start a new Web page, just open startpage.html in your text editor.

Saving Your HTML File

So you won't be resaving over your starting template later, resave your HTML file now as **scratch.html** in the HTML Tutorials folder on the Desktop. Select File and Save As; if the Desktop isn't already selected, click the Desktop button, and then click on the HTML Tutorials folder. Type **scratch.html** as the file name, and then click on the Save button.

NOTE When you save an HTML file on the Macintosh, you should not include any spaces in your file name, and you should add either an **.html** or an **.htm** file extension to the file name. You can substitute underscores (_) for spaces, if you wish, although it is a good idea to keep file names fairly short (10 or 12 characters at most, plus the file extension). It is also a good idea to use all lowercase characters in HTML file names (mypage.html, instead of MyPage.html, for instance), to help avoid problems with case sensitivity on some Web servers.

Previewing Your Work in Your Browser

Just typing the HTML codes into your text editor doesn't let you know if you're doing it right or not. To see what your work is actually going to look like, you need to open and view it in your Web browser. Just leave your HTML file open in your browser, and you'll be able to hop back and forth between your text editor and your browser, dynamically previewing your work as you go.

The steps for opening a local HTML file vary from browser to browser, and may even vary slightly from version to version. Following are the basic steps required to open a local HTML file in the versions of Microsoft Internet Explorer and Netscape Navigator included with the iMac and all G3 desktop Macs.

1. First, save your HTML file (scratch.html) so any changes you've made are saved with the file. Don't exit your text editor, but just leave your HTML file open in it (you'll be hopping right back).

2. Run your Web browser. On the iMac, you'll find the program icons for both Internet Explorer and Netscape Navigator inside the Internet folder in the Macintosh HD disk. Double-click on the icon of the browser you want to use to preview your HTML files.

3. When your computer tries to connect to the Internet, just click Cancel. Click OK to get past the message that follows (it's just telling you it can't connect to your start page on the Web).

4. In Internet Explorer, choose Open File from the File menu. In Navigator, choose Open Page from the File menu.

5. If the Desktop isn't already selected, click on the Desktop button. Double-click on the HTML Tutorials folder to open it, and then on scratch.html.

NOTE Right now, you won't see anything in the browser's window—that's because you haven't typed anything yet inside the BODY tag. On your browser's title bar, you'll see your HTML file's title displayed, as shown in Figure 2-1.

6. After checking out your HTML file in your browser, just leave it open in your browser (you'll be hopping back to it frequently during the rest of this tutorial).

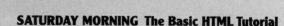

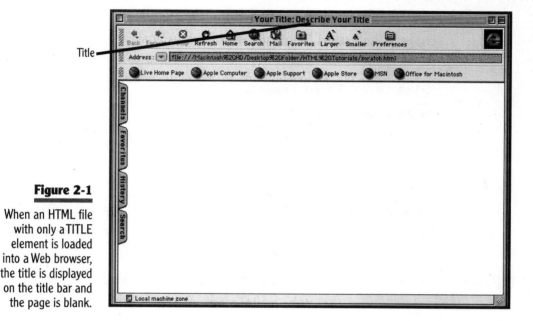

Title

Figure 2-1

When an HTML file with only a TITLE element is loaded into a Web browser, the title is displayed on the title bar and the page is blank.

7. Bring your text editor to the foreground—click your text editor's window, if visible, or choose it from the Applications menu. You can also just hold down the Command key and tap the Tab key (Command-Tab) until your text editor's window comes to the foreground.

Using Heading Level Tags

Heading level tags are used to organize the hierarchical structure of your Web page. There are six heading level tags (H1, H2, H3, and so on) that can be used in a Web page. The H1 tag is usually used only once: at the top of your page, to display a title for your page. (This is not to be confused with the TITLE tag, which defines the title that is displayed on your browser window's title bar.)

The H2 tag is generally used to define a major division in your page, while the H3 tag is used to define a sublevel division within a major division. While there are six different heading level tags, it is rare that you'll use more than the top four. Inside the BODY element you added earlier, type six heading level tags, like this:

```
<BODY>
<H1>A Level-One Heading</H1>
<H2>A Level-Two Heading</H2>
<H3>A Level-Three Heading</H3>
<H4>A Level-Four Heading</H4>
<H5>A Level-Five Heading</H5>
<H6>A Level-Six Heading</H6>
</BODY>
```

When displayed in a browser, different level headings appear as different size fonts, from large to small (although each browser decides which fonts to use).

Hopping between Your Text Editor and Your Browser

To be able to dynamically preview the results of your work as you go, you need to hop back and forth between your text editor and your browser. With your HTML file already open in both your text editor and your browser, this involves three basic steps:

1. In your text editor, press Command-S to save the latest changes to your HTML file. (Don't quit your text editor or close your file.)

2. Bring your browser to the foreground—click the browser window, if visible, or choose it from the Applications menu. You can also just hold down the Command key and tap the Tab key (Command-Tab) until your browser's window comes to the foreground.

3. Press Command-R to refresh the display of your page in your browser (or click the Refresh button in Internet Explorer or the Reload button in Navigator). The changes you saved in step 1 should now be updated in your browser (see Figure 2-2).

4. Bring your text editor back to the foreground using any of the methods described in Step 2. Make more changes to your HTML file, and then repeat steps 1 through 4 as many times as you wish while creating your HTML file.

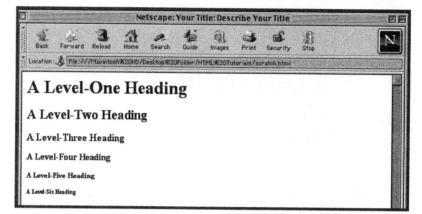

A Level-One Heading

A Level-Two Heading

A Level-Three Heading

A Level-Four Heading

A Level-Five Heading

A Level-Six Heading

Figure 2-2

Web browsers display heading levels in different font sizes.

NOTE

While doing this tutorial, or the other HTML tutorials in this book, you should hop over to your browser *frequently* to check out the results of your work. You won't know you've done it right, in other words, until you can see it in your browser. Just save your HTML file, and then hop over to your browser and click the Refresh (or Reload) button.

Creating Paragraphs and Line Breaks

The P (Paragraph) and BR (Line Break) tags let you insert paragraphs and lines of text on your page.

The P (Paragraph) Tag

You shouldn't have any untagged text in an HTML document. Any straight paragraph text you want to include in your page should be tagged with the P tag. Like the heading-level tags covered in the previous section, the P tag is a container element that uses both a start and an end tag. Type the following example of paragraph text using the P tag (see Figure 2-3):

```
<H6>This is a level-six heading</H6>

<P>This is paragraph text. This is paragraph text. This is
paragraph text. This is paragraph text. This is paragraph
text. This is paragraph text.</P>

</BODY>
```

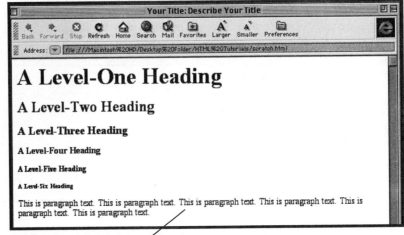

Figure 2-3

When you add a
text paragraph
using the P tag,
your browser will
automatically wrap
the lines for you
to fit its window.

Paragraph

TIP

You should just let your text editor wrap your text wherever it wants to. Where your text wraps in your text editor will have no impact on where it will wrap in your Web browser (your browser will completely ignore any hard returns you put in).

NOTE

Feel free to resize the dimensions of your browser window to more closely match what you see in the figures. To increase the font size for Internet Explorer 4.0+, just click the Larger button on the toolbar. For Netscape Navigator 4.0+, choose Preferences from the Edit menu and choose Fonts from the Category list; then reset the Size to 14 for both the Variable Width Font and the Fixed Width Font.

The reason this may be necessary (or just desirable) on a Mac is that it displays fonts at a different resolution than a Windows PC, causing fonts of the same point-size to appear smaller on a Mac than on a Windows PC. This is why some Mac browsers have Larger and Smaller buttons.

In the past it was considered okay to leave off the </P> end tag at the end of a paragraph because the P tag was considered to have an implied end tag. In most cases, this worked fine (and still does), but there are a number

of situations where you may get undesirable results in some browsers if you leave the end tag off. For that reason, it is probably a good idea to add the </P> end tag at the end of any text paragraph you want to include in your HTML file. The latest version of HTML (4.0) discourages leaving off the </P> end tag.

Besides nesting text paragraphs (P elements) inside the BODY element, you can also nest them inside a number of other HTML elements, including block quotes, definition lists, list items, and address blocks. There are actually two basic kinds of HTML elements: block elements and inline elements. A block element always forms a new "block" in your Web page, with extra vertical space added above and below it. An inline element can be directly inserted within a block element (such as a paragraph) without causing any line breaks to be inserted before or after the inserted element.

There are a number of "inline elements" that can be used to apply highlighting of one kind or another to your paragraph text, such as bolding, italics, and monospaced text. Hypertext links and inline images, both covered later in this session, are also inserted as inline elements.

NOTE Don't insert multiple blank P tags. Multiple blank P tags inserted into your HTML file should have absolutely no effect when your page is displayed in your browser. If you want to test this out, just add three blank P tags to your scratch pad file, followed by another paragraph of text, as shown here:

```
<P>This is paragraph text. This is paragraph text.
This is paragraph text. This is paragraph text. This
is paragraph text. This is paragraph text.</P>

<P></P>

<P></P>

<P></P>

<P>This is paragraph text.</P>
```

If you save your file and then hop over and refresh your browser, you'll see that multiple blank P tags have no effect, as shown in Figure 2-4.

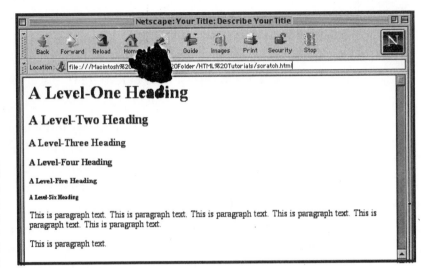

Figure 2-4

The multiple P tags inserted between two paragraphs should be completely ignored by a Web browser.

The BR (Break) Tag

The BR (Break) tag is an empty (standalone) tag that simply inserts a line break. Type three text lines separated by BR tags:

```
<P>These lines are separated by BR (Break) tags.<BR>
These lines are separated by BR (Break) tags.<BR>
These lines are separated by BR (Break) tags.</P>
```

As Figure 2-5 shows, only a single line break separates these lines when a browser displays them. (Paragraphs are separated by both a line break and an extra blank line.)

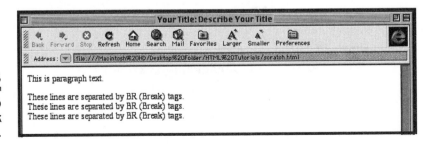

Figure 2-5

Use the BR tag to insert a line break at the end of a line.

 NOTE

You can use the BR tag almost anywhere you have text, not just inside P tags. For example, you can put one inside an H1 or H2 element to force a heading to show up on two lines.

Using Multiple BR Tags to Add Blank Lines

It is common for inexperienced Web publishers to try to add vertical blank space in a Web page by inserting multiple BR tags. Current browsers also tend to let you get away with doing this, even though it is not standard HTML. If you want to try it out for yourself, type the following example, and then hop over to your browser to check out the result:

```
<P>Four BR (Break) tags follow this line.<BR>

<BR>

<BR>

<BR>

Four BR (Break) tags precede this line.</P>
```

While you're not supposed to get away with such a maneuver (according to the official HTML specs, that is), Netscape Navigator has always let you get away with it, as does the latest version of Internet Explorer, as shown in Figure 2-6.

Figure 2-6

Both Navigator and Internet Explorer will display multiple BR tags, but in contravention of the standards for HTML.

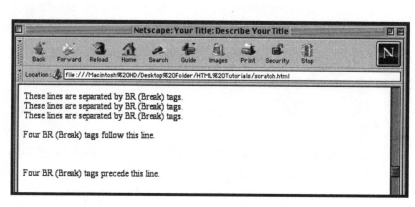

To quote from the draft specification for HTML 4.0, "a sequence of contiguous white space characters, such as spaces, horizontal tabs, form feeds, and line breaks, should be replaced by a single word space." So, should you or shouldn't you use BR tags for blank lines? Even though Netscape Navigator, Internet Explorer (versions 3.0 and 4.0), and any number of other Web browsers let you use multiple BR tags, it still doesn't constitute standard HTML. Your best bet is to avoid nonstandard HTML, even if your favorite Web browser allows you to get away with using it. There's also no guarantee how nonstandard HTML will display in future browser versions. Besides, you can get the same result in a perfectly standard way.

TIP This trick for inserting blank lines into a Web page works for all browsers. To insert blank lines into your HTML file, enclose regular hard returns inside the PRE (Preformatted Text) tags:

```
<P>Inserting a PRE tag containing hard returns will
add extra space between paragraphs.</P>

<PRE>




</PRE>
<P>This line should be three lines down.</P>
```

For more information on the PRE tag, see "Using Preformatted Text," later in this chapter.

Spacing, Tabs, and Returns

In HTML, the tags themselves do all of your page's formatting. A browser ignores more than one space inserted into text (two, five, or ten spaces all appear as if they are a single space), as well as all tabs and hard returns (unless they're inside a PRE tag). Any formatting of your HTML file using extra spaces or tabs and returns is for your eyes only. Feel free to use all the extra spaces, tabs, and returns you want to make your raw HTML files more readable as you work on them.

TIP

Other than inserting a totally transparent image, the only way to insert multiple horizontal spaces in your HTML file is to use nonbreakable space characters. You insert these into an HTML file as either   or   (which refer to the ISO 8859-1 numerical or named-entity code for the character). To simulate a paragraph tab, for example, you would insert   three times at the start of a paragraph:

This will work in virtually all Web browsers, although a few X-Windows browsers won't display nonbreakable spaces at all (instead displaying them as zero-width characters). Still, if you want horizontal space in a line of text, other than using tables, this is the only way to do it. In "Inserting Non-Keyboard Characters," you'll learn how to insert non-keyboard characters into your Web page.

Adding Comments

You can also add comments to annotate your HTML files. The *comment tag* is a standalone tag that enables you to include a message that will not be displayed in a Web browser while your HTML file is being read. Comments are useful for future reference. What's a little confusing about this tag, however, is that no "name" is included in the tag. Instead, a comment always begins with

```
<!--
```

and ends with

```
-->
```

Any text inserted between these tags is comment text, which a browser completely ignores. Here's an example of the form in which you would enter a comment into an HTML file:

```
<!--Put your comment here-->
```

Now, go ahead and type a comment between two lines of text, like this:

```
<P>This line is followed by a comment.
<!--Comments are not displayed by a browser.-->
<P>This line follows a comment.
```

These two paragraph lines appear in a Web browser without any additional vertical space between them. The browser ignores any text inside the comment tag.

Highlighting Your Text

Just as in a normal book or report, an HTML document can use highlighting to clarify the text's meaning. For instance, you can easily make text in an HTML file boldfaced or italicized.

Using Italic and Bold Highlighting

HTML has two ways to include italic or bold text on your Web page. The first way involves using "literal" tags: the I (Italic) and B (Bold) tags. The second way is to use "logical" tags: the EM (Emphasis) and STRONG (Strong Emphasis) tags. Most browsers should display the I (Italic) and EM (Emphasis) tags identically, just as they should display the B (Bold) and STRONG (Strong Emphasis) tags identically.

So what's the difference? The basic philosophy behind HTML is to logically represent the elements of a page rather than literally describe them. The browser can freely interpret the logical elements of an HTML page and display them as it sees fit. Therefore, the philosophically correct method is to always use logical tags and to avoid using literal tags. (Even though the B and I tags have the advantage of saving you some keystrokes.) As an example of using the I, B, EM, and STRONG tags for text highlighting, type the following lines of text (see Figure 2-7):

Figure 2-7

You can use literal
tags (I and B) or
logical tags (EM
and STRONG) to
italicize or bold text.

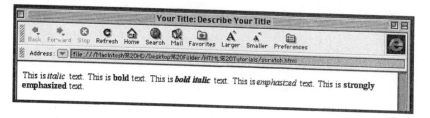

```
<P>This is <I>italic</I> text. This is <B>bold</B> text.
This is <B><I>bold italic</I></B> text. This is
<EM>emphasized</EM> text. This is <STRONG>strongly
emphasized</STRONG> text.
```

The previous example nests the I tag inside the B tag to get text that is bold and italic. You could also do it the other way around, nesting the B tag inside the I tag. (You just don't want to overlap them.) Although it is not shown in the previous example, you could also nest the EM tag inside the STRONG tag, or vice versa, to get the same result. (You can also nest the STRONG tag inside the I tag.)

You can use two other tags, CITE (Citation) and VAR (Variable), to highlight text—but because all Web browsers that I know of interpret them exactly like the I (Italic) and EM (Emphasis) tags, there's not much reason to bother using them.

Embedding Monospace Text

You may want to embed monospace text within a paragraph to request keyboard input or represent screen output. A *monospace font*, also called a *fixed-pitch font*, is a font in which all the characters occupy the same amount of space on a line (in a *proportional font* each character occupies a unique amount of space on a line):

```
This line uses a monospace font.
```

The most widely used tag for embedding monospace text is the TT (Teletype, or Typewriter Text) tag. It appears as a monospace font in all Web browsers. You can think of it as a general-purpose monospace text tag, which you can use whenever you want to embed monospace text within a paragraph. Two other tags, the CODE and SAMP tags, can embed monospaced text, but they produce the exact same result as the TT tag.

A potentially useful monospace tag is the KBD (Keyboard) tag, which should allow you to distinguish keyboard input from screen output. Unfortunately, the way in which a Web browser displays this tag is rather unpredictable. Navigator displays it the same as the TT tag. Earlier versions of Internet Explorer display it in a bolded monospace font; the latest versions follow Navigator's example. Type the following text as an example of using the TT and KBD tags:

```
<P>This text is regular text. <TT>This is an example of
the TT (Teletype Text) tag.</TT> This text is regular
text. <KBD>This is an example of the KBD (Keyboard) tag.
</KBD> This text is regular text.</P>
```

Because the latest versions of both Navigator and Internet Explorer treat these tags identically, as shown in Figure 2-8, you should probably just stick to using the TT tag and ignore the KBD tag.

TIP

By themselves, the TT and KBD tags display identically in a browser, but by using styles you can assign different display characteristics to these two tags. This would allow you to distinguish between output (the TT tag) and input (the KBD tag) in the latest browsers, for instance. For some examples of assigning styles to tags, see the Intermediate HTML Tutorial, which is scheduled for this afternoon. I've also included some examples of using styles in Appendix C, "Creating Tables."

Figure 2-8

Current Web browsers all display text marked with the TT and KBD tags identically, as monospace text.

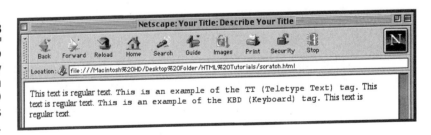

NOTE To insert monospace text as a separate text block rather than embedding it inside a paragraph, see "The PRE (Preformatted Text) Tag" section, later in this session.

Inserting Non-Keyboard Characters

You may need to enter a special code for a character into your HTML file under two different circumstances: If you want to insert a reserved character that's used to parse (interpret and display) an HTML file, and if you want to enter a special or extended character that isn't part of the regular keyboard character set. You can insert a non-keyboard character into an HTML file in two forms, as a numerical entity code or a named entity code.

Numerical entity codes are inserted in the following form, where *number* is a three-digit decimal number between 000 and 255:

`&#number;`

Named entity codes are inserted in the following form, where *name* is the name of a character as listed in the HTML specs:

`&name;`

Reserved Characters

HTML uses the <, >, &, and " characters to parse or interpret an HTML document for display. With the exception of angle brackets, these characters rarely need to be replaced with their entity codes:

- Angle brackets (< and >) should always be replaced by their corresponding entity codes if you want them to display properly in an HTML file. Use them only to signal the beginning or the end of an HTML tag.

- Double quotes (") only need to be replaced if they're part of an HTML tag that you want to appear "as is" rather than as interpreted by a browser.

✪ An ampersand (&) signals the beginning of an entity code. It only needs to be replaced if it's part of an HTML entity code that you want to appear "as is" rather than as interpreted by a browser. You never need to replace standalone ampersands.

CAUTION If you use a word processor to create HTML files, be sure to turn off the "smart quotes" feature. When creating HTML files, you always want to use regular "keyboard" quotes. In other words, each quotation mark should be straight up and down, not curled to the left or right.

You can use character entities exclusively to insert any of these characters into an HTML file when you want an HTML tag to appear on your Web page "as is" rather than as interpreted by the browser. To have a browser show "<EM>" onscreen instead of interpreting it as a formatting code, you would enter it like this:

<EM>

All Web browsers recognize the named entity codes for these characters, so you don't have to use the numerical entity codes here. For easy reference, Table 2-1 shows the named entity codes for inserting HTML reserved characters.

TABLE 2-1 HTML RESERVED CHARACTER ENTITY CODES

Character	Entity	Code
Less than	<	&lt;
Greater than	>	&gt;
Ampersand	&	&amp;
Double quote	"	&quot;

Special Characters

Suppose you want to post a page devoted to an article you've written, and you want to protect it by showing your copyright. Because the copyright symbol isn't available on the keyboard, you can't just type it into your HTML document as you would a normal keyboard character. Instead, you must use a special code that tells the browser to insert the character where you want it.

In HTML, you can enter such characters in two ways: as numerical entity codes or as named entity codes. Here, you can insert the copyright symbol by using its numerical entity code (©) or its named entity code (©).

HTML uses the ISO 8859-1 character set, which is an 8-bit character set that provides 256 positions (numbered 000, 001, 002, and so on, up to 255). Of these, 000 through 032, as well as 127, correspond to control characters (such as for designating line feeds, tabs, spaces, and so on) that do not display characters. 033 through 126 correspond to characters that can be entered from the keyboard. 128 through 159 correspond to characters that can be displayed, but that are excluded from standard HTML and are designated as "unused characters." Only the codes between 033 and 126 and those between 160 and 255 correspond to characters that you are "officially" allowed to include in an HTML file; the characters in the second range include many special symbols (copyright, degrees, cents, and so on), plus a number of accented characters (such as a capital A with an acute accent) that are commonly used in foreign languages.

For many of the characters between 128 and 159, the same character will display on both the Macintosh and Windows platforms, but there is no guarantee that other operating systems will display the same character. There are really only a few characters among the "unused characters" that you might possibly want to use, primarily the en dash (–), em dash (—), and trademark symbol (™) characters. The trademark symbol entity code is actually used quite frequently on Web pages, despite its being one of the "unused characters." Still, the Macintosh, Windows, and UNIX operating systems all will display the trademark symbol (™), which clearly has nearly universal support. If you do decide to use the trademark symbol you should stick to using the numerical entity code (™) and avoid using its named entity code (™), since many earlier browsers will display only the former.

TIP

There is a rough workaround for "legally" including a trademark symbol in an HTML document: Just insert (TM) inside a SUP (Superscript) tag. The parentheses are used to allow for browsers that don't support the SUP tag. To reduce the size of the superscripted "(TM)," also insert it inside a SMALL tag. I'll be covering using superscripts (and subscripts), as well as decreasing (and increasing) font sizes, in the Intermediate HTML Tutorial.

CAUTION

You should avoid using keyboard shortcuts to insert non-keyboard characters (such as Option-G to insert a copyright symbol, for instance) into an HTML file. The same character will show up on another platform (Windows or Unix, for instance) only if it happens to be in the same position in its native character set. Only if you stick to using numerical entity codes for the officially displayable HTML characters (160 through 255) can you have any assurance that the same character will display on different platforms, even if the character is in different positions in those systems' native character sets.

Except for the named entity codes for the uppercase and lowercase accented characters that many foreign languages require (A-grave, a-acute, and so on), the only named entity codes that have universal support in browsers are those for the copyright (©) and the registered (®) symbols. Certain Web browsers can interpret and display almost all these named entities, but in general, Netscape Navigator will not display them (other than those just mentioned). Feel free to use the named entity codes for the copyright and registered symbols, as well as for any of the accented characters; otherwise, stick to using numerical character entities.

◆ ◆

CAUTION While ISO-8859-1, the standard character set for Web pages, is also the character set used by both Windows and UNIX, it is not the native character set used by the Macintosh. (MS-DOS also uses a character set different than ISO-8859-1.) For that reason, there are a number of additional characters that should not be used, in addition to the officially designated "unused" characters. In Appendix B, "Using Special Characters," you'll find charts showing all of the "unused characters" and "special characters" that can be inserted into a Web page. I've clearly labeled all of the characters that won't display the same on the Macintosh. (The Macintosh version of Internet Explorer 4.0+ actually does display the missing Mac characters, but only because it substitutes those characters from the ISO-8859-1 character set. Other Macintosh browsers don't follow suit on this.)

◆ ◆

Table 2-2 shows some of the most commonly used special characters, their numerical and named entity codes, and support by browsers (universal support for named entities cannot be guaranteed).

Table 2-2 is just a partial list of special characters you can insert into an HTML file. For a full listing of all the special characters you can use, see Appendix B, "Using Special Characters."

Character	Number	Name	Name Support
™ (Trademark)	&#153;	&trade;	Not Navigator (prior to 4.5)
¢ (Cent)	&#162;	&cent;	Only latest 4.0+ browsers
© (Copyright)	&#169;	&copy;	All browsers
® (Registered)	&#174;	&reg;	All browsers

TABLE 2-2 SPECIAL CHARACTERS

Go ahead and enter the following example of using the numerical entity code for the copyright symbol and the named entity code for the registered symbol (see Figure 2-9):

```
<H2>&#169; Copyright 1999.</H2>

<H2>Crumbies&reg;</H2>
```

Using Block Quotes

The BLOCKQUOTE tag double-indents a block of text from both margins. You generally use it to display block quotes, as the name of the tag implies. You can use it to double-indent any block of text—you aren't limited to using it just for block quotes.

According to the specification for the tag, you aren't supposed to put raw text inside a block quote—you're only supposed to put other block elements, such as paragraphs (P tag elements) and headings, inside a block quote, and then put the text in those other elements. But no browser will display your text any differently if you do nest raw text in a BLOCKQUOTE tag. If you want to insert more than a single paragraph inside of a BLOCKQUOTE tag, you'll need to nest your text in P tags (or other block

Figure 2-9

You can insert special characters such as the copyright and registered symbols using numerical and named entity codes.

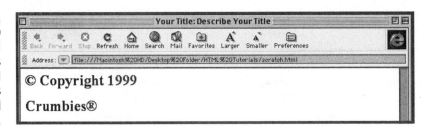

element tags). Type a paragraph of text, followed by a paragraph of text inside a BLOCKQUOTE tag:

```
<P>In <EM>Notes from Underground</EM> Dostoevsky plumbs
the depths of human psychology, revealing the complexity
and contradictions underlying even the most normal and
decent of human beings:</P>
```

```
<BLOCKQUOTE><P>Every man has some reminiscences which he
would not tell to everyone, but only to his friends. He
has others which he would not reveal even to his friends,
but only to himself, and that in secret. But finally there
are still others which a man is even afraid to tell
himself, and every decent man has a considerable number of
such things in his mind.</P></BLOCKQUOTE>
```

The BLOCKQUOTE tag displays text indented from both margins in a regular proportional font (see Figure 2-10). It has become fairly common to see the BLOCKQUOTE tag used in HTML pages as a formatting device, causing a block of text to be double-indented from the margins (even if it isn't a "block quote" per se). You can even increase the amount of the indent by nesting BLOCKQUOTE tags inside each other. With all recent graphical Web browsers this works fine, but some earlier browsers, such as Internet Explorer 2.0, may display a block quote somewhat differently. Because of how earlier browsers might display this tag you may want to consider sticking to using it just for displaying block quotes, as it was originally intended to do, rather than as a formatting device for other blocks of text. If you want to double-indent text, consider using a table (see Appendix C, "Creating Tables").

Block Quote

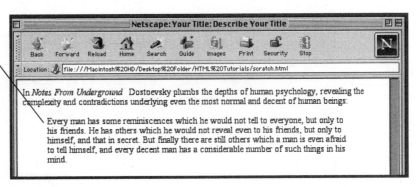

Figure 2-10

The BLOCKQUOTE tag is used to double-indent text from the margins.

Using BR (Break) Tags in a Block Quote

You can use BR (Break) tags in a block quote to display stanzas of poetry, the verses of a song, or other indented lines of text that you want separated by line breaks (rather than paragraph breaks). Type a paragraph of text, followed by a paragraph of text, using BR tags inserted inside a BLOCKQUOTE tag (see Figure 2-11).

```
<P>In <I>Porgy and Bess</I>, in the song "Summertime,"
George Gershwin evokes the hazy, lazy days of a Southern
summer:<P>

<BLOCKQUOTE>

<P>Summertime and the living is easy,<BR>

Fish are jumping and the cotton is high.<BR>

Oh your Daddy's rich and your Ma is good looking,<BR>

So hush little baby, don't you cry.</P>

</BLOCKQUOTE>
```

Using Preformatted Text

The PRE (Preformatted Text) tag is used to display text in a monospace (fixed-pitch) font. As its name implies, the PRE tag displays text "as is," including all spaces and hard returns. The primary use for this tag is to display text in a tabular or columnar format in which you want to make sure that columns are properly aligned.

Figure 2-11

By combining BR tags with the BLOCKQUOTE tag, you can create indented stanzas for a poem or song.

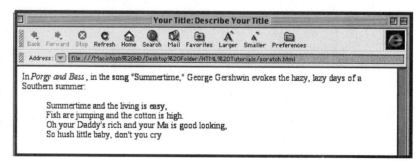

TIP
Always use spaces, not tabs, to align columns when using the PRE tag, because different browsers might display tabs in PRE-tagged text differently.

Actually, the PRE tag is the original "tables" tag for HTML. Unlike the TABLE tag (part of HTML 3.2), it is supported by all Web browsers. It can be particularly handy for displaying worksheets or reports generated by spreadsheet or database programs. Another common usage is for displaying program code or output.

TIP
When typing the following PRE tag example, you should select a monospace (fixed-pitch) font in your text editor, such as Courier or Courier New. (In the SimpleText editor, just choose Courier or Courier New from the Font menu.) If you leave the text in a proportional font, such as Geneva, you won't be able to properly line up the columns in your text editor.

For an example of using the PRE tag, type a table using rows and columns (see Figure 2-12):

<PRE>

```
             First Quarter Sales Figures for 1999
         _____

              January     February      March       Totals

    Anderson   $10,200    $ 20,015    $ 14,685    $ 44,900

    Baker       30,500      25,885      50,225     106,610

    Peterson    15,900      20,115      18,890      54,905

    Wilson      40,100      35,000      29,000     104,100

              _____

    Totals     $96,700    $101,015    $112,800    $310,515
```

</PRE>

Figure 2-12

The PRE tag displays text blocks in a monospace font, preserving all spaces and line breaks in columnar and tabular text.

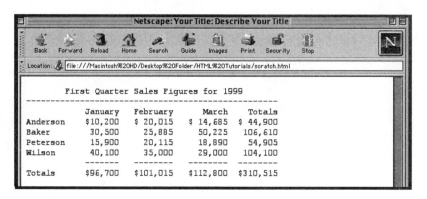

```
                First Quarter Sales Figures for 1999
          --------------------------------------------------------

                    January    February       March     Totals
          Anderson  $10,200   $ 20,015    $ 14,685   $ 44,900
          Baker      30,500     25,885      50,225    106,610
          Peterson   15,900     20,115      18,890     54,905
          Wilson     40,100     35,000      29,000    104,100
                     -------    --------    --------   --------
          Totals    $96,700   $101,015    $112,800   $310,515
```

One way to double-indent preformatted text is to put it inside a BLOCKQUOTE tag. Enclose the PRE tag text you just typed inside a BLOCKQUOTE tag, as follows:

<PRE>

<BLOCKQUOTE>

```
          First Quarter Sales Figures for 1999
   ─ ─ ─ ─ ─ ─ ─ ─ ─ ─ ─ ─ ─ ─ ─ ─ ─ ─ ─ ─ ─ ─ ─ ─

             January      February       March       Totals

   Anderson  $10,200     $ 20,015     $ 14,685     $ 44,900

   Baker      30,500       25,885       50,225      106,610

   Peterson   15,900       20,115       18,890       54,905

   Wilson     40,100       35,000       29,000      104,100


   ─ ─ ─ ─ ─ ─ ─ ─ ─ ─ ─ ─ ─ ─ ─ ─ ─ ─ ─ ─ ─ ─ ─ ─

   Totals    $96,700     $101,015     $112,800     $310,515
```

</BLOCKQUOTE>

</PRE>

Unfortunately, Internet Explorer 2.0 flubs this, continuing to display the PRE-tagged text left-flushed. You might think that you could reverse the

nesting order here, placing the PRE tags inside the BLOCKQUOTE tags, but a bug in Internet Explorer 4.0 will still cause it to be displayed flush to the left margin. This has been fixed in versions 4.01 and later of Internet Explorer, but you should just stick to putting the BLOCKQUOTE tags inside the PRE tags.

Take a Break?

This seems like a good place to take a break. Get up and stretch those arms and legs. Pour another cup of coffee or take the dog for a walk. I'll see you back in ten minutes or so for the remainder of this session.

Creating Lists

Only heading level and paragraph elements are used more commonly than lists. Many Web pages are nothing but lists of hypertext links. If you have been surfing the Web, you have probably been on that merry-go-round a few times—going from one page of lists to another page of lists to another. If you're going to create Web pages, you need to know how to make lists! HTML uses two types of lists: *ordered* and *unordered*. An ordered list is simply a *numbered* list, and an unordered list is a *bulleted* list.

TIP You don't have to physically type the numbers for the items in an ordered list or insert bullet characters for an unordered list. A Web browser automatically numbers any list items included in an OL (Ordered List) tag; when it encounters the UL (Unordered List) tag, it inserts the bullet characters for you.

The OL (Ordered List) Tag

The OL (Ordered List) tag defines a sequentially numbered list of items. The OL tag surrounds the entire list, while another tag, the LI (List Item) tag, is nested inside the OL tag to define the individual list items. Create an ordered list to see how these tags work together (see Figure 2-13):

Figure 2-13

The OL (Ordered List) tag is used to create a numbered list.

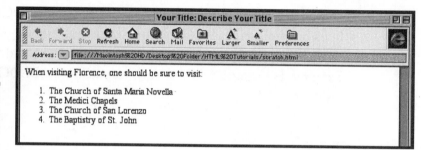

```
<P>When visiting Florence, one should be sure to visit:</P>

<OL>

<LI>The Church of Santa Maria Novella

<LI>The Medici Chapels

<LI>The Church of San Lorenzo

<LI>The Baptistry of St. John

</OL>
```

The UL (Unordered List) Tag

The UL (Unordered List) tag defines a bulleted list of items. Once again, the LI (List Item) tag is nested inside the UL tag, and defines each item within the list. Create a bulleted list (see Figure 2-14):

```
<P>In this course we will be studying the philosophical
thought of the Milesians:</P>

<UL>

<LI>Thales

<LI>Anaximander

<LI>Anaximenes

</UL>
```

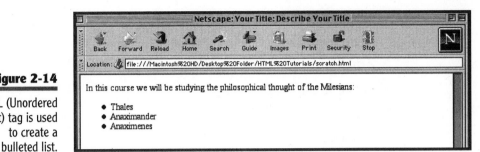

Figure 2-14

The UL (Unordered List) tag is used to create a bulleted list.

NOTE So how do you create all those fancy 3-D bullet icons you see all over the Web? Well, first of all, you don't use OL or UL tags. Those fancy bullets are actually inline graphic images that the Web author has inserted into the page. The separate lines are simply paragraphs broken up by line breaks (BR tags). I cover how to insert inline images using the IMG tag later in this tutorial. In the Intermediate HTML Tutorial, scheduled for this afternoon, I'll show you how to create link lists with fancy 3-D bullet icons. I'll also show you an even fancier way to do this using tables in Appendix C, "Creating Tables."

Nesting Lists

You can nest a list inside another list; the browser automatically indents nested list levels. You can also nest the same or different kinds of lists. In order to make it easier to see what's going on in the following example, I've added spaces to indent the different nested levels. Feel free to type in the spaces if you want, but no harm will result if you skip them. Type the following for an example of nesting lists within lists:

```
<UL>

<LI>Some Pre-Socratic Philosophers:

  <UL>

  <LI>The Milesians

   <UL>

   <LI>Thales
```

```
    <LI>Anaximander
    <LI>Anaximenes
    </UL>
 <LI>The Eleatics
    <UL>
    <LI>Parmenides
    <LI>Anaxagoras
    </UL>
    </UL>
  </UL>
```

Web browsers can vary quite a bit in how they display bullets in an unordered list. Figures 2-15 and 2-16 show how different level bullets in a nested unordered list are displayed in Internet Explorer and Netscape Navigator, respectively.

Figure 2-15

Internet Explorer displays a multi-level bulleted list like this.

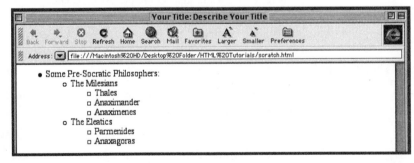

Figure 2-16

Netscape Navigator displays a multi-level bulleted list like this.

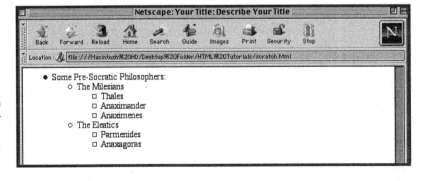

Mixing Lists

Figure 2-17 shows ordered (numbered) lists nested inside an unordered (bulleted) list. You can nest an ordered list within an unordered list (or the other way around):

```
<UL>
<LI>King-Side Openings
 <OL>
 <LI>Ruy Lopez
 <LI>King Bishop's Opening
 <LI>King's Gambit
 </OL>
<LI>Queen-Side Openings
 <OL>
 <LI>Queen's Gambit Declined
 <LI>Queen's Gambit Accepted
 <LI>English Opening
 </OL>
</UL>
```

HTML includes two other list tags: the DIR and MENU tags. The DIR tag was intended for displaying multi-column file directory lists, whereas the MENU tag was intended for displaying single-column menu lists. Most

Figure 2-17

You can nest a numbered list inside a bulleted list, and vice versa.

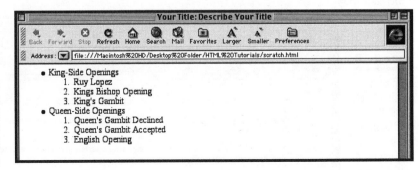

recent browsers display the DIR and MENU tags exactly the same as the UL tag. (The HTML 4.0 specification recommends that the UL tag be used instead of the DIR and MENU tags.)

Creating Definition Lists

The DL (Definition List) tag allows you to create glossaries, or lists of terms and definitions. A definition list actually consists of three tag elements that all work together: the DL (Definition List) tag to denote the list, the DT (*Definition Term*) tag to denote the terms, and the DD (Definition Description) tag to denote the definitions. Set up a short glossary now (see Figure 2-18):

```
<DL>

<DT>Appeal

<DD>A proceeding by which the decision of a lower court
may be appealed to a higher court.

<DT>Arrest

<DD>The legal apprehension and restraint of someone charged
with a crime so that they might be brought before a court
to stand trial.

<DT>Bail

<DD>A security offered to a court in exchange for a person's
release and as assurance of their appearance in court when
required.

</DL>
```

DT (Definition Term)

DD (Definition Description)

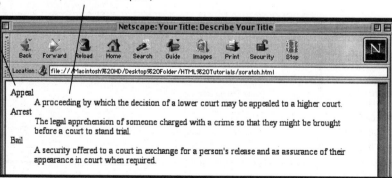

Figure 2.18

A glossary is created using three tags: the DL (Definition List), DT (Definition Term), and DD (Definition Description) tags.

As you've probably noticed, the end tags for the DT (Definition Term) and DD (Definition Description) tags are implied, as is the case for the LI (List Item) tag in a regular list. The only difference is that a glossary or definition list has a two-part item (both a term and a definition) rather than a one-part item; as long as you keep this in mind you should have no trouble creating definition lists. By itself, a glossary is a bit bland; you can dress it up by adding emphasis or tagging the definition terms with a heading tag. Here's an example of adding bold italic emphasis to a definition term:

```
<DT><I><B>Appeal</B></I>
```

Here's an example of tagging a definition term using an H3 heading tag:

```
<DT><H3>Appeal</H3>
```

Creating Hypertext Links

One of the main reasons to create a Web page is to create links to other pages, right? To do that, you need to know how to use the A (Anchor) tag. If you've surfed the Web at all, you should be quite familiar with hypertext links. You've probably used hypertext links not only to jump to and view another Web page, or jump to a specific place in either the same or another Web page, but to read a Gopher file, display an image, download a program, send an e-mail message, play an audio or video clip, run a script, access a database, telnet to a server, and so on. You can use hypertext links to jump to anything that has an address on the Internet (not just on the Web), as long as you don't need a password; of course, what happens after you make the jump depends on where you go.

In a sense, the Web is a kind of giant "What's behind door #3?" game; this perhaps helps explain much of its basic appeal. It's all quite easy and transparent: just click and go. However, explaining how to make this happen on your Web page isn't nearly as easy or transparent. This section will make the A (Anchor) tag as clear as possible. Here are the three basic kinds of hypertext links:

- **Links to other HTML documents or data objects.** These are by far the most commonly used links on the Web. They allow you to jump from one Web page to another, as well as to anything else that has an address on the Net, such as Gopher files, FTP archives, images, and so on.

- **Links to other places in the same HTML document.** These links allow you to jump from one place in a Web page to another point on the same Web page. Many Web pages have directories or "tables of contents" at the beginning of the page, allowing you to decide which part of the page you want to view. You simply click on the link to jump to that section of the page or document.

- **Links to places in other HTML documents.** These links are quite similar to links to places in the same document, except that you can jump to certain sections on other pages. If you've clicked on a hypertext link and then jumped to some point halfway down another Web page, you've used this type of link.

Anatomy of the A (Anchor) Tag

You use the A (Anchor) tag to anchor one or both ends of a hypertext link. The first kind of link, where you link to another Web page or data object, requires only one anchor. The second and third kinds of links, where you link to another place in the same or another Web page, require both ends of the link—that is, both a launch pad and a landing spot. This other end of a hypertext link, where you link a specific place in the same or another Web page, is often called a *target anchor*. Think of a hypertext link as being composed of the following three elements:

- Start and end tags that enclose the whole link

- The link target

- The link text

In Figure 2-19, the HREF (Hypertext Reference) attribute specifies the URL or address of the object of the link, which here is simply another Web page. Note that the full address (URL) is not given, just the file name. This means that the object of the link, most commonly another Web page, is located in the same folder as the Web page from which the link is being made. If you want to make a link with a Web page somewhere else on the Web, you have to include the full URL: for example, specify http://www.somewhere.com/somepage.html, rather than just the file name (somepage.html).

When using the A (Anchor) tag, you must include either an HREF attribute or a NAME attribute. If you're linking to another Web page or some other data object, you only need to use *one* anchor tag with an HREF attribute. If you're linking to a location in the same or another Web page, you need to use *two* anchor tags: the first with an HREF attribute defining the take-off location, and the second with the NAME attribute defining the target location.

If you find this a bit confusing, don't worry—at first it is. The following sections provide some hands-on examples of creating the three kinds of links, as well as using both the HREF and NAME attributes. Hopefully, learning by doing will go a long way toward dissipating your confusion.

Figure 2-19

A hypertext link has three parts: the start and end tags, the link target, and the link text.

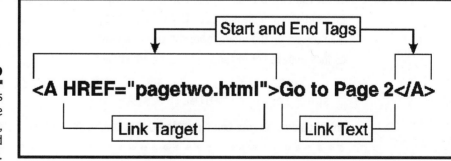

Linking to a File or Data Object

You can form an HTML link to anything on the Web that has an address. To create a hypertext link that jumps to a file that's somewhere on the Web (as opposed to in a folder in your own Web site), include the whole URL of the file to which you want to jump. Here's an example hypertext link that jumps to a real page on the Web (see Figure 2-20):

```
<P>Find out more about the Web at the <A HREF= "http://
www.w3.org/">W3 Consortium</A>.</P>
```

NOTE Most Web servers recognize one or more file names that specify a file that will automatically be opened in a browser, without having to be specified in the URL. Most commonly this is index.html, but it might also be index.htm, welcome.html, default.html, and so on. This is often called an *index page*. For instance, for my own Web site, **http://www.callihan.com/** and **http://www.callihan.com/index.html** are actually the same URL.

After you click on the hypertext link for the W3 Consortium, you will see the organization's home page, which will look like what is shown in Figure 2-21.

CAUTION When you type a URL (or Web address) in a hypertext link, you need to be aware that folder names and file names on UNIX computer systems are case sensitive. Because most Web servers on the Internet are still UNIX systems, you should always type URLs *exactly* as they appear. For instance, in the hypertext link

```
<A HREF="http://www.w3.org/MarkUp/html-spec/html-
spec_toc.html">HTML 2.0</A>
```

you should make sure you type "MarkUp" as it appears, and not as "markup."

Figure 2-20

The underlining indicates a hypertext link to the home page of the W3 Consortium.

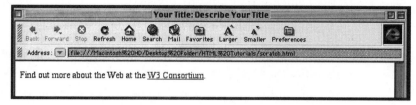

Linking to Non-Web Files

Your browser should be able to directly display any text file or GIF or JPEG graphic on a Web, FTP, or Gopher server. Other kinds of files, such as sound, animation, and video files, may require viewers or players. Real-Audio and Shockwave allow audio and animation clips to be *streamed* (played while being downloaded) rather than downloaded first and then played.

Linking to a Location in the Same HTML File

Linking to another location in the same HTML file requires two anchors: an HREF anchor and a NAME anchor. The HREF anchor creates the link (the taking-off spot), and the NAME anchor specifies the landing spot. An

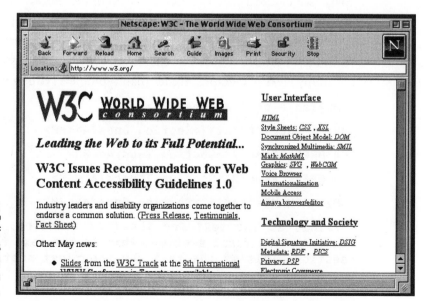

Figure 2-21

The home page of the W3C appears when you click on the link shown in Figure 2.20.

HREF anchor that links to a NAME anchor has a special form:

```
<A HREF="#anchorname">anchortext</A>
```

Notice the # sign. In an HREF anchor, the # sign is the only thing that identifies the HREF attribute value as the name of a NAME anchor rather than an address or file name. (The # sign combined with the following anchor name is sometimes called a *fragment identifier*.) The following are some of the more common uses for linking HREF and NAME anchors on the same page:

- Creating a directory or table of contents that links to the major headings of a page

- Creating "loop-back" links that jump back to the top of a page or to the table of contents at the top of a page

- Making cross-references between different points in the same Web page

- Forming links to footnotes or endnotes

The following is an example of creating a menu or table of contents for the top of a Web page, to link to subsections located lower on the same Web page (see Figure 2-22). I've included a lot of repetitious "dummy" text (the example subsections need to cover a certain amount of vertical space if you're going to be able to test out how the table of contents works in your browser). Feel free to make liberal use of copying and pasting to create the "dummy" text paragraphs, rather than typing everything in from scratch.

```
<H2>Table of Contents</H2>
<P><A HREF="#sect1">Section One</A><BR>
<A HREF="#sect2">Section Two</A><BR>
<A HREF="#sect3">Section Three</A></P>
<H2><A NAME="sect1">Section One</A></H2>
<P>This is the text for the first section. This is the
text for the first section. This is the text for the first
section. This is the text for the first section.</P>
```

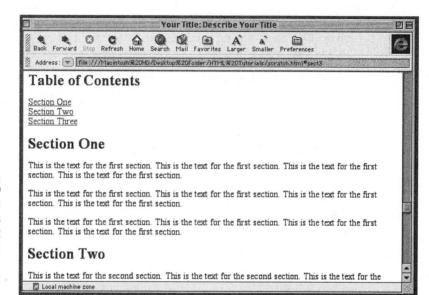

Figure 2-22

You can create a
table of contents
using hypertext
links that will
jump to subhead-
ings within
your document.

```
<P>This is the text for the first section. This is the
text for the first section. This is the text for the first
section. This is the text for the first section.</P>

<P>This is the text for the first section. This is the
text for the first section. This is the text for the first
section. This is the text for the first section.</P>

<H2><A NAME="sect2">Section Two</A></H2>

<P>This is the text for the second section. This is the text
for the second section. This is the text for the second
section. This is the text for the second section.</P>

<P>This is the text for the second section. This is the text
for the second section. This is the text for the second
section. This is the text for the second section.</P>

<P>This is the text for the second section. This is the text
for the second section. This is the text for the second
section. This is the text for the second section.</P>

<H2><A NAME="sect3">Section Three</A></H2>

<P>This is the text for the third section. This is the
text for the third section. This is the text for the third
section. This is the text for the third section.</P>
```

```
<P>This is the text for the third section. This is the
text for the third section. This is the text for the third
section. This is the text for the third section.</P>
```

```
<P>This is the text for the third section. This is the
text for the third section. This is the text for the third
section. This is the text for the third section.</P>
```

Only the first section and the start of the second section are shown in the figure. Be sure to hop over to your browser and check out how the links in the table of contents work. (Don't, however, lengthen your browser window to contain all three subheadings—if you do that, you won't be able to see how the "hop" works from the link in the table of contents to the section subheading.)

Linking to a Location in Another HTML File

Linking to a location in another HTML file is almost the same as linking to a location in the same HTML file. Both work the same way, except in the second instance, the NAME anchor (your landing spot) is placed in an entirely different file from the one where the link is being made. Here's the form for an HREF anchor that links to a place in another HTML file:

```
<A HREF="address#anchorname">anchortext</A>
```

This actually combines the forms for linking to another page and linking to a place on a page. The first part of the A tag (#*address*) links to the address of another Web page, whereas the second part (#*anchorname*) links to a place in that page marked by the specified anchor name. As an example, create a hypertext link that jumps to a place in another HTML file (see Figure 2-23):

```
<P>Go to <A HREF="links.html#part2">Part Two</A> of the
<A HREF="links.html">How to Use Links</A> page.</P>
```

I've created a file, links.html, that's included with the example files in the HTML Tutorials folder you copied to your Desktop this morning. If you click the "Part Two" link shown in Figure 2-23, you'll hop to the corresponding section of the links.html file, as shown in Figure 2-24. (Just click the Back button to return to your scratch pad file, scratch.html.)

Figure 2-23

The first link jumps to a place in the "How to Use Links" Web page, and the second link jumps to the Webpage itself.

Don't forget that in order to hop to a location in another page, the location you're hopping to has to be marked with an A tag using a NAME attribute that matches the fragment identifier (or anchor name) in the link you're jumping from. For example, the following is the anchor name that you jumped to in links.html:

```
<H2><A NAME="part2">Part Two</A></H2>
```

Creating Link Lists

So far, the discussion has focused on creating lists and creating links, but it hasn't explained creating *link lists*. A link list is a list of hypertext links, usually bulleted but sometimes numbered. Because link lists are so

Figure 2-24

A hypertext link can jump to a place, marked by a NAME anchor, that is located in the middle of another HTML file.

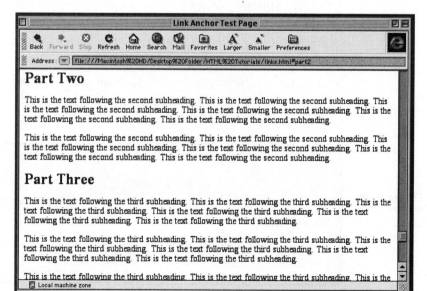

ubiquitous, everybody should know how to create them. For the example, you'll create a short list of links that link to some yo-yo Web sites. Type the following link list example (see Figure 2-25):

```
<H2>Yo-Yo Links</H2>

<UL>

<LI><A HREF="http://pages.nyu.edu/~tqm3413/yoyo/">Tomer's
Page of Exotic Yo-Yo</A>. A great Yo-Yo resource page.

<LI><A HREF="http://www.socool.com/socool/yo-yo.html">Just
Say YO!!!</A> Features the Web's first Yo-Yo animation.

<LI><A  HREF="http://www.pd.net/yoyo/">American  Yo-Yo
Association</A> Read past issues of the AYYA Newsletter.

</UL>
```

You don't have to include descriptions following your links. I like to keep the link text fairly succinct, while providing extra descriptive text following the link.

Using Inline Images

The IMG (Image) tag allows you to display *inline* images on your Web page. The term "inline" here means that an image is inserted at a particular location in a line within a Web page. You should stick to using images in either GIF or JPEG format; these two, the most commonly used formats, tend to serve different purposes. GIF images use a palette of up to 256 colors, can be interlaced and transparent, and can also be animated (include

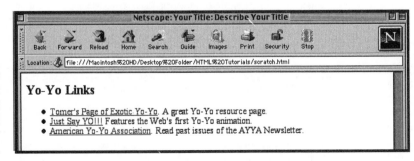

Figure 2.25

You create a link list by combining hypertext links and an unordered list (or bulleted list).

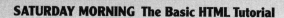

multiple image frames). JPEG images use a palette of up to 16.7 million colors, but they can't be transparent. Newer image editors may also be able to save a "progressive" JPEG, somewhat similar to an interlaced GIF, but older browsers don't support them. The general rule of thumb is that you should consider using JPEG images for photographic images or for images that include gradient fill, blend, or blur effects. If you save these images as GIF images, you may see significant dithering or color banding effects. For non-photographic images and images that don't include gradient fill, blend, or blur effects, saving your image as a GIF image may be your best bet. If you want your image to display transparently against a Web page's background color or background image, then you'll have to save it as a GIF image.

There is also another officially-approved image format, the PNG image format, that combines the best of both GIF and JPEG images. It uses a palette of up to 48 million colors, and supports transparency and progressivity. Support for this image format is still very spotty, even in the latest browsers, so you should probably avoid using it for now.

NOTE

When saving GIF or JPEG files that you want to use in Web pages, always be sure to add the file extensions. Without the file extensions, Windows and UNIX systems won't be able to identify their file types. When you save a GIF image for use on the Web, always type **.gif** at the end of the file name (myimage.gif, for instance). When you save a JPEG image for use on the Web, always type **.jpg** at the end of the file name (myimage.jpg). Also, make sure you eliminate any spaces in file names for images you want to use on the Web.

It would be premature at this point to get too deep into all of the ins and outs of creating images for display on the Web. In the Sunday Evening bonus session, "Creating Your Own Web Images," I'll be covering the different issues involved in creating your own Web images in much more detail.

Using the IMG (Image) Tag

The IMG (Image) tag is an empty, or standalone, element. It is also an inline element, rather than a block element, so it will display exactly where you put it, even in the middle of a line of text. Here is the general form of the IMG tag:

```
<IMG SRC="imagefile">
```

The SRC (Source) attribute is a required attribute. It identifies the address of the image to be displayed, which can be either a full URL (such as SRC="http://www.myserver.com/myimage.gif") or a partial Web address (you'll learn about using partial Web addresses, also called "relative URLs," in this afternoon's session). If the image file is saved in the same folder as your HTML file, you only need to include its file name as the SRC value (SRC="myimage.gif", for instance).

Until you get a little more experienced with HTML, I recommend that you save all of your HTML files and image files in the same folder; doing so will make linking to other HTML files and displaying inline images a lot simpler. Later, when you get a little more experienced, you can try your hand at using partial URLs, also called *relative URLs*; these allow you to link between files residing in different folders in your Web site, without having to specify the full URL for each. Now, insert an inline image, sample.gif, into your HTML file:

```
<P>An inline image, sample.gif, is displayed here: <IMG
SRC="sample.gif"></P>
```

Notice that the IMG tag follows a P (Paragraph) tag. That's because the IMG tag inserts an *inline* image—therefore, if you want an image to be displayed on its own line, you'll need to nest it inside its own P element (or other block element that starts a new text block). Figure 2-26 shows what this should look like in your Web browser.

Figure 2-26

All graphical
Web browsers
can display
inline images.

 NOTE

If the inline image, sample.gif, isn't showing up in your browser as shown in Figure 2-26, the most likely reason is that your HTML file (scratch.html) and the image file (sample.gif) are not saved in the same folder. As long as you've dragged and dropped the HTML Tutorials folder from the CD-ROM to your Desktop and then saved your HTML file in that folder, any of the example inline images used in this (or the next) session should show up in your browser.

Using the ALT Attribute in Inline Images

The ALT attribute can be included in the IMG tag to help identify an image. Because surfing the Web can often be more like wading through hip-deep molasses, a lot of people surf the Web with the display of images turned off in order to help speed things up. What's more, many people still use text-based browsers, such as Lynx, that don't display images at all. There are also people who are visually impaired who may want to peruse your page using a Braille or a speech browser. Using the ALT attribute will cue any of these surfers in on what an image contains or what its function is.

To create the example, copy and paste the previous example, so you have two copies of it (or you can just retype the previous example on the following line). Next, edit the copy so it matches what's shown here:

```
<P>An inline image, sample.gif, is displayed here: <IMG
SRC="sample.gif"></P>

<P>An inline image, sample.gif, is displayed here: <IMG
SRC="sample.gif" ALT="A Sample Graphic"></P>
```

Feel free to save your file and then to hop over to your browser to check out what this looks like with the display of images turned off. To turn the display of images off in Internet Explorer 4.0, choose Preferences from the Edit menu, click Web Content (in the list on the left), and then uncheck the Show Pictures check box. Click OK and then click the Refresh button. To turn the display of images off in Netscape Navigator 4.0, choose Edit from the Preferences menu, click Advanced (in the list on the left), and then uncheck the top check box (Automatically load images and other data types). Click OK and then click the Reload button. Figure 2-27 shows what the example looks like in Netscape Navigator with display of images turned off. To turn the display of images back on, just retrace your steps and recheck the appropriate check box.

NOTE

If an image is decorative and serves no informational purpose, use the ALT attribute with a blank attribute value (ALT=" ").That way, you don't clutter up a Web page in a text-only browser with [Image] references. If you're using bullet icons to create a bullet list, you might include an ALT="*" attribute value, which will allow the images to continue to function as bullets, even with images turned off.

If your graphic has informational import, you should always include an ALT attribute text string: for example, ALT="Georgy-Porgy's Home Page" or ALT="Diagram of the X-27P Circuit Board" (or something like that). Including an ALT attribute will not only allow somebody using a text-only browser or a graphical Web browser with graphics turned off to know what's going on, but also make things easier for a visually impaired person using a Braille or speech browser.

Using the ALIGN Attribute in Inline Graphics

The ALIGN attribute allows you to position an inline image relative to the line of text it's on. All current graphical Web browsers should recognize the values "top," "middle," and "bottom." Insert an inline graphic using the "top" ALIGN value (see Figure 2-28):

Figure 2-27

SAMPLE.GIF is shown here, first without the ALT attribute and then with the ALT attribute, as displayed in Navigator with the display of images turned off.

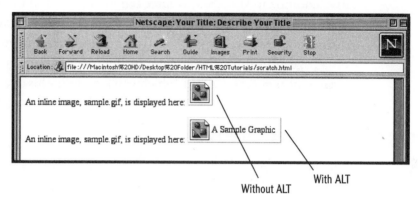

Without ALT

With ALT

```
<P>The image on this line <IMG ALIGN="top" SRC="top.gif">
is top-aligned.</P>
```

Here's an example of the "middle" ALIGN value:

```
<P>The  image  on  this  line  <IMG  ALIGN="middle"
SRC="middle.gif"> is middle-aligned.</P>
```

Insert an inline graphic using the "bottom" ALIGN value:

```
<P>The  image  on  this  line  <IMG  ALIGN="bottom"
SRC="bottom.gif"> is bottom-aligned.</P>
```

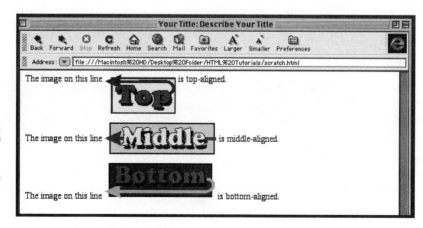

Figure 2-28

Inline images can be aligned relative to the baseline of the line on which they appear.

Two additional ALIGN attributes can be included in the IMG tag: "left" and "right." These attributes are HTML 3.2 attributes; they are used to wrap text around an image, rather than to merely align an image horizontally on a page. To simply center-align or right-align an image on a page, you need to use another method, which you'll cover in this afternoon's tutorial.

Using Horizontal Rules

The HR (Horizontal Rule) tag is a standalone element that allows you to add horizontal rules to your Web pages. To add a horizontal rule to your page, insert the following example (see Figure 2-29):

```
<P>A horizontal rule is displayed below this line.</P>
<HR>
```

Signing Your Work

HTML has a special tag, the ADDRESS tag, that is used to include information about the author or owner of a Web page, as well as information on how to contact the author or provide feedback. A horizontal rule usually separates an address from the rest of a Web page.

You can really put anything you want in your address section. If your Web page is for a business, you may want to include your name, title, company name, mailing address, and phone and fax numbers. Additionally, you might want to include your e-mail address and the URL of your business' home

Figure 2-29

Horizontal rules
are often used
in Web pages
as separators.

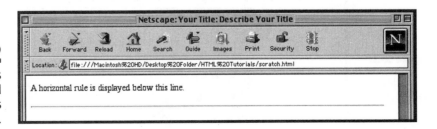

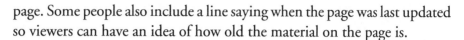

page. Some people also include a line saying when the page was last updated so viewers can have an idea of how old the material on the page is.

If you're just putting up your own personal, non-business page, you probably won't want to put up your street address or mailing address, but you should provide some means for visitors to your site to give you feedback on your page. Hey, that's half the fun of creating your own Web site: getting lots of great feedback. Visitors to your site can also let you know if there are errors on your page or when any link rot has begun to set in. The most common way of providing a means for visitors to give you feedback is to include a mailto link to your e-mail address.

Following the HR tag you created in the last example, type some address text separated into individual lines by BR tags. If you're creating a personal page, just type your name, followed by a BR tag; if you're creating a business page, type your name, company name, and phone number, following each line with a BR tag (see Figure 2-30):

```
<HR>
```

<ADDRESS>

*Type your name here
*

*Optionally, type your company name here
*

*Optionally, type your area code and phone number here
*

</ADDRESS>

```
</HTML>
```

Figure 2-30

The address section of a Web page is used to tell your visitors how they can contact you.

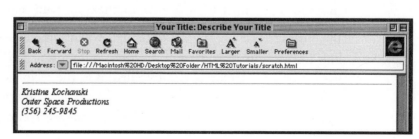

Adding a Mailto Link to Your Address

The most common way to provide visitors to your site with a way to contact you is to include what is called a *mailto link* in your address block. When a user clicks a mailto link, the browser pops up a form that allows the reader to send a message to the e-mail address in the link. To add a mailto link to your e-mail address, add the following:

```
<HR>
```

```
<ADDRESS>
```

```
Your name<BR>
```

```
Your company name (optional)<BR>
```

```
Your phone number(optional)<BR>
```

**E-Mail: <A HREF="mailto:*type your e-mail address*">*type your e-mail address*</A>
**

```
</ADDRESS>
```

Note that it's best to insert your e-mail address twice—it must follow "mailto:" (as it will not be a mailto link otherwise), and it should be repeated as the link text if you want readers to see your e-mail address rather than, for instance, "Click here to reach me via e-mail." This is because there are still a lot of people using browsers that don't support mailto links. Internet Explorer 3.0 requires that Internet Mail be installed, and Internet Explorer 4.0 requires that you have Outlook Express installed. Even if your browser supports mailto links, your e-mail program still has to be configured properly to send outgoing mail. No matter which way you cut it, you're going to have viewers who can't use your mailto link. The solution is to make sure that your full e-mail address is the link text for your mailto link.

In a browser that supports mailto links, when someone clicks on a mailto link to your e-mail address, a message composition window will pop up with your e-mail address already filled in as the recipient of the message. The user just has to type a message and click the Send button. Figure 2-31 shows a mailto link added to a Web page's address section.

Figure 2-31

Adding a mailto
link to your address
block is one way
to give visitors to
your site a way
to contact you.

```
                    Netscape: Your Title: Describe Your Title
  Back   Forward  Reload   Home   Search  Guide  Images  Print  Security  Stop        N

  Location:  file:///Macintosh%20HD/Desktop%20Folder/HTML%20Tutorials/scratch.html

  Kristine Kochanski
  Outer Space Productions
  (356) 245-9845
  E-Mail:   kkochanski@outerspaceprod.com
```

SPAM

Unfortunately, someone always comes along to spoil the party—in this case, the spammer. As a defensive measure against getting spammed, some people avoid posting either their name or e-mail address on their Web pages, providing only a guest book to allow visitors to give them feedback. Using a guest book instead of your name and e-mail address can also be a good way to help shield any children using your e-mail account from receiving pornographic, violent, or other undesirable spam messages. AOL users have to be particularly careful about revealing their screen names or other personal information (in chat rooms or message boards), because a spammer can get access to their information in AOL's member directory.

I've got my name and e-mail address on dozens of Web pages and only get what I consider to be a moderate amount (a half-dozen messages a day) of spam, most originating from providing my e-mail address in online forms (which I've stopped doing). A reader from Brazil recently posted my e-mail address on his page, and ever since, I've gotten a slow but steady trickle of spam in Portuguese!

Spam has a certain look and feel, regardless of the language. In most cases, you can identify spam by looking at the subject line. I'd hate to see everybody with a Web page end up concealing their identities and e-mail addresses, just to counter spam—such a cure would be worse than the disease, I believe. Openness is a large part of what makes the Web such a great place. Most people don't want to hide behind masks and pseudonyms—they want to be seen, read, and known. I know I do!

One alternative is to get a free Web-based e-mail address (commonly referred to as a *Web Mail* address) through Hotmail, Yahoo, NetCenter, or some other Web Mail provider. Post that e-mail address on your Web pages. You could also use it in any chat rooms that you frequent, or type it in any online forms you have to fill out. Then, if that address starts to get overly spammed, just get another one! If you're concerned about having to continually update your pages with new e-mail addresses, use a link to a contact page instead—that way, you'll only have to update it in one place. You can give real visitors (not spammers) your permanent (unpublished) e-mail address when you reply to them, so they can add it to their address books, if they wish. If you're concerned about hackers, crackers, and spoofers being able to harvest your e-mail address directly from your e-mail messages, just add "HATES SPAM" to your e-mail address (yournameHATES SPAM@yourdomain.com), or something similar, instructing the recipient to remove "HATES SPAM" when they reply.

Adding Your URL to Your Address

Once you get your Web pages up on the Web, you should include your URL (the Web address of your home page) in your address section (although your may want to skip this on your actual home page). To do this, just include a hypertext link to your home page. Because you probably don't have a home page yet, just enter the following example URL (see Figure 2-32):

```
<HR>
```

```
<ADDRESS>
```

Your name

Your company name (optional)

Your phone number (optional)

E-Mail: <A HREF="mailto:*type your e-mail address*">*type your e-mail address*</A>**
**

URL: <A HREF="http://www.yourserver.com/yoursite/">www.yourserver.com/yoursite/</A>

```
</ADDRESS>
```

Figure 2-32

You can include
your name,
company name,
phone number, an
e-mail link, your
URL, as well as
any other contact
information you
want to add to the
bottom of your page.

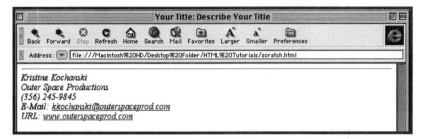

Saving Your Work

Save the HTML file you just created. When you first saved it, you named it scratch.html. If other users are going to be doing this tutorial and you want to make sure this file doesn't get overwritten, you might want to give it a new name. For instance, you could use your initials as part of the file name (jc_scratch.html, for instance).

Wrapping Up

You should now have a pretty good understanding of basic HTML if you've completed all of the examples and successfully checked them out in your browser. You should also have a good grasp of what's involved in using a text editor and a browser to create and dynamically preview your HTML files.

The more HTML you do, the more comfortable you'll get. You've also saved your scratch pad file, so you can use it as a reference later. Feel free to load it into your text editor and view it in your Web browser to familiarize yourself with how a particular tag works.

If you have the time and energy left, I encourage you to go on and do the Intermediate HTML Tutorial that is scheduled for Saturday afternoon. When you create your first Web page Sunday afternoon, you'll refer to what you learn in the Intermediate HTML Tutorial to help to make your page more attractive and visually appealing.

Another option is to skip ahead to the Saturday Evening session, "Introduction to Adobe PageMill 3.0." You might prefer learning how to use a tool that is more "mouse-centric" than a text editor. Adobe PageMill is one of the more popular HTML editors available for the Macintosh. PageMill is included with the iMac; other Macintosh users can download a try-out version from Adobe. The Saturday Evening session covers using PageMill to implement most of the HTML features that were covered in this session, plus many of the features that are covered in the Saturday Afternoon session. So take a break, stand up and stretch those muscles, and grab some lunch. I'll see you back here in an hour!

The Intermediate HTML Tutorial

- ✿ Superscripts, subscripts, and underlining
- ✿ Aligning elements and wrapping text around images
- ✿ Creating complex sites using relative URLs
- ✿ Adding pizazz with 3-D icon bullets, font changes, and background colors and images

By now, you have finished the Basic HTML Tutorial. If you haven't, you should do so before continuing with this session. Doing the Intermediate HTML Tutorial is not required for you to be able to create your first Web page on Sunday, as everything that you need to know has already been covered in the Basic HTML Tutorial. At this point, you also have the option of skipping ahead and doing the Saturday Evening bonus session, "Introduction to Adobe PageMill 3.0." PageMill is an HTML editor that is bundled with the iMac (other Mac users can download an evaluation version).

 NOTE When you did the Basic HTML Tutorial this morning, you should have already copied the HTML Tutorials folder to your Desktop. This folder contains all of the example files you'll need to do this tutorial.

Which Browser Do You Need?

Because the Basic HTML Tutorial that you did this morning dealt with HTML 2.0, it wasn't very important which browser you used to do the tutorial; pretty much any graphical Web browser could handle it. If you want to be able to do everything that's covered in this tutorial, I recommend you use Internet Explorer version 4.0 or higher, or Netscape Navigator version 4.0 or higher to preview your results.

You should by now be fairly familiar with using a text editor and a Web browser in combination to create, edit, and preview your HTML files. Feel free to go back and review the first parts of the Basic HTML Tutorial if you need to refresh your memory of the steps required to do that.

Getting Started

To get started with the Intermediate HTML tutorial, do the following:

1. If it isn't already open, run your text editor (SimpleText, for instance).

2. If it isn't already open, run the Web browser you'll be using to preview your work.

3. In your text editor, open the starting template, **startpage.html**, that you saved in the Basic HTML Tutorial. You should find it in the HTML Tutorials folder on your Desktop. (If you didn't save a starting template, you can just retype the codes as shown below.)

4. Resave your starting template as **scratch2.html** (in the HTML Tutorials folder).

Your new "scratch pad" file should look like the following listing:

```
<HTML>
<HEAD>
<TITLE>Your Title: Describe Your Title</TITLE>
</HEAD>
<BODY>
</BODY>
</HTML>
```

Working with Text

This section covers some special things you can do when working with text. These involve using some HTML 3.2 and HTML 4.0 text highlighting tags. I will also cover right-aligning and center-aligning paragraphs, headings, and other document sections.

Using HTML 3.2 Text Highlighting Tags

HTML 3.2 recognizes a number of additional tags for highlighting text, including the SUP (Superscript), SUB (Subscript), U (Underline), and STRIKE (Strikethrough) tags.

The SUP and SUB tags are highly useful tags supported by current browsers that you should use wherever you need superscripts or subscripts. The STRIKE command comes in handy mainly for using the Web or an intranet in workgroup document preparation processes, rather than for displaying final renditions. Adding underlining in HTML files doesn't make much sense; underlining is mostly a convention from the old typewriter days, when it was used to emphasize text. If you want to emphasize text, use the I or EM tags instead. If you want to check out how these tags look in your browser, enter the following (inside the BODY element):

```
<BODY>

<P>This is regular text. <SUP>Use SUP for superscripts.
</SUP> This is regular text. <SUB>Use SUB for subscripts.
</SUB> This is regular text. <U>Use U for underlining.
</U> This is regular text. <STRIKE>Use STRIKE for
strikethrough.</STRIKE></P>

</BODY>
```

To check this out in your browser, first save your file, and then hop over to your browser and open scratch2.html. If you need a refresher on how to do this, here's a quick rundown:

1. Press Command-S (or choose Save from the File menu) to save your HTML file.

2. Bring your browser to the foreground. If your browser's window is visible, just click on it to do this. You can also select it from the Applications menu at the far right of the menu bar. Another option is to use the Alt-Tab keyboard shortcut (just hold down the Alt key and tap the Tab key to cycle through all of your open applications; lift off when your browser comes to the foreground).

3. In Internet Explorer, choose Open file from the File Menu. In Netscape Navigator, choose Open Page from the File menu. Open scratch2.html from the HTML Tutorials folder. Figure 3-1 shows how this appears in an HTML 3.2–compliant Web browser.

NOTE

You may want to increase the size of your browser's text font to make the examples easier to see. In Internet Explorer 4.0+, just click the Larger button on the toolbar; this is reset to the default each time you run Internet Explorer. If you reset Navigator's font size in the Basic HTML Tutorial, it should still be set at 14 points; if you haven't reset it yet, just choose Preferences from the Edit menu, click on Fonts (in the Category list), and then change the font size settings to 14.

If you're using Netscape Navigator and if you want what you see in Navigator to match what's shown in the figures, you should make sure the default background color is set to white (Navigator's default is gray). Just choose Preferences from the Edit menu, click Colors (in the Category list), and then click the Background color rectangle. To select white as the background color, click the Crayon Picker icon on the left, and then click the white crayon in the upper-left corner. Click OK.

Figure 3-1

In HTML 3.2, you can add superscripting, subscripting, underlining, and strikethrough to text.

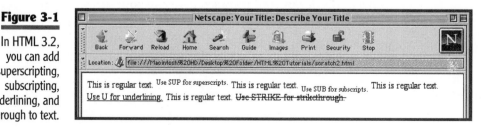

Browsers that aren't HTML 3.2–compliant generally won't display superscripts or subscripts. To account for these browsers, you may want to enclose superscripts or subscripts within parentheses to set them apart from preceding or following text. To include a superscripted trademark symbol, you might type:

```
Xerox<SUP>(TM)</SUP>
```

That way, it appears in Lynx as "Xerox(TM)" rather than as "XeroxTM." (The tradeoff here is that in a browser that does support superscripting you're stuck with the parentheses.)

Using HTML 4.0 Text Highlighting Tags

A number of new text highlighting tags have been incorporated in HTML 4.0. These include the DEL (Delete), INS (Insert), S (Strikethrough), and SPAN tags. Browser support for these tags is still a bit sketchy. Internet Explorer 4.0+ and Netscape Navigator 4.0+ both support the S and SPAN tags. Internet Explorer 4.0+ supports the DEL and INS tags, but Netscape Navigator 4.0+ doesn't.

The DEL (Delete) and INS (Insert) Tags

The DEL and INS tags allow you to mark deletions and insertions in an HTML file. Enter the following code for an example of using these tags (see Figure 3-2):

Figure 3-2

In HTML 4.0, you can mark deletions and insertions, but this only works in Internet Explorer 4.0+.

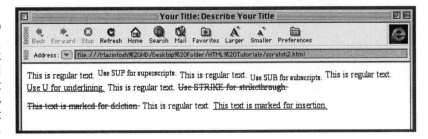

```
<P><DEL>This text is marked for deletion.</DEL> This is
regular text. <INS>This text is marked for insertion.
</INS></P>
```

The DEL and INS tags are rendered by Internet Explorer 4.0+ exactly like the STRIKE and U tags. However, you can define separate styles for these tags that will give them a unique appearance. Most likely these two tags will be useful at some point for software designed for the production and maintenance of HTML documents within a workgroup setting; the two attributes for these tags, CITE and DATETIME, are most likely intended for such use.

The S (Strikethrough) Tag

A browser supporting the S (Strikethrough) tag should display it exactly the same way as it does the STRIKE or DEL tag. STRIKE is the better choice for rendering strikethrough text, in that it's more likely to be supported by both older and newer browsers, while the S tag is supported only by the latest browsers.

TIP

Nothing stops you from using a scattergun approach to snag as many browsers as possible. For instance, `<DEL><STRIKE><S>`*strikeout text*`</S></STRIKE></DEL>` will render strikeout text in any browser that supports any of these tags.

The SPAN Tag

The SPAN tag is an inline element that functions just like any of the other inline text highlighting elements. By itself the SPAN tag does absolutely nothing. Its real value comes to light when it is mated with a style sheet. Later in this tutorial, in "Seeing What Styles Can Do," you'll apply a style to the SPAN tag.

Aligning Headings, Paragraphs, and Divisions

You can align paragraphs, headings, and other document divisions in a number of ways in HTML 3.2. In the following section, you'll learn how to do this using ALIGN attributes, the CENTER tag, and the DIV tag.

Aligning Headings and Paragraphs

You can center or right-align headings and paragraphs by including an attribute value of `ALIGN="center"` or `ALIGN="right"` in one of the heading-level tags or in a P tag. For instance, to center a level-two heading, you code your heading like this:

```
<H2 ALIGN="center">Your Heading Here</H2>
```

You right-align a level-two heading, like this:

```
<H2 ALIGN="right">Your Heading Here</H2>
```

You center or right-align paragraph text in exactly the same way as headings. For instance, to center a text paragraph, you code your paragraph like this:

```
<P ALIGN="center">Your paragraph text here.</P>
```

You would right-align a text paragraph like this:

```
<P ALIGN="right">Your paragraph text here.</P>
```

To see what this looks like in your browser, enter the following code, save your file, and then hop over to your browser to check it out (feel free to copy and paste to create the paragraph text):

```
<H2 ALIGN="right">This Heading Is Right-Aligned</H2>

<P ALIGN="right">This paragraph is right-aligned.
This paragraph is right-aligned. This paragraph is
right-aligned. This paragraph is right-aligned. This
paragraph is right-aligned. This paragraph is right-
aligned. This paragraph is right-aligned. This
paragraph is right-aligned.</P>

<H2 ALIGN="center">This Heading Is Center-Aligned</H2>
```

```
<P ALIGN="center">This paragraph is center-aligned.
This paragraph is center-aligned. This paragraph is
center-aligned. This paragraph is center-aligned. This
paragraph is center-aligned. This paragraph is center-
aligned. This paragraph is center-aligned. This para-
graph is center-aligned.</P>
```

Figure 3-3 shows how this appears in a Web browser that supports horizontal alignment of headings and paragraphs. Netscape Navigator doesn't quite right-flush the last line in a paragraph. This is a long-standing bug in Navigator (both in the Mac and Windows versions) that you'll just have to live with if you want to use this feature.

Using the CENTER Tag

One of the advantages of the CENTER tag, which is supported by all current browsers, is that you can center more than one element. Here's an example of using a single CENTER tag to center a heading, a text paragraph, and an unordered list (see Figure 3-4):

```
<CENTER>
```

```
<H2>Level-Two Heading</H2>
```

```
<P>This is some paragraph text. This is some paragraph
text. This is some paragraph text. This is some para-
graph text. This is some paragraph text. This is some
paragraph text.</P>
```

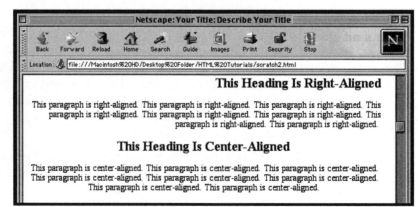

Figure 3-3

You can right-align or center headings and paragraphs.

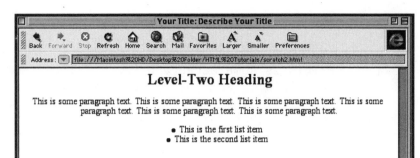

Figure 3-4

Using the CENTER tag, you can center multiple document elements.

```
<UL>
<LI>This is the first list item.
<LI>This is the second list item
</UL>
</CENTER>
```

Aligning Document Divisions

The DIV (Division) tag is an HTML 3.2 tag that defines a division within a document; within it, you can nest and align headings, paragraphs, unordered and ordered lists, definition lists, preformatted text, address blocks, tables, and even images. You can either center or right-align a document division using the DIV tag. To check out right-aligning a document division, copy and paste the codes for the last example, and then edit them to match what's shown here (see Figure 3-5):

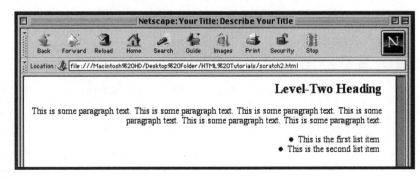

Figure 3-5

You can use the DIV tag to right-align (or center) a document division.

```
<DIV ALIGN="right">
```

```
<H2>Level-Two Heading</H2>
```

```
<P>This is some paragraph text. This is some paragraph
text. This is some paragraph text. This is some para-
graph text. This is some paragraph text. This is some
paragraph text.</P>
```

```
<UL>
```

```
<LI>This is the first list item
```

```
<LI>This is the second list item
```

```
</UL>
```

```
</DIV>
```

You can use the DIV tag to right-align (or center) a document division.

To center a document division, just use an `ALIGN="center"` attribute value in the DIV tag. If you use this tag, you should be aware that it is less likely to be supported by older browsers than is the case with using the CENTER tag to center a grouping of document elements. Also, older browsers are more likely to support using the ALIGN attribute to individually center or right-align headings and paragraphs.

Working with Images

This section of the tutorial covers several additional things you can do with inline images. These include using a banner graphic, right-aligning or centering a graphic, wrapping text around a graphic, and creating image links.

Adding a Banner Graphic

A *banner graphic* is an inline image that runs along the top of your Web page. The following example uses a sample banner graphic that is included in the HTML Tutorials folder. To add the example banner graphic to your Web page, scroll to the top of your HTML file and add the following:

```
<BODY>
<P ALIGN="center"><IMG SRC="banner.jpg"></P>
<H1 ALIGN="center">The Intermediate HTML Tutorial</H1>
```

Even if your banner graphic takes up most or all of the screen, you should place it in a centered paragraph. That way, it will always be centered, regardless of the screen resolution. The example also includes a centered level-one heading, because it's fairly common for a banner graphic to be followed by the main heading for the page. You could also nest it all inside a CENTER tag to get the same effect, rather than using the ALIGN= "center" attribute values. Figure 3-6 shows how your page should look after you add the banner graphic.

Setting Image Height and Width

HTML 3.2 and HTML 4.0 allow you to specify the height and width of an inline image. Normally, a Web browser has to download an image before allocating space for it on a Web page. This means that if you have a relatively large graphic, everything else has to wait until the image downloads. A banner graphic, usually the largest graphic on your page, can be especially guilty of holding up the show.

By including HEIGHT and WIDTH attributes that specify the size of your image, a browser can allocate space for the image and then display the

Figure 3-6

A banner graphic runs across the top of a Web page.

remainder of the page without waiting for the image to download completely. Therefore, especially if it takes longer to load than it takes ice to melt, be gracious and set the height and width of your banner graphic. Here's how to add WIDTH and HEIGHT attributes to your banner graphic:

```
<P ALIGN="center"><IMG SRC="banner.jpg" WIDTH="595"
HEIGHT="135"></P>
```

The dimensions set here are the actual dimensions of the graphic. Using dimensions other than the actual ones provides no immediate advantage in this case. Using these attributes to reduce the displayable size of your image is a waste of bandwidth and should never be done. Using them to increase the displayable size of an image, on the other hand, is the waste of a good graphic.

◀ ◀

Bandwidth is the transmission capacity of a network, but also the amount of capacity being consumed by a single connection. A Web page containing many graphics will consume more bandwidth than one containing only text, for instance.

◀ ◀

Many Web gurus will tell you to set the WIDTH and HEIGHT attributes for all images you want to include in a Web page. I don't bother doing this for small graphics such as icon bullets, but I do include them in any other images. Note that I don't bother including these attributes in the other example images used in this tutorial, because the scratch pad file you're creating will only be viewed by you locally.

Using Width Percentages

You can also specify a percentage for the WIDTH attribute in the IMG tag. For example, to set a width of 75 percent, you would use a WIDTH= "75%" attribute value, like this:

```
<P ALIGN="center"><IMG SRC="banner.jpg" WIDTH="75%">
```

This will automatically resize the graphic so it fills 75 percent of the width of the browser window, regardless of the screen resolution or the width of the browser window. Generally, you should avoid doing this, although there are a few instances where setting a WIDTH percentage can be quite handy.

Horizontally Aligning Images

In the Basic HTML Tutorial, you used the ALIGN attribute to top-align, middle-align, and bottom-align text relative to an image. Two additional attribute values, ALIGN="left" and ALIGN="right", can be included in the IMG tag. These attributes, however, are *not* used to left-align or right-align an image on the page, but instead are used to wrap text around an image (you'll cover this technique a little later in this tutorial). To right-align an image (left-alignment is the default), you need to use an entirely different method.

Right-Aligning an Image Using the P Tag

The easiest way to right-align an inline image in a Web page is to nest it in a right-aligned paragraph. In your text editor, scroll back down to the end of your file, just above the </BODY> end tag, and enter the following line of code to right-align an image using paragraph alignment (Figure 3-7 shows how a right-aligned graphic looks in a Web browser that supports paragraph alignment):

```
<P ALIGN="right"><IMG SRC="right.gif"></P>
```

Figure 3-7

You can right-align an image in an HTML 3.2–compliant Web browser by placing it inside a right-aligned paragraph.

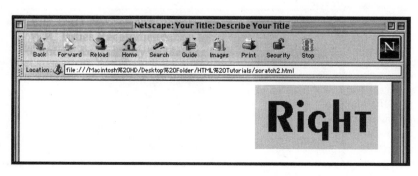

You can also right-align an image by nesting it inside a DIV tag that has an `ALIGN="right"` attribute value set. I recommend sticking to using a right-aligned paragraph for this purpose, since the chances are greater that older browsers will support it than is the case with using a right-aligned DIV tag.

Centering an Image

The IMG tag does not include an `ALIGN="center"` attribute value; if you do insert that attribute value in an IMG tag, it'll have absolutely no effect. As with right-aligning an inline image, there's more than one way to center an inline image. To center an image using paragraph alignment, enter this (Figure 3-8 shows how this appears in a Web browser that supports paragraph alignment):

```
<P ALIGN="center"><IMG SRC="center.gif"></P>
```

You can also center an inline image by nesting it inside a CENTER tag. Here's an example of how you would do that:

```
<CENTER><IMG SRC="center.gif"></CENTER>
```

You can also center an image by nesting it in a DIV tag with an `ALIGN="center"` attribute value. Since this is less likely to be supported by older browsers, I'd recommend sticking to using either a center-aligned paragraph or a CENTER tag.

Figure 3-8

You can center an image in an HTML 3.2–compliant Web browser by placing it inside a center-aligned paragraph.

Wrapping Text Around Images

Knowing how to wrap text around images is one of the keys to being able to create attractive and "flowing" Web page layouts. ALIGN="left" and ALIGN="right" allow you to do this. To wrap text around the right side of an image, you include the former in the IMG tag; to wrap text around the left side of an image, you include the latter.

Wrapping Text Around a Left-Aligned Image

Enter the following code as an example of wrapping text around a left-aligned image (feel free to use copy and paste to create the "dummy" text):

```
<P><IMG ALIGN="left" SRC="left.gif">If you set left-
alignment in an inline image, the text will wrap around
the right side of the image. If you set left-alignment
in an inline image, the text will wrap around the right
side of the image. If you set left-alignment in an
inline image, the text will wrap around the right side
of the image.<BR CLEAR="left"></P>
```

NOTE You'll learn about the `<BR CLEAR="left">` tag from the above example and similar tags used in the following examples in the "Clearing Images" section later this afternoon.

Wrapping Text Around a Right-Aligned Image

Enter the following code as an example of wrapping text around a right-aligned image (see Figure 3-9):

```
<P><IMG ALIGN="right" SRC="right.gif">If you set right-
alignment in an inline image, the text will wrap around
the left side of the graphic. If you set right-alignment
in an inline image, the text will wrap around the left
side of the graphic. If you set right-alignment in an
inline image, the text will wrap around the left side
of the graphic.<BR CLEAR="right"></P>
```

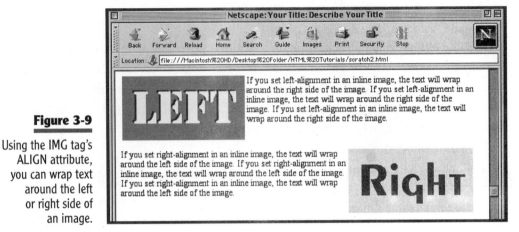

Figure 3-9

Using the IMG tag's ALIGN attribute, you can wrap text around the left or right side of an image.

Adding Spacing Between an Image and Wrapping Text

You may have noticed when you checked out the last example in your browser that there was little or no space between the image and the wrapping text. The HSPACE (Horizontal Space) attribute can be used to add space to both sides of an image. For an example of adding a horizontal space of 10 pixels to the images, edit the last two examples you created so they match what's shown here (see Figure 3-10):

```
<P><IMG ALIGN="left" SRC="left.gif" HSPACE="10">If you
set left-alignment in an inline image, the text will
wrap around the right side of the graphic. If you set
left-alignment in an inline image, the text will wrap
around the right side of the graphic. If you set left-
alignment in an inline image, the text will wrap around
the right side of the graphic.<BR CLEAR="left"></P>

<P><IMG ALIGN="right" SRC="right.gif" HSPACE="10">If you
set right-alignment in an inline image, the text will
wrap around the left side of the graphic. If you set
right-alignment in an inline image, the text will wrap
around the left side of the graphic. If you set right-
alignment in an inline image, the text will wrap around
the left side of the graphic.<BRCLEAR="right"></P>
```

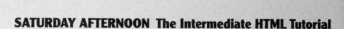

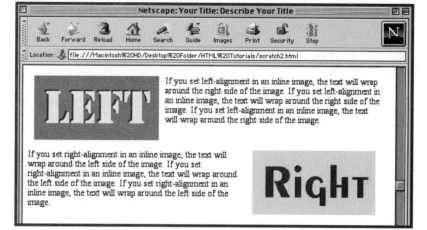

Figure 3-10

Using the IMG tag's HSPACE attribute, you can add space between an image and wrapping text.

Flowing Text Between Images

You not only can wrap text around the right or left side of an image, but you can flow text between two images as well. For example, enter the following code (see Figure 3-11):

```
<P><IMG SRC="left.gif" ALIGN="left" HSPACE="2"><IMG
SRC="right.gif" ALIGN="right" HSPACE="2">Text will flow
between a left-aligned and a right-aligned image. Text
will flow between a left-aligned and a right-aligned
image.<BR CLEAR="all"></P>
```

Figure 3-11

You can flow text between a left-aligned image and a right-aligned image in an HTML 3.2–compliant Web browser.

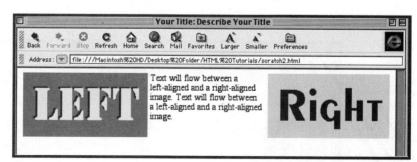

Flowing an Image Between Two Other Images

You can even flow a center-aligned image between a left-aligned image and a right-aligned image. For an example of how to do this, enter the following code:

```
<P><IMG SRC="one.gif" ALIGN="left"><IMG SRC="three.gif"
ALIGN="right"><P ALIGN="center"><IMG SRC="two.gif"><BR
CLEAR="all"></P>
```

Notice that two P (Paragraph) tags are used. The first one is used to hold the left- and right-aligned images (one.gif and three.gif), whereas the second is used to center-align the image that flows between the two other images (see Figure 3-12).

Clearing Images

The BR tag's CLEAR attribute, as its name indicates, is used to cause anything that follows to clear a horizontally aligned image. There are three CLEAR attribute values that can be included in a BR tag:

✿ `<BR CLEAR="left">` moves any following text down until the left margin is clear (is not obstructed by a left-aligned image).

✿ `<BR CLEAR="right">` moves any following text down until the right margin is clear (is not obstructed by a right-aligned image).

✿ `<BR CLEAR="all">` moves any following text down until both the left margin and the left margin are clear.

Figure 3-12

You can flow an image between a left-aligned image and a right-aligned image in an HTML 3.2-compliant Web browser.

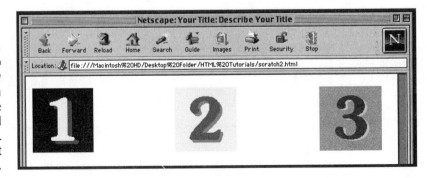

Clearing a Left-Aligned Image

To see how this works with a left-aligned image, go back to the example you created earlier for wrapping text around a left-aligned image, and move the `<BR CLEAR="left">` tag to the position shown here (or just retype the example shown here; see Figure 3-13):

```
<P><IMG ALIGN="left" SRC="left.gif" HSPACE="10">If you
set left-alignment in an inline image, the text will
wrap around the right side of the graphic. <BR CLEAR=
"left">If you set left-alignment in an inline image,
the text will wrap around the right side of the graphic.
If you set left-alignment in an inline image, the text
will wrap around the right side of the graphic.</P>
```

Clearing a Right-Aligned Image

To see how this works with a right-aligned image, go back to the example you created earlier for wrapping text around a right-aligned image and move the `<BR CLEAR="right">` tag to the position shown here (or just retype the example shown here; see Figure 3-14):

```
<P><IMG ALIGN="right" SRC="right.gif" HSPACE="10">If you
set right-alignment in an inline image, the text will
wrap around the left side of the graphic. <BR CLEAR=
"right">If you set right-alignment in an inline image,
the text will wrap around the left side of the graphic.
If you set right-alignment in an inline image, the text
will wrap around the left side of the graphic.</P>
```

Figure 3-13

A BR tag with `CLEAR="left"` set will cause following text to break past a left-aligned image.

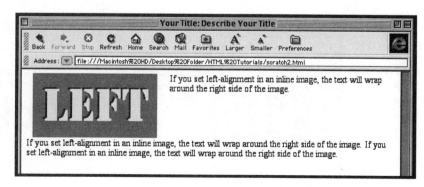

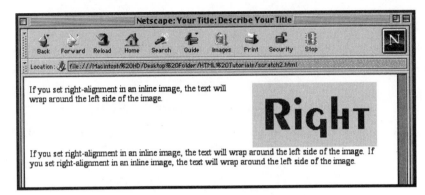

Figure 3-14

A BR tag with
`CLEAR="right"`
set will cause
following text to
break past a right-
aligned image.

Clearing Both Left-Aligned and Right-Aligned Images

To see how this works with flowing text between a left-aligned and a right-aligned graphic, go back to the example you created earlier for flowing text between a left-aligned image and a right-aligned image and move the `<BR CLEAR="all">` tag to the position shown here (or just retype the example shown here; see Figure 3-15):

```
<P><IMG SRC="left.gif" ALIGN="left" HSPACE="2"><IMG
SRC="right.gif" ALIGN="right" HSPACE="2">Text will flow
between a left-aligned and a right-aligned image. <BR
CLEAR="all">Text will flow between a left-aligned and a
right-aligned image.</P>
```

Figure 3-15

A BR tag with
`CLEAR="all"`
set will cause
following text to
break past both
a left-aligned
image and a right-
aligned image.

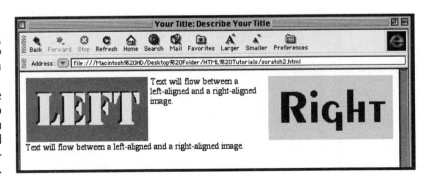

Creating Image Links

In the Basic HTML Tutorial, you learned how to place inline images in your page, and you also learned how to create hypertext links. What you haven't learned yet is how to create an *image link*, an inline image that functions as a hypertext link, so that a link will be activated when you click on the image. Hey, if you want to brag about knowing HTML, you've got to know how to create image links!

Creating a Simple Image Link

To create an image link, just nest an image (using the IMG tag) inside a hypertext link (using the A tag). Here's a simple example:

```
<P><A HREF="link.html"><IMG SRC="link.gif"></A></P>
```

You'll notice that the IMG tag is positioned inside of the </A> tag. While text inserted as link text is underlined in blue in a browser (unless you've changed the defaults), an image link is outlined with a blue border (see Figure 3-16).

Including Both an Image and Text in a Link

You can include both an image and text in the same hypertext link. Just copy and paste the previous example and then edit it so it looks like this:

```
<P><A HREF="link.html"><IMG SRC="link.gif">The image
and the text are a link.</A></P>
```

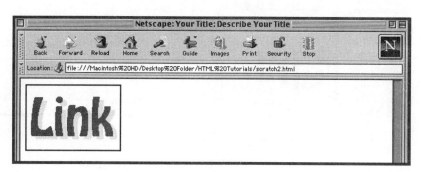

Figure 3-16

An image link is outlined with a blue border when displayed in a browser.

Copy and paste this example and then edit it so the text is outside the link, like this:

```
<P><A HREF="link.html"><IMG SRC="link.gif"></A>The
image is a link, but not the text.</P>
```

Figure 3-17 shows how these two examples appear in a browser. Because in the second example the text has been moved after the </A> end tag, it is no longer part of the link.

The HTML file link.html, used in the previous examples, is included with the example files in the HTML Tutorials folder. To check out how either of the image links works, click on one or the other "Link" image. Just click on your browser's Bac1k button to return to your scratch pad file (scratch2.html).

Controlling Image Link Borders

The IMG tag's BORDER attribute allows you to specify a custom width for the border that is displayed around an image link. The default border width may vary from browser to browser.

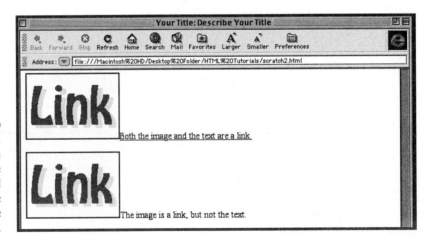

Figure 3-17

The image, displayed with a blue border, and the link text, underlined with a blue line, are both part of the same hypertext link.

Setting a Custom Image Link Border Width

Press Command-V to paste in the example that you previously copied to the Clipboard, then increase the width of the border around the image link to 10 pixels, like this (see Figure 3-18):

```
<P><A HREF="link.html"><IMG SRC="link.gif" BORDER="10">
</A>The border is set to 10 pixels.</P>
```

NOTE

If you previously clicked on the link to link.html, the border around your image link may no longer be blue. It will be whatever color is set for displaying visited links.

Turning the Image Link Border Off

You can also turn off the image link border entirely by setting the border width to zero (BORDER="0") in the IMG tag. This is often done to add navigation icons to a Web page. Just copy and paste the previous example, and edit it so it matches what is shown here (see Figure 3-19):

```
<P><A HREF="link.html"><IMG SRC="link.gif" BORDER="0">
</A>Turning off the border doesn't turn off the link.
</P>
```

Figure 3-18

By using the BORDER attribute in the IMG tag, you can increase the width of the border around an image link.

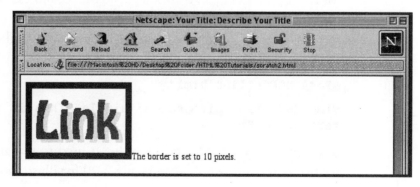

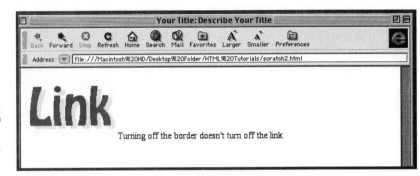

Address: file:///Macintosh%20HD/Desktop%20Folder/HTML%20Tutorials/scratch2.html

Link

Turning off the border doesn't turn off the link.

Figure 3-19

Even without a border, the image here is still a link.

NOTE   It is a good idea to include ALT attributes in the IMG tags for any image links or navigation icons you create. They'll help describe the purpose of the link to surfers who have image display turned off, or to visually handicapped surfers using Braille browsers. For more info on the IMG tag's ALT attribute, see "Using the ALT Attribute in Inline Images" in the Basic HTML Tutorial.

Aligning Image Links and Text

There are many ways to align image links relative to associated link text or descriptive text; the following are just some of the possibilities. Create the first example. Then you can just copy and paste it to create the base code for the second example, copy and paste the second example to create the base code for the third example, and so on. In the first example, an ALIGN="middle" attribute value is used to middle-align the link text relative to the image link:

```
<P><A HREF="link.html">
<IMG SRC="link.gif" ALIGN="middle">This is the link
text.</A></P>
```

Then an ALIGN="top" attribute value is used to top-align the link text relative to the image link. (See Figure 3-20 for illustrations of both kinds of alignment.)

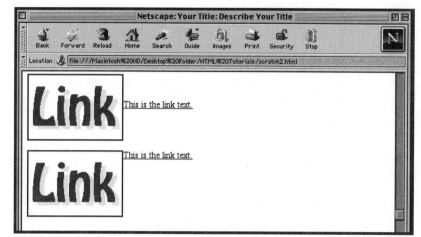

Figure 3-20

The link text is
middle-aligned and
top-aligned relative
to the image link.

```
<P><A HREF="link.html">
<IMG SRC="link.gif" ALIGN="top">This is the link text.
</A></P>
```

In the next example, the image link and the link text are centered, and a
BR tag is inserted, to display the link text under the image link:

```
<P ALIGN="center"><A HREF="link.html">
<IMG SRC="link.gif"><BR>.This is the link text.</A></P>
```

Now the positions of the image link and the link text are reversed, so that
the link text is displayed to the left of the image link, with both centered on
the page. (See Figure 3-21 for illustrations of the two examples.)

```
<P ALIGN="center"><A HREF="link.html">
This is the link text.<IMG SRC="link.gif"></A></P>
```

In this example, inserting a BR tag after the link text causes the link text to
be displayed above the image link, with both centered on the page (see
Figure 3-22):

```
<P ALIGN="center"><A HREF="link.html">
This is the link text.<BR><IMG SRC="link.gif"></A></P>
```

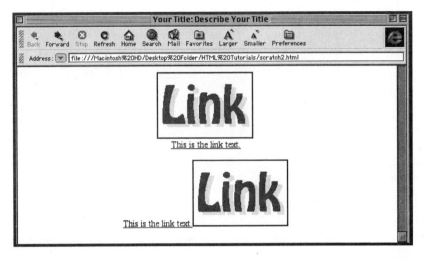

Figure 3-21

The link text is displayed below and to the left of the image link; in each case, both are centered on the page.

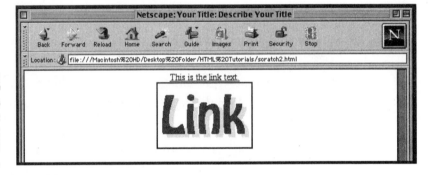

Figure 3-22

The link text is displayed above the image link; both are centered on the page.

Working with Lists

The Basic HTML Tutorial covered creating ordered (numbered) lists and unordered (bulleted) lists. It also covered nesting lists, and mixing and matching lists. This section of the Intermediate HTML Tutorial covers some additional ways you can control the display of ordered and unordered lists.

Specifying Number Types

To use the TYPE attribute to specify the number type for an ordered list, you can pick one of these values: "A" (uppercase letters), "a" (lowercase

letters), "I" (uppercase roman numerals), "i" (lowercase roman numerals, or the default "1" (Arabic numbers). Enter the following code for an example of specifying uppercase roman numerals for an ordered list (see Figure 3-23):

```
<OL TYPE="I">
<LI>This is item one.
<LI>This is item two.
<LI>This is item three.
<LI>This is item four.
</OL>
```

NOTE Whenever adding an OL or UL element immediately following a P element, you should make sure that the </P> end tag is added to the end of the paragraph. Internet Explorer 2.0 fails to add any vertical space between the paragraph and a following list if the </P> end tag is missing. In Internet Explorer 3.0, if the paragraph is centered or right-aligned, any following list is similarly aligned if the </P> end tag is missing.

Creating Multilevel Outlines

When bulleted lists (with UL tags) are nested, most browsers vary the bullet types for different bullet levels. However, no current Web browser automatically varies the number type in nested numbered lists. In HTML 3.2, you can use the TYPE attribute to specify the number type for each level of the ordered list. Enter the following code as an example of using TYPE attributes in the OL tag to create a multilevel outline:

Figure 3-23

The TYPE="I" attribute value causes an ordered list to be displayed with roman numerals.

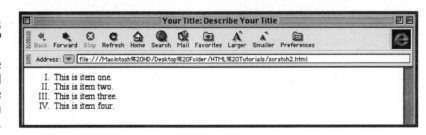

NOTE This example and two of the next three examples utilize spaces to indent the nested list levels, making it easier for you to visually recognize the different list levels. Feel free to space over to create the indents, but realize that this is for your eyes only; it will have no effect when displayed in a browser. Your browser will automatically indent nested ordered lists. Also, be careful to nest the different list levels, rather than overlapping them.

```
<OL TYPE="I">
<LI>Level-one outline level.
  <OL TYPE="A">
  <LI>Level-two outline level
    <OL TYPE="1">
    <LI>Level-three outline level
      <OL TYPE="a">
      <LI>Level-four outline level
      <LI>Level-four outline level
      </OL>
    <LI>Level-three outline level
    </OL>
  <LI>Level-two outline level
  </OL>
<LI>Level-one outline level
</OL>
```

Figure 3-24 shows how this appears in an HTML 3.2–compliant Web browser. Remember, the indenting you see in the figure (or in your browser) comes from nesting the OL tags; it has nothing to do with any spaces or tabs you may have added here.

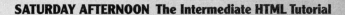

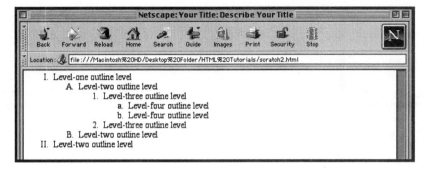

Figure 3-24

By using the
TYPE attribute to
assign different
number types, you
can create a
multilevel outline.

TIP

Browsers don't display any additional space between list items in an unordered or ordered list. To add blank lines between the list items in the previous example, just insert a BR tag at the end of each list item.

There are a lot of ways that you can dress up your outline (which looks a bit bland as it is). For instance, you could bold your level-one list items. You could also apply heading-level tags (H2, H3, and so on) to the different outline-level list items. Later in this session, you'll learn how to use the FONT tag to change the size, color, and typeface of your text; this too can be used to differentiate the appearance of the different outline levels. Still another option is to use styles (see "Working with Styles" later in this session).

CAUTION

You should be aware that a multilevel outline can look utterly awful in an older Web browser that doesn't support the TYPE attribute for ordered lists; therefore, if you use this feature, you might want to label your page as "HTML 3.2 or later only."

Including Paragraphs in a Multilevel Outline

You can insert paragraphs inside a multilevel outline by inserting a paragraph following a list item. The paragraph will automatically line up vertically with the text of the preceding list item. For instance, insert the following code (see Figure 3-25):

Figure 3-25

Paragraphs included in a multilevel outline automatically line up vertically with the preceding list item.

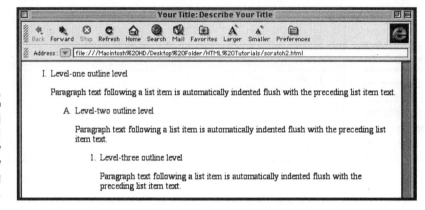

```
<OL TYPE="I">

<LI>Level-one outline level

<P>Paragraph text following a list item will auto-
matically be indented flush with the preceding list
item text.</P>

   <OL TYPE="A">

<LI>Level-two outline level

<P>Paragraph text following a list item will auto-
matically be indented flush with the preceding list
item text.</P>

      <OL TYPE="1">

<LI>Level-three outline level

<P>Paragraph text following a list item will auto-
matically be indented flush with the preceding
list item text.</P>

         <OL TYPE="a">

         <LI>Level-four outline level

         <LI>Level-four outline level

         </OL>

<LI>Level-three outline level

</OL>
```

```
    <LI>Level-two outline level
  </OL>
```

<LI>Level-one outline level

</OL>

> **NOTE**
>
> When inserting paragraphs inside ordered (or unordered) lists, be sure to add the </P> end tag at the end of the paragraph. Otherwise, no intervening space will be added between the paragraph and a following list item.

Using START and VALUE Attributes

You can use the START attribute in an OL start tag to start the numbering sequence at a particular number. You can use the VALUE attribute in an LI tag to restart the numbering sequence at a particular number. For an example of first starting the numbering sequence at 3 and then restarting it at 8, enter the following code (see Figure 3-26):

```
<OL START="3">
<LI>This should be numbered as 3.
<LI>This should be numbered as 4.
<LI VALUE="8">This should be numbered as 8.
<LI>This should be numbered as 9.
</OL>
```

Figure 3-26

You can use the OL tag's START attribute and the LI tag's VALUE attribute to start or restart the numbering of an ordered list.

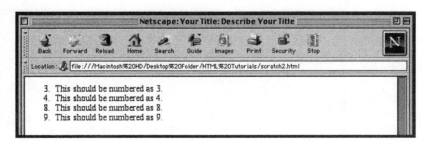

The numbering sequence will be started or restarted using the current TYPE attribute value. For instance, if TYPE="A" is used in the OL tag, then START="3" in an OL tag or VALUE="3" in an LI tag would start or restart the numbering at C.

Specifying Bullet Types

You can also use the TYPE attribute with unordered (bulleted) lists to specify the type of bullet to display. The TYPE attributes you can use are "disc," "circle," and "square." Navigator and Internet Explorer (4.0 or greater) display nested bullet lists with the progression of disc, circle, and square. Enter the following code for an example of specifying a bullet-type sequence other than the default for a bulleted list three levels deep (see Figure 3-27):

```
<UL TYPE="square">
<LI>First-level bullet
<LI>First-level bullet
  <UL TYPE="disc">
  <LI>Second-level bullet
  <LI>Second-level bullet
    <UL TYPE="circle">
    <LI>Third-level bullet
    <LI>Third-level bullet
    </UL>
  </UL>
</UL>.
```

Figure 3-27

Using the TYPE attribute, you can specify the bullet types for different nested levels in a bulleted list (unordered list).

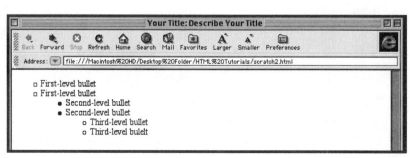

Take a Break?

You've been going at this most of the day, so you're probably ready for a breather, right? If it is already past dinner and your eyes are starting to droop, feel free to call it a day. You can come back and do the remainder of the Intermediate HTML Tutorial any time you want.

However, if the afternoon is still young, or you're just gung ho to learn some more HTML, get up and take a much deserved break. Stretch to uncramp those muscles, stare at the horizon to relax your orbs, grab a snack or a sip. I'll see you back in 10 or 15 minutes, when you'll learn about creating icon link lists using fancy 3-D bullets.

Creating Icon Link Lists

An *icon link list* is a list of hypertext links that uses colorful 3-D graphical icon bullets (inline images), rather than plain black-and-white bullets like those you get when you create an unordered list using the UL tag. This is a good way to add some pizazz to your Web page.

Creating Left-Aligned Icon Link Lists

There are several different ways to create an icon link list. The method I'll be showing you here allows you to create a link list using colorful 3-D bullet images that will indent one line of following text. In Appendix C, "Creating Tables," I'll show you another method that can indent an unlimited number of following lines.

For this example, use the same list of yo-yo links you typed in the Basic HTML Tutorial as an example of creating a regular link list. If you want, you can open scratch.html, copy the yo-yo link list, and then paste it into scratch2.html. To create the base code for this example, just edit the link list you pasted in so the code matches what is shown here (you can also just type in the codes, if you wish):

```
<A HREF="http://pages.nyu.edu/~tqm3413/yoyo/">Tomer's
Page of Exotic Yo-Yo</A>. A great Yo-Yo resource page.
```

```
<A HREF="http://www.socool.com/socool/yo-yo.html">Just
Say YO!!!</A> Features the Web's first Yo-Yo animation.

<A HREF="http://www.pd.net/yoyo/">American Yo-Yo
Association</A> Read past issues of the AYYA
Newsletter.
```

NOTE

In the first link example, don't mistake the tilde (~) for a hyphen (-). Tildes are often used in URLs to indicate a shortcut to a user's folder on a Web server, so the full folder path to where a user's folder is actually located on a server doesn't have to be included in the URL.

Right now, these are just the links. You still need to add in the left-aligned bullet images and the BR tags needed to create the list. Also, to see the indent for the following line, you need to add some extra text to the last link's description text. Just edit the base code you've created so it looks like this (see Figure 3-28):

```
<P><IMG SRC="redball.gif" ALIGN="left" HSPACE="3"
VSPACE="3">

<A HREF="http://pages.nyu.edu/~tqm3413/yoyo/">Tomer's
Page of Exotic Yo-Yo</A>. A great Yo-Yo resource
page.<BR CLEAR="left">

<IMG SRC="redball.gif" ALIGN="left" HSPACE="3"
VSPACE="3">

<A HREF="http://www.socool.com/socool/yo-yo.html">Just
Say YO!!!</A> Features the Web's first Yo-Yo
animation.<BR CLEAR="left">
```

Figure 3-28

You can create an indented icon bullet list by using left-aligned bullet images and BR tags with the CLEAR attribute.

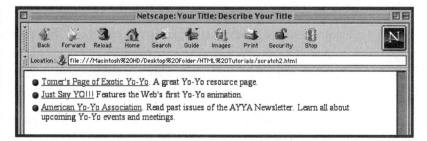

```
<IMG SRC="redball.gif" ALIGN="left" HSPACE="3"
VSPACE="3">
```

```
<A HREF="http://www.pd.net/yoyo/">American Yo-Yo
Association</A> Read past issues of the AYYA
newsletter. Learn all about upcoming Yo-Yo events
and meetings.<BR CLEAR="left"></P>
```

Notice that this is really one paragraph with BR (Line Break) tags using CLEAR="left" attributes to separate the different icon link list items. Create any additional icon links in the same way. If you want a blank line between your icon links, just use a P tag instead of the BR tag to separate the lines.

The amount of VSPACE that you should add to cause the indent of the following line will depend somewhat on the actual bullet image you're using. You may need to open a bullet image in an image editor and increase the amount of white space below the bullet relative to that above the bullet, to get the bullets to line up right. You should also be aware that different browsers may display the bullet images in a higher or lower position relative to the link text; for instance, the Macintosh versions of both Netscape Navigator 4.05 and Internet Explorer 4.01 display the bullet images about a pixel lower than do the Windows versions of these same browsers.

TIP

Someone using a text-only browser or a graphical Web browser with graphics turned off might not realize that the graphics are icon bullets. To clue them in, you might want to edit the IMG tags for the previous icon bullets by adding ALT="*":

```
<IMG SRC="redball.gif" ALIGN="top" HSPACE="3" VSPACE=
"3" ALT="*">
```

FIND IT ON ▶
THE CD

If you're wondering where to get more graphic icons to spice up your Web pages, you can find a collection of public domain graphic icons and other Web art on the CD-ROM. At the Web site for this book, you'll find additional Web art available that you can download and use, as well as links to other places on the Web where you can find lots more Web art that you can download and use.

Using Relative URLs

When creating a hypertext link or inserting an inline image, you don't always need to specify a full, or *absolute*, URL or Web address. If a Web page or other file to which you are linking—or a graphic file you're inserting into your Web page—is in the same folder, folder structure, or server (or in the same domain), you can leave off those parts of the URL that are common to both. A *relative* URL is also called a *partial* URL because it provides only those parts of a Web address that are not common to both the linking and the linked file. (You've actually used quite a few relative URLs in these tutorials; if an HTML file or image is located in the same folder as the linking HTML file, then you only need to include the file name as the URL.)

 NOTE •
Feel free to skip this section and jump ahead to "Working with Rules." You won't need to read this section to plan and create your first Web page on Sunday, since you'll save all of your HTML files and images in the same folder. If you want to go beyond creating anything more than just a simple Web page with a few graphics, you'll want to read this section to understand how to create relative links.
• •

The main advantage of relative URLs, apart from their being shorter than absolute URLs, is *portability*. By always using relative URLs for links that are internal to your own Web site, you can create and test out your whole Web site on your local computer's hard drive, and then transfer the whole thing to your folders on your Web server, without having to change a single link. If you were to use absolute URLs pointing to files on your own hard drive, those links would still work for you after you transferred your pages to the Web, but they would not work for anyone else (they don't have access to your hard drive).

Assume that you have a folder, My Pages, in which you are going to store all of your Web pages, inline images, and related files. If your Web site is fairly simple and only composed of a few pages, storing all the files for your site in one folder works just fine. If you go beyond just creating a simple

Web site, however, you'll soon find that keeping track of all the files saved in that folder can present a bit of a challenge. The solution is to organize the files for your Web site into subfolders.

You might want to put your images into a separate subfolder, while also creating separate subfolders for the different main sections of your Web site, leaving only your home page (or "index page") in the main folder for your site (which will act as the root folder).

ALL IN THE FAMILY

The phrase *child folder* refers to a folder that is inside (a child of) the linking file's folder. In Figure 3-29, the images, products, and support folders are all child folders of the My Pages folder. The phrase *parent folder* refers to the folder in which a linking file's folder is located. In Figure 3-29, the My Pages folder is the parent folder of the images, products, and support folders. The phrase *grandparent folder* refers to the parent folder of a parent folder. In Figure 3-29, the My Pages folder is the grandparent folder of the technical and sales folders. The phrase *grandchild folder* refers to the opposite relation—in Figure 3-29, the technical folder is the grandchild folder of the My Pages folder. The phrase *sibling folder* refers to child folders located in the same parent folder. Other relationships can be set up here, such as between two cousins, between an aunt (or uncle) and a niece (or nephew), and so on.

Figure 3-29

The images, products, and support folders are subfolders of the My Pages folder, while the technical and sales folders are subfolders of the support folder.

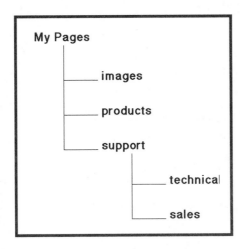

Linking to a File in a Child Folder

Now, suppose you want to link from your home page (My Pages > index.html) to an inline image stored in the images folder (My Pages > images > headline.gif). In that case, the IMG tag would need to look like this:

```
<IMG SRC="images/headline.gif">
```

Linking to an HTML file in a subfolder works exactly the same way. Suppose you want to link from your home page (My Pages > index.html) to a product catalog you've saved in the products folder (My Pages > products > catalog.html). In that case, the hypertext link would need to look like this:

```
<A HREF="products/catalog.html">
```

That's pretty simple. If you want to link to a file that is in a child folder (or subfolder) of the linking file's folder, you only need to include the name of the child folder, a forward slash, and the file name of the file you're linking to. A common mistake is to insert a forward slash in front of the child folder (in Unix forward slashes come after, not before, folder names). Another common mistake is to use backward slashes (\) instead of forward slashes.

Linking to a File in a Grandchild Folder

But what if you want to link to a file that's located in a subfolder of a subfolder (a grandchild folder, in other words) of the linking file's folder? Suppose that you want to link from your home page (My Pages > index.html) to a page of support phone numbers you've saved in the technical folder that is in the support folder (My Pages > support> technical > numbers.html). In that case, the hypertext link would need to look like this:

```
<A HREF="support/technical/numbers.html">
```

Linking to a File in a Parent Folder

Linking back up, from a child folder to a parent folder, gets a little trickier. For instance, assume that you want to link in your catalog page (My Pages > products > catalog.html) to your home page (My Pages > index.html). In that case, the hypertext link would need to look like this:

```
<A HREF="../index.html">
```

Notice the two dots and the forward slash ("../"). In Unix, this refers to a parent folder of the current folder. So, this URL tells the browser to step up one level (to the parent folder of the linking file's folder) and then to open index.html.

Linking to a File in a Grandparent Folder

What if you want to link back up to a file stored in a parent of the parent of the linking file's folder? For instance, suppose you want to create a link in your page of support numbers (My Pages > support > technical > numbers.html) that links back to your home page (My Pages > index.html). In that case, the link would need to look like this:

```
<A HREF="../../index.html">
```

In other words, for each level you want to step back up, you just insert two dots and a forward slash ("../").

Linking to a File in a Sibling Folder

What about linking between files located in separate child folders of the same parent folder? Assume, for instance, that you want to add a link to your product catalog page (My Pages > products > catalog.html) that links to a FAQ (*frequently asked questions*) page, faq.html, that you've saved in the support folder (My pages > support > faq.html). That requires stepping up one level (to the parent folder) and then stepping back down one level (to the sibling folder). To do this, the link would need to look like this:

```
<A HREF="../support/faq.html">
```

Linking to a File in a Child Folder of a Sibling Folder

What if you want to link to a file located in a child folder of a sibling folder? That is, to a nephew (or niece) folder? Assume, for instance, that you want to create a link in your product catalog page (My Pages > products > catalog.html) to a page of technical support numbers, numbers.html, that you've saved in the technical folder (My Pages > support > technical > numbers.html). In that case, the link would need to look like this:

```
<A HREF="../support/technical/numbers.html">
```

Now, assume that you want to make a link in the other direction, from numbers.html (in My Pages > support > technical) to catalog.html (in My Pages > products). That link would need to look like this:

```
<A HREF="../../products/catalog.html">
```

Here you're actually stepping back up two levels ("../../") on the tree, and then walking down another branch (the products folder).

TIP

When creating subfolders in a multi-folder Web site, you should avoid using uppercase letters in your folder or file names. This is because file and folder names on Unix servers are case sensitive. If you make a habit of always using lowercase letters in file and folder names that are part of your Web site, you'll run into a lot fewer problems if you later transfer your Web site up onto a Unix server. You must also eliminate any spaces in your Web site's file and folder names (you can substitute underscores ("_") in their place, if you wish).

Working with Rules

You learned how to use the HR (Horizontal Rule) tag in the Basic HTML Tutorial. In the following section, I'll show you how to create custom horizontal rules by changing their height, width, alignment, and shading. I'll also show you how to use inline images as fancy, colorful graphic rules.

The default horizontal rule looks rather bland. Though it does have some shading to give it a bit of a 3-D look, in most browsers, this shading barely shows up if a browser's background is set to white (which it usually is). This section covers some things you can do to dress up your horizontal rules, including changing their height, width, and alignment; you'll also learn how to use some 3-D graphic rules. The attributes used here in the HR tag were all originally Netscape Navigator extensions; HTML 3.2 includes them, and most current Web browsers support them.

Setting the Height of a Horizontal Rule

To change the height of a horizontal rule, set the SIZE attribute value in the HR tag. The value you set is the rule's height, or *thickness*, in pixels. Enter the following code for an example of creating a horizontal rule that has a thickness of 10 pixels, and another one that has a thickness of 15 pixels (along with a regular rule so that you can see the difference; see Figure 3-30):

```
<P>This is the default horizontal rule:</P>
<HR>
<P>This is a 10-pixel horizontal rule:</P>
<HR SIZE="10">
<P>This is a 15-pixel horizontal rule:</P>
<HR SIZE="15">
```

The amount of space inserted above and below a horizontal rule may vary from browser to browser. Internet Explorer 4.01, included with the iMac, fails to insert any space below a horizontal rule. The fix for this is to insert a BR tag following the HR tag, which will add the necessary extra space below the horizontal rule in the one browser that needs it:

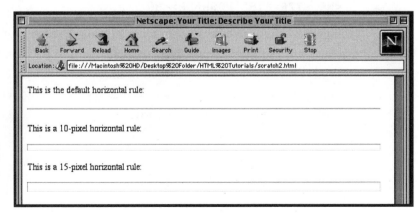

Figure 3-30

You can vary the thickness of a horizontal rule.

```
<P>This is the default horizontal rule:</P>
<HR><BR>
<P>This is a 10-pixel horizontal rule:</P>
<HR SIZE="10"><BR>
<P>This is a 15-pixel horizontal rule:</P>
<HR SIZE="15"><BR>
```

You might think that this would add even more space below a horizontal rule in browsers other than Internet Explorer 4.01. In Netscape Navigator, which does add sufficient vertical space following a horizontal rule, adding the BR tag after the HR tag doesn't have any effect at all.

Turning Shading Off

You can also turn a horizontal rule's shading off by including a NOSHADE attribute in the HR tag (the default setting for a horizontal rule is that it is shaded). The shading is actually a thin drop shadow at the bottom and to the right of the horizontal rule and not the shade of the rule itself. In fact, when shading is turned off, most browsers will fill the horizontal rule with a black or gray shade. To set an unshaded horizontal rule, just add the NOSHADE attribute to the HR tag, as shown here:

```
<P>This is an unshaded 15-pixel horizontal rule:</P>
<HR SIZE="15" NOSHADE><BR>
```

Figure 3-31 shows how this looks in Internet Explorer, where it is filled in black, with square corners. Netscape Navigator 4.05 (which ships with the iMac) also displays this rule filled in black, with square corners. This very same rule, when displayed in any Windows version of Netscape Navigator, is filled in gray, with rounded corners.

Figure 3-31

Internet Explorer displays an unshaded horizontal rule filled in black and with square corners.

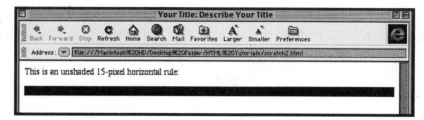

Controlling the Width and Alignment of a Horizontal Rule

You can change the width and alignment of a horizontal rule. The width can be set either as a percentage value (for instance, WIDTH="75%") or as a straight pixel value. Rules can also be left-aligned or right-aligned (center-alignment is the default). Following are a couple examples of controlling the width and alignment of a horizontal rule (see Figure 3-32). This is an example of a 15-pixel unshaded horizontal rule set to a width of 75 percent:

```
<P>This is a 75% wide, 15-pixel high, "unshaded"
horizontal rule:</P>

<HR WIDTH="75%" SIZE="15" NOSHADE><BR>
```

This example is left-aligned, with the width set to 50 percent and the size changed to 10 pixels:

```
<P>This is a left-aligned, 50% wide, 10-pixel high,
"unshaded" horizontal rule:</P>

<HR ALIGN="left" WIDTH="50%" SIZE="10" NOSHADE><BR>
```

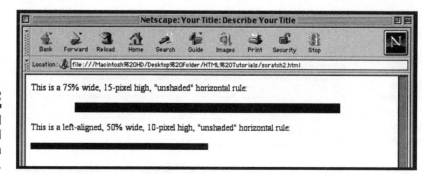

Figure 3-32

You can control the width and alignment of a horizontal rule.

◆ ◆

CAUTION   You might be tempted to stack up horizontal rules of different widths to generate an effect similar to this:

_____

_____

_____

Be advised that in a Web browser that doesn't support setting the WIDTH attribute for the HR tag, your effect will turn out something like this:

_____

_____

_____

This is a good example of a situation in which both Navigator and Internet Explorer support a certain feature that you should probably avoid using. The general rule is not to do tricks specific to only a few browsers if they're likely to mess up other browsers. One way around this is to provide alternative pages, or at least label your page as requiring an HTML 3.2-compliant Web browser.

◆ ◆

Using Graphic Rules

Instead of using the HR tag, you can use a graphic rule, which is simply a graphic of a rule that you can insert on your page as an inline image. Enter the following code as an example of inserting a graphic rule on your Web page (see Figure 3-33):

Figure 3-33

Instead of a plain horizontal rule, you can use a fancy graphical horizontal rule.

> **Your Title: Describe Your Title**
>
> Back Forward Stop Refresh Home Search Mail Favorites Larger Smaller Preferences
>
> Address: file:///Macintosh%20HD/Desktop%20Folder/HTML%20Tutorials/scratch2.html
>
> This is a graphic rule:
>
> _____

```
<P>This is a graphic rule:</P>
<P><IMG SRC="rain_lin.gif"></P>
```

Controlling the Width, Height, and Alignment of a Graphic Rule

You can control the width, height, and alignment of a graphic rule just the same as with any other inline image. This is an example of setting a width of 65 percent, a height of 10 pixels, and center-alignment:

```
<P ALIGN="center"><IMG SRC="rain_lin.gif" WIDTH="65%"
HEIGHT="10"></P>
```

As Figure 3-34 shows, the graphic rule is now center-aligned and extends across only 65 percent of the browser's window. The impact is further enhanced with an increase of the graphic rule's height to 10 pixels.

It's okay to set a WIDTH percentage for a graphic rule, but I recommend avoiding this for other inline images. Don't set the height as a percentage (you can set the height in pixels, though).

Working with Fonts

The FONT tag allows you to change font sizes, colors, and faces. In the following sections, I'll show you how to apply the FONT tag's SIZE, COLOR, and FACE attributes.

Figure 3-34

Just as with any other inline image, you can control the width, height, and alignment of a graphic rule.

Changing Font Sizes

The FONT tag allows you to specify the size and color of a section of text. The FONT tag uses the SIZE attribute to change the size of a font. You can set font sizes using *absolute* or *relative* size values.

You can set seven absolute (or fixed) sizes, numbered from 1 to 7, using the SIZE attribute of the FONT tag. The default is 3, which is the same as regular paragraph text; 1 is the smallest and 7 is the largest, so you can set two absolute font sizes that are smaller than normal paragraph text and four sizes that are larger. Each Web browser determines the sizes of these fonts. To see what these different font sizes look like in your Web browser, enter the following code and then hop over to your browser:

```
<P><FONT SIZE="1">Font Size 1</FONT><BR>
<FONT SIZE="2">Font Size 2</FONT><BR>
<FONT SIZE="3">Font Size 3 (the default)</FONT><BR>
<FONT SIZE="4">Font Size 4</FONT><BR>
<FONT SIZE="5">Font Size 5</FONT><BR>
<FONT SIZE="6">Font Size 6</FONT><BR>
<FONT SIZE="7">Font Size 7</FONT></P>
```

As you can see in Figure 3-35, the font sizes you can set range from very small to quite large.

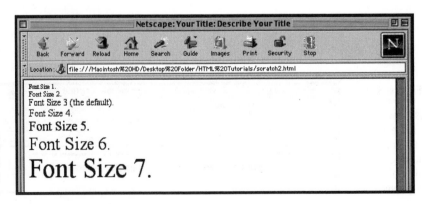

Figure 3-35

You can set seven different absolute font sizes.

NOTE

• •

If you clicked the Larger icon on Internet Explorer's toolbar to increase the size of the text font, the browser stepped up a font size level. Font size 3 (the default font size) is displayed at the same size as font size 4, while font size 4 is displayed at the same size as font size 5 . This isn't a problem until you get up to font sizes 6 and 7. There is no font size 8, so if the Larger icon has been clicked, font size 6 and font size 7 are displayed as the same size. If you click the Larger icon twice to really boost the size of the text font, it actually jumps up two font sizes, so font sizes 5, 6, and 7 are all displayed at the same size. This is a characteristic only of the Macintosh version of Internet Explorer. H1 elements are rendered in a font size of 6, while H2 elements are rendered in a font size of 5. H1 and H2 elements will only be displayed in the same size font in the Mac version of Internet Explorer if you click on the Larger icon twice.

• •

TIP

■ ■

You can also nest font tags inside each other; therefore, you could do something like the following to switch back to the default font size in the middle of a larger set font size:

```
<FONT SIZE="4">This is Font Size 4. <FONT SIZE=
"3">This is the default size font.</FONT> This is
Font Size 4 again.</FONT>.
```

■ ■

Setting Relative Font Size Changes

You can also set relative font sizes. Relative font size changes are indicated by a plus (+) or minus (–) sign preceding the font size number. For instance, FONT SIZE="+1" indicates a font size that's one size larger than the base font size. Because the default base font is the same as a Size 3 absolute font size, a Size +1 relative font would be the same as a Size 4 absolute font (3+1=4). Enter the following code for an example of using relative font size changes to indicate the seven possible font sizes (see Figure 3-36):

```
<P><FONT SIZE="-2">Font Size -2.</FONT><BR>
<FONT SIZE="-1">Font Size -1.</FONT><BR>
Default Font Size.<BR>
```

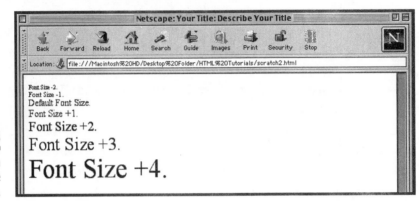

Figure 3-36

You can set seven different relative font sizes.

```
<FONT SIZE="+1">Font Size +1.</FONT><BR>

<FONT SIZE="+2">Font Size +2.</FONT><BR>

<FONT SIZE="+3">Font Size +3.</FONT><BR>

<FONT SIZE="+4">Font Size +4.</FONT></P>
```

You'll notice that a relative –2 is the same as an absolute 1, –1 is the same as 2, +1 is the same as 4, and so on. The default font size, which requires no font size change, is the same as 3.

Setting the Base Font Size

The BASEFONT tag, an empty (standalone) tag, allows you to change the size of the *base font* (the font size used in paragraph text). You can set it to any of the absolute font sizes, 1 through 7. You set the base font size the same way you set an absolute font size. For instance, to increase the base font size one notch (from 3, the default), set the base font to an absolute font size of 4:

```
<BASEFONT SIZE="4">
```

When you change the base font size using the BASEFONT tag, all following relative font sizes will change relative to the new base font. For instance, if you change the base font size to 4 (as in the previous example), then a following relative font size of +1 would have the same effect as setting an absolute font size of 5 (4+1=5).

You can insert the BASEFONT tag at any point within a Web page to set the base font to any of the absolute font sizes. It stays in effect until another BASEFONT tag changes the base font size. If you want the BASEFONT tag to reset the base font size for your whole page, you need to insert it at the top of your page following the BODY tag. The BASEFONT tag affects not only relative font sizes but also any SMALL and BIG font changes , as well as the size of all paragraph text, character rendering (italic, bold, and so on), list elements, definition lists, block quotes, predefined text, and address blocks that follow it. Headings and text set with absolute font size tags are not affected, however.

CAUTION

♦ ♦

You should stick to setting BASEFONT sizes as absolute font sizes. Some browsers won't recognize relative font sizes set in the BASEFONT tag.

♦ ♦

Changing Font Colors

The FONT tag uses the COLOR attribute to change the color of a font. To specify a font color, you can use one of 16 color names, or you can use RGB hex codes. (The latter is more difficult, but gives you access to a much wider range of colors.)

Setting Colors Using the 16 Color Names

The 16 color names are black, white, aqua, blue, fuchsia, gray, green, lime, maroon, navy, olive, purple, red, silver, teal, and yellow. Enter the following code for an example of specifying font colors using color names (this example omits "black" and "white"):

```
<P><FONT SIZE=7>

<FONT COLOR="aqua">Aqua </FONT><FONT COLOR="blue">Blue
</FONT>

<FONT COLOR="fuchsia">Fuchsia </FONT><FONT
COLOR="gray"> Gray </FONT>
```

```
<FONT COLOR="green">Green </FONT><FONT
COLOR="lime">Lime </FONT>

<FONT COLOR="maroon">Maroon </FONT><FONT COLOR="navy">
Navy </FONT>

<FONT COLOR="olive">Olive </FONT><FONT COLOR="purple">
Purple </FONT>

<FONT COLOR="red">Red </FONT><FONT COLOR="silver">
Silver </FONT>

<FONT COLOR="teal">Teal </FONT><FONT COLOR="yellow">
Yellow </FONT>

</FONT></P>
```

The illustration in Figure 3-37, shown here in monochrome, gives only a rough idea of what this looks like in a browser. Be sure to hop over to your browser to see what the colors really look like. Recent browser versions actually support many additional color names, but these should be avoided, since many HTML 3.2-compliant Web browsers won't display them. If you want to display more colors than the 16 standard color names allow, you should stick to using RGB hex codes.

TIP

You may have noticed that there's no "orange" in the 16 official color names you can use to specify font colors. The only way to specify an "orange" color is to use an RGB hex code, covered next.

Figure 3-37

There are 16 standard color names, including black and white (not shown here), that you can use to set font colors.

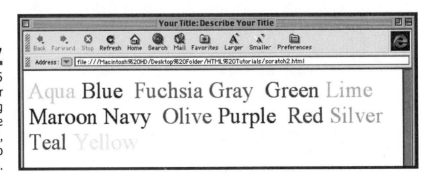

Setting Colors Using RGB Hex Codes

Setting the font color using RGB hex codes involves specifying values from 0 to 255 (00 to FF, in hexadecimal) for the red, green, and blue components of a color, providing you with a grand total of no less than 16.7 million different colors from which to choose.

If you're wondering why the RGB codes are set as hexadecimal, rather than decimal, values, the reason is that you can count in hexadecimal from 0 to 255 using only two-digit numbers. The hexadecimal equivalent to 159, for instance, is 9F.

You set the RGB hex code for a color in the FONT tag in this general form, where *rr* is the hex value for red, *gg* the hex value for green, and *bb* the hex value for blue:

```
<FONT COLOR="#rrggbb">This is the text to be colored.
</FONT>
```

For instance, a red color here could be specified as #FF0000, a lime green color as #00FF00, and a blue color as #0000FF. (FF is the highest hexadecimal number, equaling 255, whereas 00 is the lowest, equaling 0.) Enter the following example of assigning font colors using RGB hex codes (the example also sets the font size so it will be more visible in your browser; see Figure 3-38):

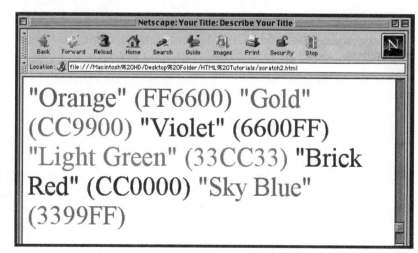

Figure 3-38

Here are just some of the wide range of colors you can set using hex codes.

```
<P><FONT SIZE="7">
<FONT COLOR="#FF6600">"Orange" (FF6600) </FONT>
<FONT COLOR="#CC9900">"Gold" (CC9900) </FONT>
<FONT COLOR="#6600FF">"Violet" (6600FF) </FONT>
<FONT COLOR="#33CC33">"Light Green" (33CC33) </FONT>
<FONT COLOR="#CC0000">"Brick Red" (CC0000) </FONT>
<FONT COLOR="#3399FF">"Sky Blue" (3399FF) </FONT>
</FONT></P>
```

On systems that can only display 256 colors, browsers convert all colors to a palette of 216 colors that are composed of all the RGB combinations of the 00, 33, 66, 99, CC, and FF hex codes (now known as a "browser-safe palette").

Browsers on systems that can only display 256 colors use dithering to display colors that aren't included in the browser or system palette that is used for those systems. Sometimes this is fine, other times decidedly not. The only colors that definitely won't be dithered on 256-color systems are those included in the 216-color browser-safe palette (often referred to as the "Netscape palette," since that's where this started, but other browsers now also use the same palette). Other colors, if they aren't also included in a particular system's 256-color palette, will be dithered on 256-color systems.

◄ ◄

BUZZ WORD To *dither* means to create a new color by interspersing pixels of multiple colors so that the human eye "mixes" them and perceives the intended color. This effect is referred to as *dithering*.

◄ ◄

If you want to make sure that your colors don't turn to mud on 256-color systems, you should stick to setting RGB hex codes that are included in the browser-safe palette. (To do this, stick to using only combinations of these RGB hex codes: 00, 33, 66, 99, CC, and FF).

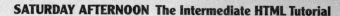

Showing you how to count in hexadecimal or explaining how an RGB color scheme works is beyond the scope of this book. Quite frankly, unless you already know hex and RGB color theory, the only practical way is to use some kind of color chart, wheel, or cube that allows you to select the color you want and get the corresponding hex code.

FIND IT ON ▶
THE WEB

There are a number of places on the Web that have color cubes or charts that show you all of the browser-safe colors and their RGB hex codes. Here are two of the best:

✿ Victor Engel's No Dither Netscape Color Palette at **www.onr.com/ user/lights/netcol.html**

✿ Doug Jacobson's RGB Color Chart at **www.phoenix.net/ ~jacobson/rgb.html**

I've also included a file, colors.html, with the example files in the HTML Tutorials folder. Just open it in your browser to see a sampler of browser-safe colors and their corresponding RGB hex codes.

Many HTML editors also have color pickers, which allow you to choose the color you want, and which then insert the RGB hex code into your Web page for you. Generally, however, they won't identify which are the browser-safe colors.

Changing Typefaces

The FACE attribute for the FONT tag was originally a Microsoft extension, but it's now part of HTML 4.0. It allows you to specify a typeface or a list of typefaces in which to have text displayed. A browser that supports this attribute will check to see if any of the typefaces specified are present on a local computer, and then display the text in that typeface if it's available. (If not, it will display the text in the default typeface the browser uses to display text, or in whichever typeface the user has selected in its preferences.)

One of the tricks to using this attribute is to specify a list of fonts that will snag as many computers as possible. You should realize that just because a font is available on your system, this doesn't mean it will be available on someone else's system. (It must have the exact same name, not simply the

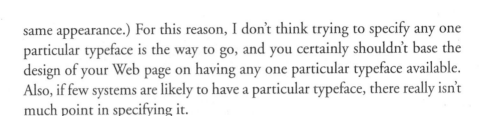

same appearance.) For this reason, I don't think trying to specify any one particular typeface is the way to go, and you certainly shouldn't base the design of your Web page on having any one particular typeface available. Also, if few systems are likely to have a particular typeface, there really isn't much point in specifying it.

A good way to use this attribute is to specify a list of typefaces that fit into the same category, such as serif, sans serif, monospaced, and display fonts. For instance, to maximize the chances that the next example will be displayed in a sans serif font, enter the following code (see Figure 3-39):

```
<P><FONT SIZE="6" COLOR="blue" FACE="Verdana, Arial,
Helvetica">This text will be in either Verdana, Arial,
or Helvetica, depending on which fonts are installed on
a local system.</FONT></P>
```

If Verdana is not available on a particular system, then the text will be displayed in Arial. If Arial is not available, the text will be displayed in Helvetica. You could also include Geneva or Swiss in your list. Alternatively, you could specify a monospaced font for a different effect (see Figure 3-40).

LISTING POSTSCRIPT FONTS

Even though PostScript fonts are native to the Macintosh system, they aren't necessarily native to other systems. Windows users, for instance, must purchase Adobe Type Manager if they want to display smoothly rendered PostScript fonts on their systems. If they don't have Adobe Type Manager installed (and most of them won't), they will see a very poor quality bitmap version of your PostScript font.

For this reason, in a list of typefaces for the FONT's FACE attribute, you should always list one or more True-Type fonts in front of any PostScript fonts you may also want to list. For instance, if you want to list the Courier typeface, always insert the New Courier typeface first; if you want to insert Helvetica, always insert Arial and/or Verdana first; if you want to insert Times, always insert Times New Roman first.

Figure 3-39

The FONT tag's
FACE attribute is an
HTML 4.0 feature
that can be used to
display text in a
font (here, Verdana)
that's different from
the default font.

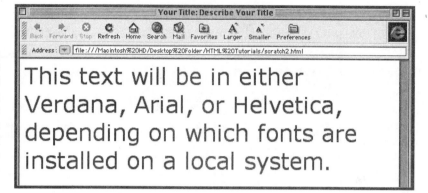

Figure 3-40

Here, the FACE
attribute specifies a
monospaced font
(Courier New).

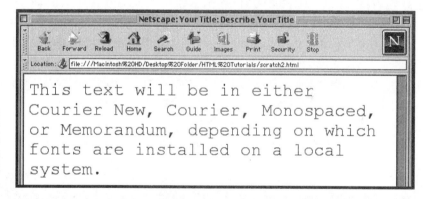

```
<P><FONT SIZE="6" COLOR="blue" FACE="Courier New,
Courier, Monospaced, Memorandum">This text will be in
either Courier New, Courier, Monospaced, or Memorandum,
depending on which fonts are installed on a local
system.</FONT></P>
```

For an example of specifying a "display" font, enter the following (see
Figure 3-41):

```
<P><FONT SIZE="7" COLOR="blue" FACE="Broadway, Impact,
Techno">This text will be in either Broadway, Impact, or
Techno, depending on which fonts are installed on a local
system.</FONT>
```

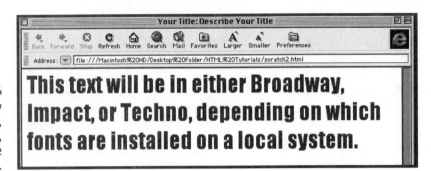

Figure 3-41

If the Broadway font isn't available, the second font, Impact, will be displayed.

CAUTION When using the FONT tag to assign sizes, colors, or faces, you may incur possibly deleterious results. Not everyone uses a graphical browser. Avoid using the FONT tag as a substitute for any of the heading level tags (H1, H2, and so on); text-based and Braille browsers rely on the heading level tags to convey the structure and order of precedence within a document. That doesn't mean that you can't combine the two, either nesting a heading level tag inside a FONT tag, or vice versa (you'll get somewhat different results—one bold and the other not—depending on which way you do it).

Using Background Colors and Images

Using a background color or image is a great way to dress up your Web page. In the following sections, you'll learn how to use a background color (as well as matching text and link colors) and how to use a background image with your Web page.

Using a Background Color

Using the right background color is a simple and easy way to make your Web page look really great (or really horrible, depending on the color you

choose). Background, text, and link colors for the entire page are set with the following attributes in the BODY tag: BGCOLOR sets the background color, TEXT sets the text (or foreground) color, LINK sets the color of unvisited links, VLINK sets the color of visited links, and ALINK sets the color of activated links (where you hold down the mouse button on a link but haven't released it). As with the FONT tag's COLOR attribute, you can set these attributes using any of the 16 color names (black, white, aqua, blue, fuchsia, gray, green, lime, maroon, navy, olive, purple, red, silver, teal, and yellow) or by using RGB hexadecimal codes. The general form for entering these attributes as color names is shown here, where *colorname* refers to one of the 16 color names:

```
<BODY BGCOLOR="colorname" TEXT="colorname" LINK=
"colorname" VLINK="colorname" ALINK="colorname">
```

The general form for entering these attributes as RGB hexadecimal codes is shown here, where *rrggbb* is three pairs of hexadecimal digits forming the code for setting the red, green, and blue components of an RGB color:

```
<BODY BGCOLOR="#rrggbb" TEXT="#rrggbb" LINK="#rrggbb"
VLINK="#rrggbb" ALINK="#rrggbb">
```

The following example sets the colors for the background, the text (or foreground), and the three varieties of links (regular links, visited links, and activated links). Go to the top of the Web page, and then add the following code to the BODY tag, as an example of setting these attributes:

```
<BODY BGCOLOR="#003366" TEXT="#FFFFCC" LINK="#FF9900"
VLINK="#FF6666" ALINK="#FF0000">
```

This sets the background color to slate blue, the text to light yellow, the links to yellow orange, visited links to a salmon peach (or something like that), and activated links to bright red (see Figure 3-42).

Figure 3-42

You can set a background color as well as matching text and link colors (hop over to your browser to see this in color).

TIP

If you stick to hexadecimal codes 00, 33, 66, 99, CC, and FF when inserting RGB hex codes, you can reduce the total number of colors from which you must select to 216. The background, text, and link colors set in the example are all combinations of these codes. This will have the added benefit of making sure that your colors will display as anticipated on a 256-color system.

CAUTION

If you decide to set colors, avoid color combinations that render your text font less readable. The wrong color combination can make your Web page entirely unusable. The important thing is to develop and organize your content first, and then hone the appearance of your Web page. Setting the colors for a badly conceived and poorly organized Web page can only make it worse. Make sure that there is plenty of contrast between your background color and your text and link colors. Also, be sure that your text and link colors don't clash with your background color (like bright red text against a bright blue background).

Using a Background Image

The BACKGROUND attribute of the BODY tag allows you to specify a background image. The background image can be a GIF, JPEG, or PNG file. The general format for entering this attribute is shown as follows, where *filename* is a graphic file that's in the same folder as the Web page, and *URL* is a relative or absolute address of a graphic file that's in a folder other than the Web page:

```
<BODY BACKGROUND="filename or URL">
```

When using background images avoid busy or high-contrast images. If you're going to use a dark background image, you should set the color of your text and links to a lighter color. Go to the top of the Web page and then, as shown in the following example, comment out the previous BODY start tag. Next, add a new BODY start tag using the BACKGROUND attribute to assign BACKGRND.GIF as the background image (see Figure 3-43):

```
<!--<BODY BGCOLOR="#336699" TEXT="#FFFFCC" LINK=
"#FF9900" VLINK="#FF6666" ALINK="#FF0000">-->

<BODY BACKGROUND="backgrnd.gif">
```

Figure 3-43

One of the more effective ways to add visual appeal to your Web page is to use a background image.

Although this example doesn't include them, along with the BACK-GROUND attribute, you can use the TEXT, LINK, VLINK, ALINK, and BGCOLOR tags as well.

TIP

If you specify a dark background image (using the BACKGROUND attribute) in conjunction with light text and link colors, you should be aware that your text and links may not be readable in a browser that has the display of images turned off. To make sure that your page will be readable against a white or light browser background, use the BGCOLOR to set a background color against which the text will still be readable.

Background images are actually pretty small, often no bigger than 100x100 pixels. A browser *tiles* a background image so it covers the entire background of a Web page. This means that a background image can be a great way to add some punch to your page, without adding significantly to its bandwidth usage. Some image editors can create background images, causing all four sides of an image to match up, so that no seams are visible between the tiled images.

FIND IT ON ▶
THE WEB

Many background images that you can use to enhance the look of your Web pages are available on the Web. Here are just a few places where you can download background images:

- ✿ The Background Sampler by Netscape at **home.netscape.com/ assist/net_sites/bg/backgrounds.html**

- ✿ Backgrounds by NCSA at **www.ncsa.uiuc.edu/SDG/Software/ mosaic-w/coolstuff/Backgrnd/**

- ✿ Rose's Backgrounds Archive at **www.wanderers2.com/rose/ backgrounds.html**

FIND IT ON ▶
THE CD

You'll also find many background images included with the Web art collections included on this book's CD-ROM.

Using a Transparent Banner Image

In the previous example, the background of the banner graphic wasn't transparent, but stood out as a white rectangle against the background image. Being a JPEG image, it couldn't be set to be transparent. I've included a GIF version of the same banner image, with the background set to transparent. To check it out, just edit your banner image's IMG tag in your scratch pad file so it matches what's shown here (see Figure 3-44):

```
<BODY BACKGROUND="backgrnd.gif">

<P ALIGN="center"><IMG SRC="banner.gif" WIDTH="595"
HEIGHT="135"></P>
```

The transparent banner image, banner.gif, uses a shadow effect that fades to white. As such, it'll only look good when displayed against a background color that is set to white or a background image within which the primary color is white (such as backgrnd.gif, for instance). In the Sunday Evening session, "Creating Your Own Web Images," you'll learn the various steps involved in creating your own transparent GIF images.

Figure 3-44

If you want your background to show through your banner image, you need to use a transparent GIF image for your banner.

◆ ◆

CAUTION You can't depend on a browser's background automatically being white. While the Macintosh version of Internet Explorer defaults to a white background, many browsers, including the Mac version of Netscape Navigator, default to a gray background. Users can also set whatever color they prefer to be displayed in their browsers' backgrounds. If your Web page will look unattractive (or be unreadable) with a background color other than white, you should specifically identify white as your background color, like this:

```
<BODY BGCOLOR="white" BACKGROUND="backgrnd.gif">
```

This will catch everyone except for folks who've told their browsers to only use their preferred background color, overriding any other background color specified by a Web browser.

◆ ◆

● ●

NOTE Save the HTML file you just created. You can use it later as a reference. When you first saved it, you named it scratch2.html. If more than one person will be doing this tutorial and you want to make sure that this file doesn't get overwritten, you might want to give it a new name.

● ●

Working with Styles

This section is an extra bonus section, so if the dinner bell is ringing or you're just plain running short on time and energy, feel free to come back and do this section at another time.

Style sheets for HTML files are a fairly recent development. Only Internet Explorer 4.0+, Netscape Navigator 4.0+, and some other recent browsers support using styles in Web pages. (In browsers that don't support styles, any styles you set will simply be ignored.)

NOTE

This section contains some examples of how to use styles with the SPAN and other HTML tags. Just type the examples in as shown and then check out the results in your browser. If you like what you see and want to experiment further with styles, I've included some links at the end of this session to assist you in finding out more about using styles.

Saving Your "Styles" Scratch Pad File

Some of the style examples will affect the entirety of your page, so to keep these examples separate from what you've already done in this session, go ahead and resave scratch2.html as scratch2a.html in the HTML Tutorials folder on your Desktop. That way you'll also have a separate file that you can come back to later and use as a quick reference on using styles. You can also use it as a practice file for trying out new style effects in the future.

Applying Styles to the SPAN Tag

By itself, the SPAN tag (a new HTML 4.0 tag) does absolutely nothing. Its whole purpose is to allow you to apply style characteristics to a "span" of text; in other words, applying styles to the SPAN tag allows you to create your own custom text highlighting effects. Edit the paragraph at the top of your scratch pad file to insert an example SPAN tag. It should look like this:

```
<P>This is regular text. <SUP>Use SUP for superscripts.
</SUP> This is regular text. <SUB>Use SUB for subscripts.
</SUB> This is regular text. <U>Use U for underlining.
</U> This is regular text. <STRIKE>Use STRIKE for
strikethrough.</STRIKE></P>

<P>This is regular text. <SPAN>This is SPANNED text.
</SPAN> This is regular text.</P>
```

Don't bother yet to hop over to your browser to check this out. Until you create the style for your spanned text, it'll just be displayed as regular text. To create a sample style for your spanned text, insert the following codes in the HEAD section of your Web page, just below the TITLE tag (see Figure 3-45):

Figure 3-45

The SPAN tag comes to life when a style is applied to it.

> # The Intermediate HTML Tutorial
>
> This is regular text. Use SUP for superscripts. This is regular text. Use SUB for subscripts. This is regular text. Use U for underlining. This is regular text. Use STRIKE for strikethrough.
>
> This is regular text. *This is SPANNED text.* This is regular text.
>
> This text is marked for deletion. This is regular text. This text is marked for insertion.

```
<TITLE>Your Title: Describe Your Title</TITLE>

<STYLE TYPE="text/css">

<!--

SPAN {font-family: sans-serif; font-style: italic;
font-size: 125%; font-weight: bold; color: blue;
background: yellow}

-->

</STYLE>

</HEAD>
```

Applying Styles to Other Tag Elements

You can apply styles to any tag element you can create in an HTML file. For an example of creating styles that can globally affect the appearance of your Web page, add the following example styles to your style sheet (see Figure 3-46):

```
<STYLE TYPE="text/css">

<!--

BODY, OL {font-family: Verdana, sans-serif; font-size:
14pt; color: #CC0000}

H1 {font-family: Verdana, sans-serif; font-weight: 900;
font-size: 32pt; color: blue}
```

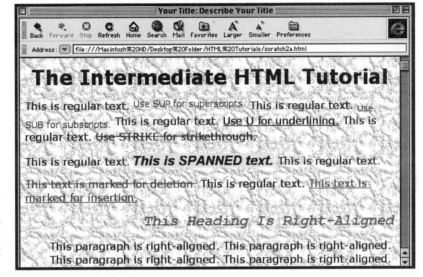

Figure 3-46

You can set styles
for any tag element
in a Web page.

```
H2, H3, H4, H5 {font-family: monospace; font-style:
italic; color: #FF6600}

UL {font-family: Verdana, sans-serif; color: #CC0000;
list-style: url(redball.gif)}

U {color: purple}

STRIKE {color: green}

PRE {color: blue}

DEL, INS {color: fuchsia}

A {color: #339900}

HR {color: #66FFCC}

SPAN {font-family: sans-serif; font-style: italic;
font-size: 125%; font-weight: bold; color: blue;
background: yellow}

-->

</STYLE>
```

If you view this example in Netscape Navigator 4.0+, you'll notice that a couple of things don't quite work. If you set a BODY style, Navigator will apply those settings to any FONT elements in your page, wiping out any font color, size, or face changes that you've set. The other thing you'll notice is that applying a style property to the HR tag (in this case, setting the color) doesn't work.

There's nothing you can do about the HR tag issue, but here's a workaround that'll get Navigator to recognize both your styles and your font color, size, and face changes:

1. Delete the BODY style from the style sheet (just leave the first style set for the OL tag), like this:

   ~~BODY,~~ OL {font-family; Verdana, sans-serif; font-size: 14pt; color: #CC0000}

2. Insert a FONT start tag at the top of your Web page, setting the size, color, and face for paragraph text in your page. For example, type this at the top of your page:

   ```
   <BODY BACKGROUND="backgrnd.gif">

   <FONT SIZE="4" COLOR="#CC0000" FACE="Verdana, Arial, Helvetica">
   ```

3. Insert a FONT end tag at the bottom of your Web page, like this:

   ```
   </FONT>
   ```
   ```
   </BODY>
   ```

Here are some additional pointers to help you understand some of what's going on in the sample style sheet, as well as to show you some alternative property values you can try out:

○ The comment tags (<!-- and -->) that are nested inside the STYLE tag hide its content from browsers that don't recognize the STYLE tag. Browsers that do recognize the STYLE tag will ignore the comment tags.

- Be sure you enclose the properties (`color: green`, for instance) for each style inside the curved brackets ("{" and "}"), not inside of parentheses. Multiple style properties are separated by semicolons.

- For the *font-family* style property, you can specify either specific font family names (like Verdana, Gill, Helvetica), or a generic font family (like sans serif, serif, or monospacee). The first listed font present on a system will be displayed.

- The available *font-style* values are italic, oblique, and normal. The available font-weight values are normal, bold, bolder, lighter, or numerical values incremented by 100 from 100 to 900. For example, a normal value corresponds to a numerical value of 400, while a bold value corresponds to 700.

- You can specify *font-size* values in various fashions. 12pt specifies a 12 point font. You can also specify the font size in pixels (14px, for instance). 150% increases the font's size to 150 percent of a font's default size in points. 2.5em increases the font size two and a half times relative to its actual size (if a user has universally increased the font size, its new size will be set relative to the increased size, not relative to the default size in pixels). You can also specify these font-size values: xx-small, x-small, small, medium, large, x-large, and xx-large.

- You can specify *color* values using either a color name or an RGB hex value. The color names are the same 16 standard color names discussed previously. RGB hex values are also the same discussed previously (#CCFF00, and so on). To set the background color for any element, add a background property (`background: navy`, for example).

Finding Out More About Styles

FIND IT ON ▶
THE WEB

If you want to find out more about using styles, check out these resources on the Web:

- ✿ Cascading Style Sheets by W3C at **www.w3.org/Style/CSS/**

- ✿ WebDeveloper.com's Guide to Cascading Style Sheets at **www.webdeveloper.com/html/html_css_1.html**

- ✿ Cascading Style Sheets by Web Design Group at **www.htmlhelp.com/reference/css/**

- ✿ Creating Your First Style Sheet by Eric Meyer at **webreview.com/wr/pub/97/10/10/style/**

- ✿ Web Review's CSS Browser Compatibility Charts at **webreview.com/wr/pub/97/10/10/style/index.html**

Wrapping Up

If you've made it this far and finished both the Basic HTML Tutorial this morning and the Intermediate HTML Tutorial this afternoon, you're doing great! If you've finished only part of the Intermediate HTML Tutorial, or even if you've barely skimmed it, that's perfectly OK; everything in this afternoon's tutorial was frosting on the cake.

Take a dinner break and then, if you've got the energy, come back in an hour or so for the Saturday Evening bonus session, "Introduction to Adobe PageMill 3.0." If your brain is fried and your fingers are cramped, feel free to come back to do that session some other time and I'll see you bright and early tomorrow morning, when you'll start planning your first Web page.

Introduction to Adobe PageMill 3.0 (Bonus Session)

- Setting up your Web site
- Creating link lists
- Changing font colors and sizes
- Dragging and dropping images
- Using background colors and images

This is a bonus session, so you don't have to do it this weekend. If you haven't done the Saturday Morning session, "The Basic HTML Tutorial," I recommend that you complete it before moving on to this session. If you haven't yet done the Saturday Afternoon session, "The Intermediate HTML Tutorial," that's fine—you've got the option of doing this session in its place.

Adobe PageMill is a premier Web authoring software program that combines HTML editing, site management, and some image manipulation capabilities. In this session, you will learn about PageMill's HTML editing capabilities.

Getting the Software

Adobe PageMill 3.0 has the following system requirements:

- PowerPC Mac

- OS System 7.5 or later

- 5 MB application RAM/16 MB system RAM

FIND IT ON ▶
THE WEB Adobe PageMill 3.0 comes bundled with the iMac, so if you have an iMac you can install the application from the wallet of CD-ROMs that came with your computer. After inserting the CD-ROM disc, just double-click on its icon on the Desktop; then run the installer. You can also download a 30-day try-out version at **www.adobe.com/newsfeatures/tryadobe/ main.html**.

Getting Started

After installing PageMill, you need to create a new PageMill Web site. In the following sections, you'll create a folder, PageMill Tutorial, on the Desktop, and then designate it as the local root folder of your PageMill Web site.

◄ ◄

In a Web site, whether it is located on your own computer or up on the Web, the *root folder* is the folder inside of which all files and any other folders in your site are located.

◄ ◄

In the following steps, you'll create a PageMill Web site for doing this tutorial. Tomorrow, if you decide to use PageMill to create your first Web page, you should create another PageMill Web site to hold the Web site you'll ultimately be transferring to the Web.

Creating Your Root Folder

Just follow these steps to create the root folder for your PageMill Web site:

1. If it isn't already selected, choose the Finder in the Applications menu. If you have any application windows open, choose Hide Others in the Applications menu. Close any file folders that are open on the Desktop.

2. With the Finder selected in the Applications menu, choose File and New Folder from the File menu.

3. On the Desktop, click on the name of the new folder ("untitled folder") to highlight it and type **PageMill Tutorial** as the new folder name (if more than one person will be doing this tutorial on the same computer, you may want to give this folder a unique name, such as **John's PageMill Tutorial**).

Creating and Naming Your New PageMill Site

Next, create and name your PageMill Site:

1. Run PageMill (click on the application's icon in the Adobe PageMill 3.0 folder).

2. In PageMill, choose New and New Site from the File Menu.

3. In the Name box, type a name for your site (this doesn't have to be the same as the name of the folder you just created). For example, call it **My PageMill Tutorial**.

4. Click on the Local Site Location button. Click the PageMill Tutorial folder (if that's what you named it) and click on the Choose button.

5. Click on the Create button to create a default home page (index. html) in your site's root folder. A dialog box showing the folder tree and file list for your new site should be displayed, as shown in Figure 4-1.

Specifying a Resources Folder

You should specify a folder within your site where PageMill will save any GIF files converted from imported PICT images and other external files (media and other files imported from outside of your PageMill site) when

Figure 4-1

A new PageMill site, PageMill Tutorial, has been created.

you upload your page to your Web server. (PageMill will create this folder when it is necessary). To do this:

1. Choose Preferences from the Edit menu; then in the window on the left, scroll down to and click on the Site icon.

2. In the Site Resources Folder Name box, type a name for the folder (**images,** for example, although you can name this folder whatever you want) and click on the OK button.

3. To ensure that converted images are placed in the site, even if the site isn't loaded, choose Preferences from the Edit menu, and then click on the Resources icon.

4. Under the Resource Folder, click on the folder button. Double-click the local root folder you created for your site (the PageMill Tutorial folder, for instance) to open it.

5. Click on the New button, and type the same folder name (**images**, for instance). Click on the Create button.

6. Click on the Choose button, and the OK button.

Opening Your Index Page

Your index page (index.html) will automatically be opened when your Web site is accessed in a Web browser. Go ahead and open your index page in PageMill:

1. Double-click on **index.html** to open it in PageMill.

2. In the Title box, delete "Untitled Document"; then type a new title for the page. For instance, type **My PageMill Tutorial**).Then hit the Return key (see Figure 4-2).

Using the Sample Text

You can type text directly into PageMill's document window, or you can drag and drop text into it. To make things a bit easier for you, I've included

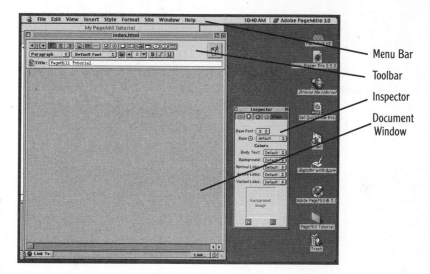

Menu Bar

Toolbar

Inspector

Document Window

Figure 4-2

The site's default page, index.html, is opened in PageMill.

a text file, sample.txt, in the HTML Tutorials folder you copied to the Desktop in the Saturday Morning session.

1. Open sample.txt in your text editor.

2. Position your text editor's window so that PageMill's document window is also visible.

3. Click and drag with the mouse to select all of the text in sample.txt; click and hold the mouse down on the selected text, and then drag and drop it into PageMill's document window. (See Figure 4-3.)

4. Close or hide your text editor's window. Click inside PageMill's document window (index.html) to deselect the text you just dragged and dropped.

TIP

When creating text to be imported into PageMill, separate text paragraphs with two hard returns. A single return between text paragraphs is converted to a line break, not a paragraph break.

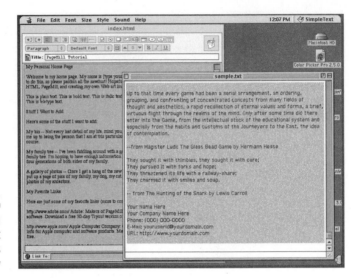

Figure 4-3

You can drag and drop text into PageMill's document window

TIP

You can view and directly edit the source HTML code that PageMill creates, by selecting View and Source Mode; to return to the regular edit mode, just click on Source Mode again. You can also press Command+H to toggle Source Mode on and off. (If dragging and dropping text or images messes up the page display in the document window, you can just toggle Source Mode on and off to fix it.)

Setting Heading Levels

The headings you set determine the hierarchical structure of your Web page. To structure and organize your Web page, you should always use headings (selected from the Change Format menu), instead of simply changing the font size. You can select from six different headings, although only the first four are commonly used: Largest, Larger, Large, Small, Smaller, and Smallest.

• •

It is good practice in most cases to include only one level-one heading (Largest Heading), at the top of your Web page. Some Web page designs may substitute a banner graphic for a level-one heading, either eliminating the level-one heading altogether or using it for section headings. This is perfectly standard HTML, if you want to do it that way. Many search engines give special weight to your level-one heading and may not index your page the way you want, if more than one level-one heading is present or if it is absent.

You should also avoid using the heading formats for purely decorative, rather than structural, purposes. If you just want to increase the size of some text, change the font size instead of using one of the heading formats.

• •

Major sections should be set using a level-two heading (Larger Heading), and subsections using a level-three heading (Large Heading).

Set one level-one heading and two level-two headings:

1. Click on the text line, "My Personal Home Page." Pull down the toolbar's Change Format menu (see Figure 4-4) and choose the Largest Heading format.

2. Click on the text line, "Stuff I Want to Add"; choose Larger Heading from the Change Format menu.

3. Click on the text line, "My Favorite Links"; choose Larger Heading again from the Change Format menu (see Figure 4-5).

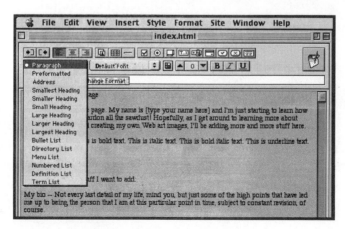

Figure 4-4

A variety of formats can be applied to paragraphs in PageMill.

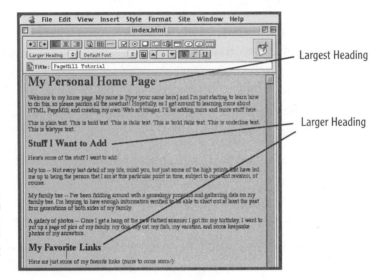

Largest Heading

Larger Heading

Figure 4-5

Organize a
Web page by
setting different
heading levels.

Aligning Headings and Other Paragraphs

By default, headings and paragraphs are left-aligned. You can also right-align or center headings and paragraphs. The second group of icons on the toolbar show the alignment of the current paragraph, where the cursor is located. To center the level-one heading:

1. Click on the level-one heading ("My Personal Home Page") at the top of the page. You should see the Left Align Text icon selected on the toolbar.

2. Click on the Center Text icon on the toolbar to center the heading (see Figure 4-6).

Increasing the Base Font Size

With larger monitors becoming standard, most surfers now have a screen resolution of 800 × 600 pixels. This suggests that the default base font size displayed in most browsers may be a little smaller than it should be. It is

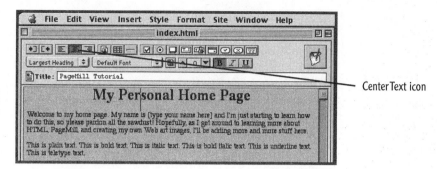

Center Text icon

Figure 4-6

You can center and right-align headings and paragraphs.

not a bad idea to increase the base font size for your Web page to help make it more readable:

1. If the Inspector window is not visible, choose Show Inspector from the Window menu on the menu bar.

2. In the Inspector, change the Base Font setting from 3 to 4.

Highlighting Text

You can apply bold, italic, underline, teletype and other styles to text. Apply the following highlighting styles to the text in the second paragraph:

1. Select the text, "This is bold text." Click the Bold icon on the toolbar.

2. Select the text, "This is italic text." Click the Italic icon on the toolbar.

3. Select the text, "This is bold italic text." Click the Bold icon and then click the Italic icon.

4. Select the text, "This is underline text." Click the Underline icon.

5. Select the text, "This is teletype text." Choose Teletype from the Style menu (see Figure 4-7).

Figure 4-7

You can easily apply bold, italic, bold italic, underline, teletype, and other text highlighting styles.

There are a variety of additional highlighting styles you can apply to your text from the Style pull-down option on the menu bar. These include the Strong, Emphasis, Citation, Sample, Keyboard, Code, and Variable styles. The Strong style displays exactly the same as the Bold style, and the Emphasis style displays exactly the same as the Italic style. The only difference is that Bold and Italic are descriptive names, while Strong and Emphasis are logical names. In most browsers, the Citation and the Variable styles display exactly the same as the Italic or Emphasis styles, while the Sample, Keyboard, and Code styles display exactly the same as the Teletype tag (in a monospaced font). Unless you want to create a Cascading Style Sheet to differentiate the display of these additional highlighting styles, you should probably just stick to using the Bold, Italic, Underline, and Teletype highlighting styles.

Creating a Numbered List

You create a numbered list by using the Numbered List format style:

1. Click and drag with the mouse to select the last three paragraphs (starting with "My bio" and ending with "A gallery of photos").

2. Choose the Numbered List format from the Change Format menu. As shown in Figure 4-8, the three selected paragraphs have been indented, with "#." inserted where the list numbers will be displayed.

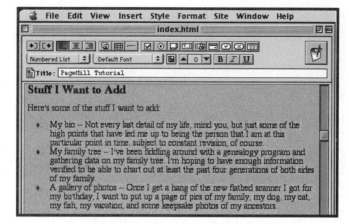

Figure 4-8

Numbered lists are
easy to create.

3. To dress up your numbered list a bit, you can apply a Bold highlighting style to "My bio," "My family tree," and "A gallery of photos."

Checking It Out in Your Browser

You can't actually see what your numbered list is going to look like until
you see it in your browser. To check it out:

1. Press Command-S to save your page.

2. Choose Switch To from the View menu, and then click on your
   browser (Netscape Navigator or Internet Explorer, for instance). You
   should see your page in your browser, as shown in Figure 4-9.
   Choose Quit from your browser's File menu to quit your browser.

TIP

To edit which browsers are listed in the Switch To menu, select Preferences from the Edit
menu and click on the Switch To icon. To add a browser, click on the Add icon, locate the
browser's program file, and then click Open.

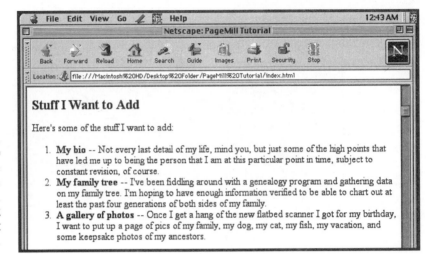

Stuff I Want to Add

Here's some of the stuff I want to add:

1. **My bio** -- Not every last detail of my life, mind you, but just some of the high points that have led me up to being the person that I am at this particular point in time, subject to constant revision, of course.
2. **My family tree** -- I've been fiddling around with a genealogy program and gathering data on my family tree. I'm hoping to have enough information verified to be able to chart out at least the past four generations of both sides of my family.
3. **A gallery of photos** -- Once I get a hang of the new flatbed scanner I got for my birthday, I want to put up a page of pics of my family, my dog, my cat, my fish, my vacation, and some keepsake photos of my ancestors.

Figure 4-9

To actually see the numbers in a numbered list, you have to check your page out in a browser.

NOTE You can also get a rough idea of what your page will look like in a browser by viewing it in PageMill's Preview mode. To toggle the Preview mode on and off, just click the Toggle Preview Mode icon (in the upper-right corner of your page's window). You can also choose Preview Mode from the View menu. In this example, there is no difference between how your page is displayed in Edit or Preview mode (you just can't edit your page in Preview mode). The numbers for the numbered list you just created, for instance, are still displayed as "#" characters in Preview mode.

Creating a Bulleted List

It is just as easy to create a bulleted list as it is to create a numbered list. To do this you use the Bullet List format:

1. Under the "My Favorite Links" heading, click and drag to select all four paragraphs beginning with "http://. . ."

2. Choose the Bullet List format from the Change Format pull-down menu. As shown in Figure 4-10, the three selected paragraphs have been changed to the desired format.

> **My Favorite Links**
>
> Here are just some of my favorite links (more to come soon!):
>
> - http://www.adobe.com/ Adobe: Makers of PageMill 3.0, PhotoShop, Illustrator, and other software. Download a free 30-day Tryout version of PageMill 3.0.
> - http://www.apple.com/ Apple Computer Company: Get the latest updates, suport info, and product info for Apple computer and software products. Mac OS 8.5 users can download Mac OS 8.6 for free.
> - http://www.imac2day.com/ iMac2day: A great resource page for iMac users, including articles, reviews, message board, and where to get the best iMac deals.
> - http://www.w3.org/ World Wide Web Consortium: This is where to find out all about the official specs for HTML, CSS, XML, XSL, XHTML, SMIL and other Web acronyms!

Figure 4-10

Bulleted lists are also easy to create.

Creating Hypertext Links

In the text for the list you just created, some Web addresses are included that you can use to practice creating hypertext links. When you're done, the result will be a link list, which combines a bulleted list with a list of hypertext links. Create the first hypertext link:

1. Click and drag to select the first Web address and the following space ("http://www.adobe.com/ ").

2. Press Command-X to cut the selected text. (Or choose Cut from the Edit menu.)

3. Click and drag to select the text ("Adobe:") at the start of the first list item (don't select the following space).

4. Click inside the Link To box at the bottom of the PageMill window. Press Command-V to paste in the Web address you cut in Step 2 (or select Paste from the Edit menu). Hit the Delete key to delete the following space, and then hit the Return key to create the link (see Figure 4-11).

5. Repeat these steps to create the hypertext links for the next three bulleted list items. When you're finished, the result should look like what's shown in Figure 4-12.

Figure 4-11

To create a
hypertext link, just
highlight the text
you want for the
link, and then
type or paste in
the Web address in
the Link To box.

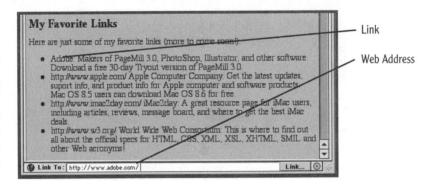

Link

Web Address

Figure 4-12

A Web page
without any
hypertext links
just isn't a
Web page!

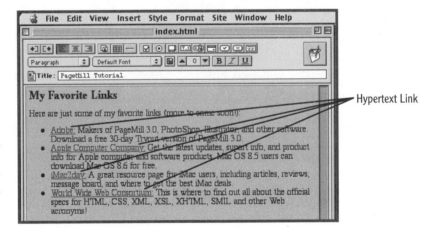

Hypertext Link

To test out any of these links, save your page (Command-S) and switch to
your browser (choosing Switch To from the View menu). For instance, if
you click on the "Adobe" link you added, your dialer will connect you to
the Internet (unless you're already connected), and Adobe's home page will
be opened in your browser, as shown in Figure 4-13. When finished checking
out Adobe's home page, just choose Quit from your browser'sFile menu;
then disconnect from the Internet. That's it. You've just created and tested
out your very first list of links in PageMill.

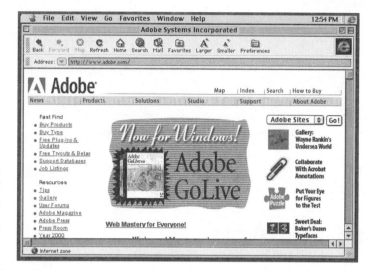

Figure 4-13

You can switch to your browser and check out any links you've added in PageMill.

Creating Definition Lists

Another kind of list you can create in PageMill is a definition list. This is sometimes also called a "glossary" list, because it is used most often to create a glossary (or list of terms and definitions). A definition list can also be used to create a Q&A (*Questions & Answers*) list or a FAQ list. To create a "glossary" definition list:

1. Click and drag to select the six paragraphs starting with "Appeal" and ending with "when required."

2. Choose the Definition List format from the Change Format menu.

3. Click on "Appeal"; then choose the Term List format from the Change Format menu. Repeat for "Arrest" and "Bail."

4. Definition lists by themselves are a bit blank. To dress up the list a bit, apply Bold highlighting to "Appeal," "Arrest," and "Bail" (see Figure 4-14).

NOTE

There are two other list types, menu and directory lists, that can be created in Page-Mill. However, in almost all browsers, these list types display exactly the same as a bulleted list.

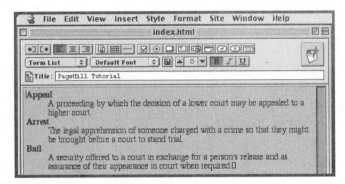

Figure 4-14

Definition lists are often used to create glossaries.

Creating Block Quotes

In HTML, the BLOCKQUOTE tag is used to indent "block quotes" in from the left and right margins. Many Web publishers, however, use this tag to double-indent a text block on a Web page. In PageMill, you can click on the Increase Indent icon on the toolbar to create a block quote. Clicking on the Increase Indent icon again increases the double-indent (it actually nests your text within two BLOCKQUOTE tags). Clicking on the Decrease Indent icon decreases the double-indent. To create a double-indented block quote, do the following:

1. Click anywhere in the paragraph starting "Up to that time. . ." Click on the Increase Indent icon on the toolbar.

2. Click anywhere in the following paragraph ("—from Magister Ludi. . ."). Click on the Increase Indent icon.

3. To increase the double-indent for any paragraph, click again on that paragraph and on the Increase Indent icon (see Figure 4-15).

4. To decrease the double-indent for the first paragraph ("Up to that time. . ."), click on it and on the Decrease Indent icon.

5. To complete the look of a "block quote," click on the second paragraph, and then on the Right Align Text icon on the toolbar. Additionally, if you want, italicize the title of the book (see Figure 4-16).

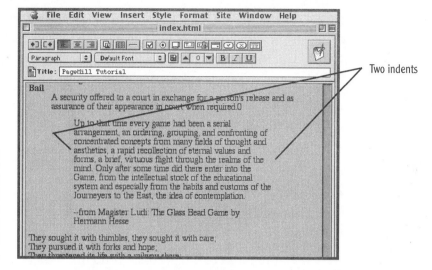

Two indents

Figure 4-15

The Increase Indent icon can be used to create block quotes or to just double-indent text on a Web page.

Figure 4-16

Creating a real "block quote," including the citation line, is easy.

NOTE

While recent browsers just double-indent block quotes, some older browsers add additional formatting, such as italicizing or bolding the block quote text. As these older browsers go out of use, this becomes less of a concern, but you may want to take it into consideration if you want to use this feature just to create double-indents on a Web page.

Creating Indented Poetry Stanzas Using a Block Quote

Much poetry put up on the Web is created just using a left-aligned paragraph, with line breaks added to single-space the poetry lines. Using a block quote to indent a poem can add a nice touch:

1. Click anywhere in the next text example (starting with "They sought it with thimbles. . ."). Click on the Increase Indent icon on the toolbar.

2. Click on the following paragraph ("--from The Hunting. . ."), and then click twice on the Increase Indent icon. Click the Right Align Text icon. To complete the look, italicize the title of the work (see Figure 4-17).

When you drag and drop text into PageMill's document window, any single hard returns between lines of text are automatically changed to line breaks (double hard returns are changed to paragraph breaks). When typing in your own raw text, you may want to insert your own line breaks. To check out adding your own line break:

1. Click at the start of the poem's second line, and press the Delete key to delete the line break.

2. Choose Special Character and Line Break from the Insert menu. (You can also just press Shift-Return to get the same result.)

Using Preformatted Text

The default font for paragraph and other text in Web pages is a proportional font. To line up columns, such as figures in a chart, you need a font for which the various characters and numbers all have a single width. The solution is the Preformatted format style, which allows you to set a block of text in a monospace (*or fixed-pitch*) font such as Courier New or Courier. (If you're preparing your text in your text editor, be sure to do your typing

Figure 4-17

You can also use a block quote, with line breaks, to indent a stanza of poetry.

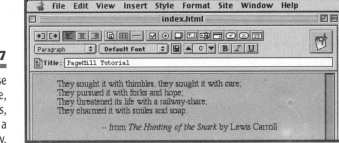

in a monospace font. Otherwsie, you won't be able to accurately line up the columns of your table.

To save you some time, I've already prepared an example of preformatted text that you can drag and drop into your Web page. I didn't include it with the first batch of example text because PageMill generally collapses extra spaces if you save and reopen your page, unless you apply the Preformatted format style right away. To drag and drop the preformatted text example into your Web page, do the following:

1. In PageMill, position the cursor at the start of the line, "Your Name Here," and hit the Return key to insert a line.

2. In your text editor, open **sample2.txt** from the HTML Tutorials folder.

3. Arrange your text editor's window and PageMill's document window so both are visible. You should be able to see in PageMill's window the location (just above the line "Your Name Here") where you want to drag and drop the text from your text editor.

4. Click and drag to select all of the text in sample2.txt. Click on the selected text, and drag it to the PageMill document window, dropping it onto the blank line you added in Step 1. (You don't want to drop it into the block quote you created above. If you drop your text in the wrong place, choose Undo Drag from the Edit menu and try again.) Quit your text editor.

5. In PageMill, your dropped text should still be selected. Choose Preformatted from the Change Format pop-up menu (see Figure 4-18).

Figure 4-18

The Preformatted style formats text in a monospace font (such as Courier New).

```
First Quarter Sales Figures for 1999 ($000)
--------------------------------------------
              Jan       Feb       Mar     Totals
Adams     $ 1255    $ 2345    $ 5250    $ 8850
Baker       2690      1525      3650      7865
Caldwell    3235      2575      2400      8210
Peters      1525      2165      1250      4940
Wilson      1755      1585      1045      4385
            ------    ------    ------    ------
Totals    $10460    $10195    $13595    $34250
          ======    ======    ======    ======
```

Using Horizontal Rules

Horizontal rules are often used to separate different sections of a Web page. To create an example of adding a horizontal rule, do the following:

1. Click at the start of the line, "Your Name Here," and hit the Return key to add a blank line. Press the left-arrow key on the keyboard to reposition the cursor at the start of the blank line.

2. Choose Horizontal Rule from the Insert menu. You'll notice that a horizontal rule has been added.

3. Click on the horizontal rule. In the Inspector window, change the Width to **85**, but leave Percent selected, to set the rule to a width of 85 percent of the browser window. In the Size box, type **5** to increase the height of the rule to five pixels. Check the No Shade check box. To center the rule, click on the Center Align Text icon on the toolbar.

4. To see what your horizontal rule looks like, just click the mouse above the horizontal rule to deselect it (see Figure 4-19).

Creating an Address Block

One of the most common uses of a horizontal rule is to set off the address block at the bottom of a Web page. I've already included some example text for your address block at the bottom of the page, just below the horizontal rule you just added. To create your address block, just do the following:

Figure 4-19

Horizontal rules are often used to separate different sections in a Web page.

1. Select the five lines starting with "Your Name Here."

2. Click on the Change Format pop-up menu and on Address. You'll notice that text included in an address block is automatically italicized.

3. To center your address block, click on the Center Align Text icon on the toolbar.

4. Type your own name in place of "Your Name Here." Type your company name in place of "Your Company Name Here" (or delete it if you don't want to add a company name). If you're planning on creating a business site, you can type your phone number in place of "(000) 000-0000" (otherwise, if you'll be creating a non-business site, delete this line). If you have an e-mail address, type it in place of "yourname@yourdomain.com." If you already have a Web address, type it in place of "www.yourdomain.com."

Adding an E-mail Link

An e-mail link is a hypertext link that pops up a window allowing someone to send a message to your e-mail address. To add an e-mail link, do the following:

1. If you typed in your own e-mail address, select it with the mouse (or just select the dummy e-mail address in the example).

2. Press Command-C to copy your e-mail address. Click inside the Link To box at the bottom of PageMill's window, type **mailto:**, press Command-V to paste in your e-mail address, and then hit the Return key (see Figure 4-20).

Figure 4-20

It is a good idea to add an e-mail link to your address block

Adding Inline Images

There are several different ways you can add inline images to your Web pages: inserting, copying and pasting, and dragging and dropping them. You'll learn how to insert a banner graphic at the top of your Web page, and then how to drag and drop an image into your Web page.

Inserting a Banner Graphic

A banner graphic usually runs across the top of a Web page. I've included an example banner graphic, mybanner.gif, in the HTML Tutorials folder. To add a banner graphic to the top of your page, just do the following:

1. At the top of your page in PageMill, add a blank line.

2. Click on the blank line; then select Insert, Object, and Image from the menu bar.

3. In the Insert dialog box, open the HTML Tutorials folder. Double-click on mybanner.gif to insert it into your page (see Figure 4-21).

Because mybanner.gif is outside of your Web site, when you use PageMill to transfer your page to the Web, it'll automatically transfer mybanner.gif to the Resources folder (**images**) you set up at the start of this session.

Figure 4-21

A banner graphic runs across the top of a Web page.

CAUTION ◆◆◆◆◆◆◆◆◆◆◆◆◆◆◆◆◆◆◆◆◆◆◆◆◆◆◆◆◆◆◆◆◆◆◆◆◆

Whenever you link to an image (or any other external resource) that is outside of your PageMill site, PageMill will transfer it to your Resources folder (images, for instance) when you use PageMill to transfer your site to the Web, but not before. If you do choose to link to images or other resources that are outside of your PageMill site, you should make sure not to alter, move, delete, rename, or otherwise change the image or resource, at least until you've transferred your site to your Web server. This is only for practice, since when you create a real site in PageMill, it is a good idea to first copy an image or other resource into a folder in your site before linking to it from a page in your site.

◆◆◆

Making a Color Transparent

When using a GIF image for your banner graphic, in PageMill you can set one of the colors in the graphic (usually the background color) so that it'll be transparent. To set the background color of your banner graphic to be transparent, just do the following:

1. Click on your banner graphic to select it.

2. Choose Image and Open Image Window from the Edit menu.

3. In the image window, click on the Make Transparent icon (the "wand") and then on the color you want to be transparent (the background color). You'll notice that the background color has been changed to a shade of gray to indicate that it is now transparent (see Figure 4-22).

4. Close the image window. At the prompt, click the Save button to save the changes to your image.

Dragging and Dropping an Inline Image

You can drag and drop an image from a Web page, an image editor window, or any other application that allows dragging and dropping of images. For this example, you'll drag and drop an image from the Adobe PageMill 3.0 CD-ROM:

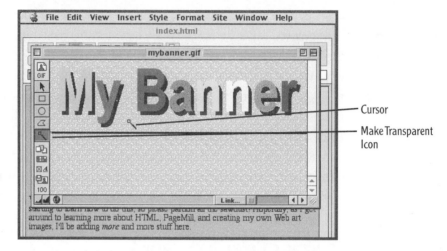

Cursor

Make Transparent Icon

Figure 4-22

You can change a color in a GIF image to be transparent.

NOTE

If you're using the tryout version of PageMill, you won't have the PageMill CD-ROM available. Instead, you can open tutor2.html from the HTML Tutorials folder and then drag and drop rain_lin.gif from that file into your PageMill page.

1. In PageMill, click at the start of the first paragraph ("Welcome to. . ."); then hit the Return key to add a blank line.

2. Insert the PageMill CD-ROM in your CD-ROM drive. Double-click on the CD-ROM's icon once it appears on the Desktop (if you can't see the CD-ROM icon, just hide PageMill in the Application menu).

3. Double-click on the Web Pages and Content folder, on the WebMorsels folder, and then on **index.html**.

4. In your browser, click on the top banner ("WebMorsels catalog").

5. In the WebMorsels Catalog page, if necessary, scroll the page down so that the list of links is visible under WebMorsels Image Index. Click on the Rules link (under WebMorsels Image Index), and then click the Marble link.

6. Resize and position the browser window so that both it and PageMill's document window are visible (close some folder windows, if you need to).

7. Click on one of the "marble" graphic rules, drag it over to PageMill's window, and drop it on the blank line you added. Quit your browser.

8. If the graphic rule isn't already centered, just click on it and then on the Center Align Text icon on the toolbar (see Figure 4-23).

Flowing Text Around an Image

You can flow text around either the left or right side of an inline image. For an example of doing this, just do the following:

1. Click at the start of the first paragraph ("Welcome to. . .").

2. Choose Object and Image from the Insert menu. Open the HTML Tutorials folder, and double-click on **logo.gif**.

Graphic rule

Figure 4-23

A graphic rule has been dragged and dropped into the page.

3. Click on the image; then choose Align Object from the Format menu. Choose Left to align the image at the left side of the page (and wrap the text around the right). (Choosing Right does it the other way around, aligning the image at the right side of the page and wrapping the text around the left.)

4. Click at the end of the first paragraph (". . .more stuff here.") and then on Insert and Margin Break (see Figure 4-24).

Take a Break?

You are well on your way through the basics of PageMill. If you've done everything up until now, then you may be starting to get the yawns, unless of course you're now on your fifteenth cup of coffee! Even if you've just done the Saturday Morning session and the first part of this session, that's still a lot of ground covered. If your battery is running low and the clock is creeping toward (or has already crept past) midnight, feel free to call it a day. Just save your page before exiting PageMill, so you can pick up later where you left off.

However, if you're primed to learn even more now about using PageMill, take a quick break. Stretch those muscles, maybe get a breath of the fresh night air. I'll see you back here in ten minutes or so, when you'll learn about changing font sizes, colors, and faces, using background images, and creating a table of contents for your page.

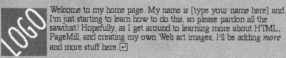

Figure 4-24

You can flow text around an image.

Changing Font Sizes and Colors

A good way to dress up the look of your page is to change font sizes and colors. For an example of changing the size and color of a font, do the following:

1. In the first paragraph, replace the text "[type your name here]" with your own first name (if you haven't already done so).

2. Click and drag with the mouse to select your name. Choose Size from the Style menu, and then choose +2 to increase the size of the text up two notches. Since you earlier set the base font size to 4, this will increase the size of the selected text to a font size of 6. (You can also click on the Increase Relative Font Size icon on the toolbar to increase the font size.)

3. With your name still selected, choose Color from the Style menu (you can also click on the Set Color icon on the toolbar). Click on one of the 16 listed colors. To make the color a bit more noticeable, click the Bold icon on the toolbar (see Figure 4-25).

You can also select a custom color. To select a color other than the basic 16 colors listed, select the text you want to color, and then choose Color from the Style menu, and then choose Custom.

Changing Fonts

You can change the font for selected text. (If a font is not available on someone's computer system, they won't be able to see your font change in their browser. Arial, Courier New, and Verdana, available with the iMac,

Figure 4-25

You can change the size and color of any text in your page.

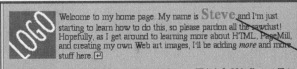

Size and color change

are the only fonts you can also reliably expect to be present on a Windows system. These fonts may not, however, be present on many other Mac systems. In the following, you'll apply a font to text and edit the source code for your page in order to include a list of fonts to be displayed (which increases the changes that at least one will be present on other systems). For an example of changing the font, do the following:

1. Select your level-one heading ("My Personal Home Page").

2. Choose Font from the Style menu (you can also pull down the Set Font menu on the toolbar). If available, choose Arial, and if Arial isn't on your system, choose Helvetica. (In the next section, you'll learn how to manually add a list of fonts in place of the single font you just chose—that way you could manually insert Arial in front of Helvetica, although you'd still see Helvetica on your system, as would other Mac users without Arial.)

3. While you're at it, change the font color: choose Color from the Style menu, and then choose one of the 16 listed colors (or choose Custom to pick a custom color). The font and color is applied to the level-one heading, as shown in Figure 4-26 (you'll have to preview this in your browser to see the color, however).

Figure 4-26

The font for the level-one heading, "My Personal Home Page," has been changed to Arial.

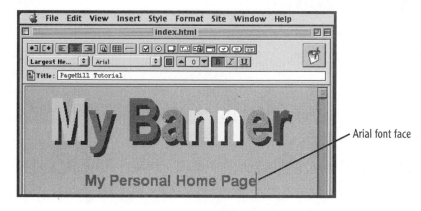

Arial font face

> ### Making Wise Font Selections
>
> Even though PostScript fonts are native to the Macintosh system, they aren't necessarily native to other systems. Windows users, for instance, must purchase Adobe Type Manager as a separate product if they want to be able to display smoothly-rendered PostScript fonts on their systems. If they don't have Adobe Type Manager installed (and most of them won't), they will see a very poor quality bitmap version of your PostScript font.
>
> For this reason, if you want to apply a typeface in PageMill using the Set Font control on the toolbar (or by choosing Style and Font from the menu bar), you should avoid selecting PostScript fonts. Instead, select True-Type fonts that have a good chance of being present on both Macintosh and Windows systems. This largely narrows your choices down to Arial or Verdana (instead of Helvetica), Courier New (instead of Courier), and Times New Roman (instead of Times).
>
> For a way to specify both True-Type and Postscript fonts at the same time, see the next section, "Editing the Source Code to Include a List of Fonts."

Editing the Source Code to Include a List of Fonts

While you can't depend on any one font being present on all computer platforms, you can include a list of fonts that will cover as many bases as possible. For instance, if you want to have your selected text displayed in a sans serif font, you could list not only Arial, but also Helvetica, Verdana, AvantGarde, and Geneva. If you want to have it displayed in a monospaced font, you could list not only Courier, but also Courier New. You're also not limited to only listing fonts that are included on your own system—if you know the name of a font that is generally available to Windows users, but not to Mac users, you can still include it in your list of fonts (you just may not be able to see it yourself). There are also cases where the same font will be present on both Mac and Windows systems, but won't be spelled the same. In those cases, you could include both spelling variants in your list of fonts—for instance, Gill Sans Condensed Bold is available on the iMac, while Gill Sans Ultra Bold Condensed may be available on a Windows computer.

To include a list of fonts, instead of using just a single font for your level-one heading, do the following:

1. Choose Source Mode from the View menu (or press Command-H).

2. If your level-one heading was still selected, it should still be selected (highlighted) in Source mode. Within the highlighted code, locate the FACE="Arial" code (or FACE="Helvetica", if you specified that font).

3. Edit the FACE attribute you just located, replacing the original single typeface name with a list of typefaces. For instance, edit the FACE attribute so it matches what's shown here: FACE="Arial, Helvetica".

NOTE By inserting Arial in front of Helvetica, you ensure that Windows users will see Arial and not a bitmap version of Helvetica if they don't have Adobe Type Manager installed. Macintosh users without Arial on their systems will see Helvetica instead.

The same holds true for specifying other PostScript fonts, such as Courier, Times, Avant Garde, Helvetica Narrow, and so on. You should always insert appropriate True-Type fonts in front of any PostScript fonts you want to include in a list of typefaces. For instance, if you want to list the Courier typeface, always insert the New Courier typeface first; if you want to insert Helvetica, always insert Arial first; if you want to insert Times, always insert Times New Roman first.

4. Choose Source Mode again from the View mode to toggle it off.

Changing Text, Links, and Background Colors

To really change the look of your page, you can change the colors of the text, links, and background. To change these colors, just do the following:

1. Change the color of the background (it is easier to set the background color first, and then to set the other colors to match). Click on the Background pop-up menu in the Inspector, and on a darker color, such as navy blue.

2. Change the colors of the rest in the Body Text, Normal Links, Active Links, and Visited Links pop-up menus (see Figure 4-27).

SELECTING COLORS

Sometimes the 16 standard colors aren't enough for you to do everything you want with your Web pages. If you want to create a more subtle and appealing color scheme, you'll need to select at least some custom colors (choose Color from the Style menu, and then choose Custom). It is beyond the scope of this short tutorial to explain how to select custom colors, but you can find lots of guidance on doing this in PageMill's help files.

This does, however, open up another can of worms. Any custom colors you choose may end up getting dithered on systems that can only display 256 colors, turning a color that looks great on your system into one that looks terrible on someone else's system.

A workaround is to avoid using PageMill's custom colors. Instead, in Source mode, manually insert RGB hex color codes that are part of the browser-safe palette (the 216 colors that will display undithered on 256-color systems). For more inform-ation on doing this, see "Setting Colors Using RGB Hex Codes" in the Intermediate HTML Tutorial (the Saturday Afternoon session).

Figure 4-27

You can change the colors of the text, links, and background.

Setting a Background Image

You can also set a background image. To tile a background image behind your page, do the following:

1. In the Inspector (under the Page tab), click the icon located on the left under the "background image" square.

2. For a background image example, open the HTML Tutorials folder, and double-click 3dgreen.gif (see Figure 4-28).

Feel free to try out other background images. Depending on the background image you select, you may have to reselect the colors of your text and links to complement your background image. When using a textured background image (such as 3dgreen.gif), you may also want to increase the base font size another notch (to 5, for instance) to help ensure that the text will be easily read against the background.

It is also a good idea to set a background color that is at least close to the primary color of your background image. That way, if someone has display of graphics turned off, they won't end up seeing (or not seeing) white text

Figure 4-28

Using a background image can give your page a more dramatic look.

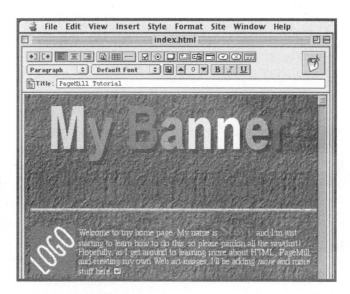

against a white background. To get a match that is close, you may need to select one of PageMill's custom colors or manually insert an RGB hex color code in Source mode.

Using Anchors to Create a Table of Contents

You've created a link list to other sites on the Web, but you can also create a link list (a table of contents) that links to locations inside your Web page. Doing this is a two-step process:

1. Create anchors marking the locations you want the links in your table of contents to jump to.

2. Create a link list (table of contents) with links that jump to the anchors created in Step 1.

Creating the Anchors

For this example, insert anchors to mark the two headings, "Stuff I Want to Add" and "My Favorite Links":

1. Scroll back up to the top of your page, and click at the start of the "Stuff I Want to Add" heading. Choose Anchor from the Insert menu.

2. Click the anchor icon that has been inserted. In the Inspector dialog box, delete the contents of the Name box, and type a name for your anchor. For this example, type **Part1** in the Name box.

3. Click at the start of the "My Favorite Links" heading. Choose Anchor from the Insert menu.

4. Click on the inserted anchor icon, and type a name for the anchor in the Inspector's Name box. For this example, type **Part2** in the Name box.

Creating the Table of Contents

Now, create the table of contents:

1. Click at the start of the second paragraph ("This is plain text. . .") and hit the Return key to add a paragraph break. Click on the blank line you just added.

2. Type **Table of Contents**, and hit Return. Type **Stuff I Want to Add** and hit Return. Type **My Favorite Links** (don't hit Return).

3. Click on the first line ("Table of Contents"). Choose the Larger Heading format from the toolbar's Change Format menu.

4. Select the following two lines of text. Choose the Bullet List format from the toolbar's Change Format menu.

5. To create the first link, click and drag to select the text ("Stuff I Want to Add") that you will use for the first table of contents link. Scroll down so that the text you've selected and the first anchor you created are both visible. Next, click on the first anchor icon (to the right of the "Stuff I Want to Add" heading), then drag and drop it onto the text you've selected. You'll see "#Part1" displayed as the link in the Link To box at the bottom of PageMill's window.

6. To try an alternative method for doing the same thing, select the text ("My Favorite Links") that you will use for the second table of contents link. Click inside the Link To box at the bottom of PageMill's document window, type **#Part2**, and hit Return. This method can be handy if the linking text or object and the anchor are not both visible at the same time in PageMill's window, precluding dragging and dropping the anchor icon on the linking text.

NOTE

You may be wondering why you typed "Part2" in the "Creating the Anchors" section earlier, but "#Part2" in the previous step in this section. The first names the anchor, while the "#" is included in the link to tell a browser to jump to the anchor name that follows. If you switch to Source mode, you can see how these two different codes are inserted by PageMill.

Figure 4-29 shows the finished table of contents. It only has two entries in it, but you could add as many more entries (or "jumps") to it as desired. To test out your table of contents, switch to your browser (choosing Switch To from the View menu). In your browser, click on either of the two links to jump to their respective anchors.

Wrapping Up

This session has just been an introduction to using PageMill. There's much more that you can do using the application, including adding tables, forms,

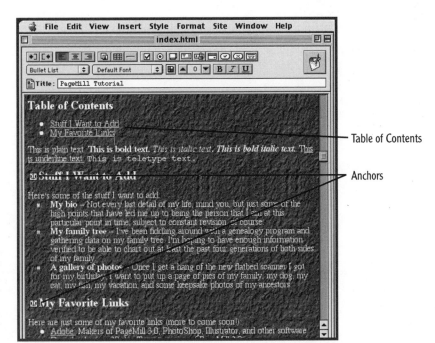

Figure 4-29

A table of contents lets visitors to your page jump to different locations in your page.

frames, and image maps. (To cover all that would take a weekend in itself!) Later in this book, in Appendix D, "Putting It Up on the Web," you'll learn to use PageMill to transfer your Web site up to a server on the Web, as well as how to maintain your site after transferring it.

If you want to continue to play around with PageMill a little longer tonight, either trying some different permutations of what you've already done or trying out some new stuff, go ahead, but don't stay up too late! You've got another big day tomorrow, when you'll plan and create your first Web page.

Planning Your First Web Page

- ✿ Defining your objective
- ✿ Creating an outline
- ✿ Choosing an example Web page
- ✿ Getting your materials together

Before you actually start creating your first Web page, you need to do some planning. You only have one morning for this, so what you'll do here is a kind of "mini-planning" session. It is intended to give you a taste of what a real planning process might be like, and is not presented as the one and only way to plan a Web page. I've broken down the planning process into a series of practical stages, which you should follow, in order, for the time being; later, when you get into planning more Web pages, feel free to rearrange these steps as you see fit, or to devise an entirely different planning process.

To make things easier, and to narrow down the possibilities, there are three generic example Web pages on the CD-ROM; later in this session, you can select one as a guide for planning and organizing your own material. You won't actually work with these example Web pages in this session. When you get around to selecting the Web page example you want to use as a model, you will want to pull it up in your browser and take a closer look at it because you'll use it later as a template for your own Web site.

You can copy the folder that includes the Web page examples from the CD-ROM directly to your Desktop, and then use that folder as your working folder for both planning and creating your first Web page. To copy the folder of Web page examples to your Desktop, just do the following:

1. Insert the CD-ROM disc in your CD-ROM drive. When the disc has been mounted on your Desktop, double-click it to open it in the Finder.

2. Double-click the Book Examples folder. Drag and drop the Web Page Examples folder onto your Desktop.

NOTE All the example files are available for download at **www.callihan.com/create_imac/.** Just download the Web page examples.sit file, drag and drop it to your Desktop, and then double-click it to unstuff it.

Getting Oriented

Feel free to use your text editor or your favorite word processor while planning your first Web page. You can start out using whatever works best for you: a yellow legal pad, the back of an envelope, a restaurant napkin, a whiteboard, or butcher paper taped to the wall. For this morning's session, you won't do any HTML, and you'll focus on the concept, organization, and content of your page. At the end of this process, you will pull it all together in your text editor or word processor; the latter can be especially effective if it has a good outlining tool.

The final product of your planning process will be what you could call a "mock-up text file." This file will include both the text that you want to use and references to anything else that you want to have in your Web page. These may identify, for instance, the name of your banner graphic and any other graphics you are including, URLs for hypertext links, and your e-mail address. Organize your mock-up text file according to the relative order, precedence, and position in which you want text or other objects to appear in your Web page. Here's a breakdown to give you a better idea of what you'll do this morning:

✿ **Defining Your Objective.** You begin by defining your objective, that is, what you want to do. If you don't already have a pretty good idea of what you want to do, you might follow one of the suggestions for brainstorming provided in this section.

- **Doing an Outline.** You then take your objective and break it down into its main constituents; create an outline, defining the basic structure and order of precedence of your material.

- **Selecting a Web Page Example.** I've included three generic Web page examples that you can use as guides or templates in planning and creating a Web page. For a fairly simple page with a list of links, choose the first Web page example; for a more complicated page with subsections, choose the second Web page example. After you have created your first Web page, you can come back and use the third Web page example to help plan and create your first multi-page Web site; still later, once you've become more adept at creating your own Web page designs, you can dispense with this step and design your own examples (or work designing your Web pages directly in HTML without using an example or template).

- **Assembling Your Materials.** You then sketch out what you want to do in more detail, developing and writing some text to go with your outline. You also have the option to decide on a banner or logo graphic for your page, but I've provided a sample banner graphic in the Web page examples that you can use as a placeholder, if you want to hold off selecting or creating your own banner graphic for now. After you become a more sophisticated and experienced Web publisher, this is the stage where you'll do things like select or create a background image; create and convert graphs, charts, or diagrams; define a form; design a table; delineate frames; create an animated GIF; decide on streaming audio, animation, or video; and so on. For right now, you should just focus on the basics.

- **Gathering Your URLs (Optional).** Part of what makes a Web page a Web page is links to other Web pages. Before including a list of links to other Web pages, you need to gather the URLs you want to use. This section will cover some methods to easily assemble a collection of URLs for your Web page. If you want, you can skip doing this for today's planning and creating sessions—I've included a sample list of hypertext links in the first Web page example that

you can use instead. Eventually you'll want to grab your own URLs, so be sure
to come back and do this section later if you decide to skip it.

- **Creating Your Mock-Up Text File.** Here you'll pull together in a single text file a mock-up of the different elements you want to include in your Web page. Place them in the rough position and order in which you want them to appear, including any text you want to use, references to any graphics you want to use, and URLs for any hypertext links you want to include.

- **Drawing a Map (Optional).** You don't need a map for a single page. Once you start planning and creating a multi-page Web site, this section may come in handy. Although an outline captures the static structure of a Web page or Web site, a map delineates the dynamic relationships within and between your Web pages.

Don't get bogged down! You need not take more than 20 to 40 minutes on any one task. If you get stuck, just move on to the next step. The main point here is not to plan your Web page in depth, but to get a taste of what a real planning process might be like.

NOTE For the following sections, first read and think about the information. When you get to the end of each section, the task area will provide instructions as to what you'll need to perform.

Defining Your Objective

First, you must define what you want to do. Boil it down to an objective: the purpose of your undertaking. (This is sometimes called a mission statement, but that just seems a bit too formal for this activity.) *Don't assume that you already know your objective.* The questions you need to identify are short (in fact, you can put them each in one word: Why? Who? What? and How?), but not easy to answer.

Your first question should simply be, "Why do I want to create a Web page?" In answering this question, you should try to think of all the reasons you might want to create a Web page. Write them down in a list. These reasons may be fairly general at the start; you can refine it to something more specific as you go along. For instance, you may simply want to communicate and express yourself. Or you may primarily want to sell a product or offer a service. You may just want to experiment, to stretch and challenge yourself. You may want to connect and network with colleagues and associates. Or you may simply want to have fun! Define your larger frame focus. And don't just stop at the first answer. Think up at least three reasons for creating a Web page, prioritizing them in a list.

Your second question should be, "Who am I trying to reach?" The Web is all about connecting, but nobody is compelled to connect with anyone else. People need to have a reason to want to connect to your Web page or site. Pull promotion strategies (unlike push strategies) are what tend to work best on the Web, so plan on offering information, resources, even entertainment to those you want to reach. What pulls people to your site or page and keeps them coming back generally isn't that you happen to be selling a product or offering a service, but that you offer value-added resources. Think of what you can offer, what you have to give. Target that relative to the audience you would like to attract. Then provide links to descriptions of your company, products, and services.

NOTE

You shouldn't confuse this with all the talk about "push" technologies that you hear about on the Web. Although they are somewhat related, what I'm referring to are a couple of old-line marketing terms that predate the Web or the Internet. Cold calling, for instance, is a push strategy, as are putting up a billboard, advertising in a magazine, distributing a catalog, and so on. A pull strategy, on the other hand, might involve a sidewalk sale, free entertainment (along with hot dogs and balloons), sponsoring a public service announcement, distributing a brochure on health risks, etc.

A Web page is not just a billboard that surfers are going to simply look out their browser windows and see while driving down the Information Superhighway. It is more like a store located five miles off the exit ramp. Just telling people where you are won't necessarily cut it—you need to give them a positive reason to go out of their way and come visit your page. You need to offer something that will pull the people you want to reach (potential customers and clients, for instance) to your page. Think in terms of what you have to offer to the people that you most want to visit your page, and not just of what you are trying to sell or promote.

The third question should be, "What am I trying to achieve?" It is very easy to confuse this question with the first question, the Why question. The Why question has to do with reasons, with what impels you in a particular direction, while the What question has to do with zeroing in on specific actions or results you want to facilitate. Perhaps you want not only to sell a product or increase sales, but also to facilitate communication with clients or potential customers; or you may want to disseminate industry information, educate and inform the public, receive feedback from customers or clients, display your talents or skills, lobby for a political position (or argue for a philosophical one), or network with professional colleagues or associates.

As with the Why question, don't just stop with a single answer, but make a list of at least three fairly specific things (actions or results) you'd like to see happen, then prioritize them. And don't forget the Who! Correlate the Why with the Who to help formulate what your What is.

The fourth question should then be something like, "How do I want my page to implement my Why, Who, and What?" The How here will be the actual form that your Web page will take to achieve the ends you want.

This can be fairly complex, if you wish to make it so. For instance, if you're primarily interested in expressing yourself and in putting down your welcome mat on the Web, you may decide that a personal Web page containing your interests and values will fill the bill. You may want to share information and news with other family members, friends, co-workers, or neighbors. You might create a page about your family, with pictures of the

kids and pets, or maybe the story of last summer's vacation. If you want to link with neighbors, or with others who might share your community concerns, you might create a page for your local community.

You may want to create or contribute to a *virtual community*. Putting up a page on a hobby shared by others can help populate a virtual community centered and focused on that interest. If you're interested in advancing your career or finding a job, then you might decide to create an online résumé or a page focused on your career interests and involvements. You might want to interact with others in your field or profession by creating a FAQ (Frequently Asked Questions) page or online newsletter to share your professional knowledge and expertise.

There is no shortage of possibilities, and in defining your How, you just want to try to narrow them down. Let your How flow from your Why, Who, and What.

Again, make a list of at least three ways in which you would like to achieve your desired results, then prioritize them from the one you think would be the most effective. You don't have to implement all of these in the page you're planning and creating today, but filtering out some of your choices can be a good way to see what direction you want your future pages to go.

Finally, try pulling it all together in a single concise statement. In one sentence, correlating the Why and the Who to come up with your What, and then let that What determine your How. Put it all together and you have your objective.

Stay flexible and open! Don't spend so much time creating an objective that you end up being hesitant to change or alter it in response to changing realities. Make your objective an aiming point, a working hypothesis, and not a stone around your neck; feel free to change it as you go. Don't be afraid to retrace your steps, revising your Why, Who, What, and How in light of further understandings. Remember, right now you're creating an objective for only one page. You probably would come up with a different objective if it were for an entire Web site; tie that into the mission statement of your organization, and you'll probably come up with yet another objective.

TASK #1: Define Your Objective

Ask yourself the four one-word key questions, and then utilize the answers you've come up with as the basis for forming a single statement; this statement then becomes your objective. Develop this statement in a medium with which you're comfortable—your text editor or your word processor, or on a pad of paper, whatever works. Don't take forever or get hung up doing this, though. This is just a starting point, not a destination. The idea is to get some kind of grip on where you're coming from and where you're trying to go.

Doing Your Outline

Whereas an objective expresses the intentions, purposes, and goals of your project as a whole, an outline organizes it into divisions and subdivisions, establishing the hierarchy and sequence of the material you want to present. Your outline doesn't have to be complicated or even complete, but it should at least break your objective down into its basic components. As with your objective, your initial outline should not be carved in stone. It may not take full form until you are well into the next phase, assembling your materials.

TASK #2: Do Your Outline

For now, use your objective as the top level of your outline, then break out beneath it the different parts or components. These components define and order how you want to execute your objective, providing a structure for the information you're going to present to a viewer of your Web page. If you want, write a brief description of each component.

Selecting an Example Web Page

This step should help you visualize the Web page you are going to plan and create. At the start of this session, you copied three Web page examples from the CD-ROM to your working folder. This afternoon, you'll use one of these as a template or guide as you create your first Web page. Although you won't actually be working with the files themselves this morning, you should pull them up and review them in your browser. (Once you become more adept at designing your own Web pages, you can skip this particular step; think of the Web page examples presented here as training wheels that you can dispense with once you learn to ride on your own.) Here is a summary of what the three examples are about:

○ **A Web Page Using a Link List.** This is the simplest of the three example Web pages. It includes a list of external links connecting to other pages on the Web.

○ **A Web Page Using Subsections.** This example Web page is a little more complex, providing a table of contents (a *menu*) of internal links that jump to different subsections within the same page.

○ **A Web Site Using Subpages.** You should use this example Web page only after trying out one of the first two. It provides a menu of external links that functions as an index to a multi-page Web site, allowing the user to jump to different subpages.

NOTE All the whiz-bang graphics aside, what still matters more than anything else is simply content—straightforward, honest information. The Web already has plenty of self-congratulatory Web pages. Before doing a Web page on a certain subject, do a few searches on the Web, using AltaVista, Lycos, Yahoo!, or some other search engine to find out whether someone with a credible site has already done what you want to do; if so, just create a link to that site, rather than cover the same ground. Create a site that'll complement, rather than merely duplicate, the efforts of others.

TASK #3: Select Your Web Page Example

Choose one of the following Web page examples to use as a model to use in assembling the materials for your Web page. Use the third example only if you have already created your first Web page using one of the first two, and are ready to plan and create your first multi-page Web site.

Example #1: A Web Page Using a Link List

This very basic Web page example includes a banner graphic, level-one and level-two headings, an introductory paragraph, a list, and an address block. The list can be either a "list of particulars" or a link list to other Web pages. An example of using this with a plain list (no links) would be to create a "business card" where you describe your business in the introductory paragraph, then follow that with a list of products, services, or qualifications. A different kind of page using a link list with other pages on the Web would be a page that describes a hobby or an area of professional expertise, followed by a list of links to other pages on the Web that share the same theme (see Figure 5-1). Go ahead and pull this up in your browser to get a closer look. You can find it as basic-1.html in the Web Page Examples folder on your Desktop (if you followed the instructions earlier for dragging and dropping this folder from the CD-ROM).

Example #2: A Web Page Using Subsections

This is a more complex example, but it's still just a single page. Like the first Web page example, it includes a banner graphic, level-one and level-two headings, and an introductory paragraph. However, the link list here, instead of linking to other Web pages, functions as a table of contents that jumps to the subsections of the document, using internal links rather than external ones. You'll probably want to use this example if your outline is more complicated. Think of the subsections as corresponding to the subsections of your outline (see Figure 5-2). Pull this up in your browser to

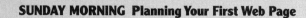

Figure 5-1

Best for a relatively simple page, this example contains a banner graphic, level-one and level-two headings, an introductory paragraph, a link list, and an address block.

A Web Page Using a Link List

This is an example of a basic web page. It contains a banner graphic, level-one and level-two headings, an introductory paragraph, a short list of links, a horizontal rule, and an address block. The address block contains the name of the author of the page, a Mailto e-mail link, and a date reference.

A List of Links

- Create Your First Web Page In a Weekend (iMac/Mac Edition): HTML is for everyone!
- World Wide Web Corsortium: Find out the latest about the Web and HTML.
- The Bandwidth Conservation Society: Save bytes -- don't be a bandwidth hog.

Your Name Here
E-Mail: your@address.com
Last Modified: Current date here

Figure 5-2

The second Web page example, best for a more complex page, contains a banner graphic, level-one and level-two headings, an introductory paragraph, a table of contents that jumps to a series of subsections, and an address section.

A Web Page Using Subsections

This is an example of a Web page using subsections. It is similar to the first Web page example, except that the list of links jumps to subsections within the same page, instead of to other pages out on the Web.

- First Subsection: This link jumps to the first subsection.
- Second Subsection: This link jumps to the second subsection.

First Subsection

This is the text for the first subsection. This is the text for the first subsection. This is the text for the first subsection. This is the text for the first subsection. This is the text for the first subsection. This is the text for the first subsection. This is the text for the first subsection.

Second Subsection

This is the text for the second subsection. This is the text for the second subsection. This is the text for the second subsection. This is the text for the second subsection. This is the text for the second subsection. This is the text for the second subsection. This is the text for the second subsection.

Your Name Here
E-Mail: your@address.com
Last Modified: Current date here

get a closer look. Test drive the table of contents, jumping to the different subsections. You can find it as basic-2.html in the Web Page Examples folder on your Desktop.

Example #3: A Web Site Using Subpages

I don't recommend that you use this Web page example the first time through. Get your feet wet first with one of the first two Web page examples, and then try this one out. Generally, if the material you want to present is extensive, you should consider breaking the page's subsections into separate subpages; any time a page extends beyond three or four screens, you should consider breaking it up into more than one page. One of the advantages of breaking up a long Web page into a main page and subpages is that visitors to your Web site need only load the home page and the particular subpage they're interested in seeing, rather than wait for the whole document to load.

On the other hand, breaking up the whole document into pieces can penalize visitors who want to view the whole thing, forcing them to reconnect to the server to retrieve each subpage. Another disadvantage is that a Web document that's broken up into a main page and subpages can't be printed or saved in a single operation. The longer a Web document (especially if it includes a lot of text), the more likely it is that a viewer will want to print it out for future reference or to read it in a more eye-friendly medium (paper). A compromise that you see fairly frequently on the Web is to do both— that is, to break up the site into subpages, but include a link to another version that is all in one page and that uses subsections.

You might also want to create a home page linked to subpages if you've created a number of loosely related or unrelated Web pages that you want to link together through an index page. It's fairly common on the Web to see personal pages done this way, linking to and serving as indexes for more specialized pages, possibly created for business or other purposes. (See Figure 5-3 for an example of a home page linked to a number of subpages.)

Pull the example up in your browser to get a closer look. Test drive the index link list, clicking on the first link in the list to check out the jump to the subpage. Check out the loop-back link from the subpage to the main

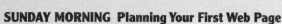

Figure 5-3

The third Web page example, best for an even more complex multi-page Web site, contains a banner graphic, level-one and level-two headings, an introductory paragraph, and an "index" link list that jumps to a series of subpages.

A Web Site Using Subpages

This is an example of Web site using subpages. It is similar to the first two Web page examples, except instead of a link list that jumps to other pages out on the Web or that jumps to subsections within the same page, it has a link list that jumps to subpages that are part of the same Web site.

Table of Contents

- First Subpage: This links to the first subpage.
- Second Subpage: This links to the second subpage.

Your Name Here
E-Mail: yourname@yourdomain.com
Last Modified: Current date here

page. This example includes only one subpage, so the links to the other subpages in the list won't work unless you create additional subpages. You can find it as basic-2.html in the Web Page Examples folder on your Desktop.

A subpage is just another Web page. Figure 5-4 shows a basic subpage, which doesn't even have a banner graphic. If you use a subpage rather than add subsections to your home page, what would have been the level-two subheadings serve as the level-one headings at the top of your subpages. On the CD are two examples of subpages that allow you to test the links to the main page (basic-3.html). You can find these subpages as basic-3a.html and basic-3b.html in the Web Page Examples folder on your Desktop. You'll get a good idea of how they work if you click on one of the subpage links in the main page.

First Subpage

This is the text for the first subpage. This is the text for the first subpage. This is the text for the first subpage. This is the text for the first subpage. This is the text for the first subpage. This is the text for the first subpage. This is the text for the first subpage.

Return to Home Page.

Your Name Here
E-Mail: your@address.com

Figure 5-4

A subpage of the Web site introduced in Figure 5-3

TIP

The sample subpage does not include a banner graphic. Coordinating the graphics between your main page and your subpages, however, is a good way to give a Web site a common look and feel. One trick is simply to use a smaller version of the banner graphic that heads your main page.

Notice that the subpage example includes a loop-back link at the bottom of the page; it returns viewers to the main page from which the subpage is linked. Check it out to see how it works. When you use a subpage, always include a loop-back link that'll take a viewer back to the home page. Visitors don't necessarily come through the home page to get to a subpage. If they have the URL on their hotlist or bookmark list, or have gotten it from a search engine, they may go directly to your subpage. Without a loop-back link they would have no way to get back up to that page's home page—just hitting the Back button won't work.

Take a Break?

You've defined your objective, done your outline, and selected the Web page example you want to use—hey, that's a lot of brain work! Time for a break. If you haven't eaten anything yet, you might want to get a bowl of cereal or some other sustenance, because there's plenty more to do if you want to plan *and* create your first Web page today. So, give the noggin a short rest, get a bite if you're hungry. I'll see you back in ten minutes or so, when you'll assemble your materials and pull together your mock-up text file.

Assembling Your Materials

At this point, you should start to put together the different bits and pieces that will compose your Web page. For instance, you may want to think of a title and write your level-one heading and an introductory paragraph, as well as any other text you want to create. For this first time through, I

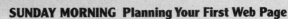
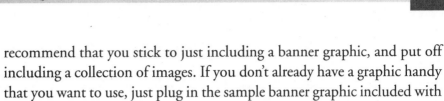

recommend that you stick to just including a banner graphic, and put off including a collection of images. If you don't already have a graphic handy that you want to use, just plug in the sample banner graphic included with the example Web pages as a placeholder until you get around to creating a more personalized banner graphic for your page.

TASK #4: Write a Title, Level-One Heading, and Introductory Paragraph

Think of a title that you want to have displayed at the top of your Web page, then write an introductory paragraph; this should describe your Web page in a nutshell. One thing you may want to keep in mind here is that many search engines give special weight to your title, level-one heading, and the initial text on your page when indexing your page; try to include keywords and key phrases in all three (title, level-one heading, and introductory paragraph) that you think people might use in doing a search for a page like yours. If you chose the second Web page example to use as your model, you should also think of some subsection headings to use, and write a short introductory paragraph for each.

Go ahead and save your file in the Web Page Examples folder with a name that you'll remember. At this point, it really doesn't matter which format you save it in, but at the end of this session, you'll want to save it as a straight text file.

NOTE

If you have already created your first *single* Web page and have come back to try your hand at creating a multi-page site, you should create separate text files containing the title and the introductory paragraph for each separate Web page you want to create.

TASK #5: Create Your Banner Graphic (Optional)

I've provided a sample banner graphic for you, so if you don't have one of your own and don't want to take the time right now to create one, feel free to skip this. You can use the sample banner graphic that is included in the Web page example you've selected as a placeholder until you get around to scanning or creating the graphic you want to use.

To create your own banner graphic, you'll need an image editor that can save JPEG and GIF graphic files. If you have an iMac, feel free to use the painting module included in the AppleWorks suite. If you need to convert an image from another format (PICT, TIFF, and so on), check out the CD-ROM for GraphicConverter and CompuPic, for converting and manipulating images. Also, see Appendix A, "Resources," for links to where on the Web you can find Macintosh Web publishing software tools, including image editing and conversion software.

Don't try to create a masterpiece just for this session. Just create a quick JPEG or GIF image that'll give you a taste of what a banner graphic is. To learn how to use the AppleWorks Painting and Drawing modules to create your own Web art images, see the Sunday Evening session, "Creating Your Own Web Images."

To create a quick banner graphic, just make sure your graphic is less than 500 or 600 pixels wide. For a banner graphic, generally you'll want to keep the height to 200 pixels or less. When you save your image, save it as a JPEG or GIF file. Because you'll be using this image in a Web page, for your image's file name, follow these guidelines: Use only lowercase letters, omit any spaces, and add a .jpg file extension (for a JPEG file) or a .gif file extension (for a GIF file) at the end of the file name. Go ahead and save it in the Web Page Examples folder, just to keep everything together in one place.

Gathering Your URLs (Optional)

This is really part of the "assembling your materials" process, but it is important and involved enough to deserve breaking out as a separate step. If you're running short on time, feel free to skip this step for now. If you're using the first Web page example, you can use the sample list of links as placeholders. I've also included a number of URLs in Appendix A,

"Resources," that you can use as sample URLs in your Web page (just add "http://" to the beginning of each URL to get the full URL). Eventually, however, you'll want to know how to gather your very own URLs, so be sure to come back and do this section after you've planned and created your first Web page.

If you have chosen to follow the first Web page example, you'll probably want to insert a list of links to other Web pages, either the one included in the example or another. If you have chosen one of the other Web page examples, you may still want to include links to other Web pages, either as link lists or as *in-context* links inserted in your text.

FIND IT ON ▶
THE WEB

■ ■

You may not have the slightest idea what hypertext links you want to include in your Web page. A good way to gather a list of URLs to use in your Web page is to go to Yahoo! (**www.yahoo.com**) and do a search using a keyword or keywords that describe your page. Yahoo! should return one or more categories of links that match your query.

■ ■

Gathering URLs While Surfing

The easiest way to gather your URLs is simply to connect to the Web, go to the Web page you want to link to, and grab its URL. Here's how to do it.

1. Run your text editor or word processor, so you'll have a place to paste your URLs as you gather them.

2. Run your browser and connect to the Internet. Display the Web page you want to link to in your Web browser (see previous tip for using Yahoo! to find links).

3. Highlight the URL in your browser's Address box (Internet Explorer) or Location box (Navigator), and press Command-C to copy it (or choose Copy from the Edit menu on the menu bar).

4. Bring your text editor or word processor to the foreground (by using the Applications menu or by pressing Command-Tab to cycle through your open applications). Click the cursor in your text editor's or word processor's file window and press Command-V to paste in the URL you just copied (or choose Paste from the Edit menu on the menu bar).

5. Following the URL, type in the title of the Web page you are linking to (you can copy and paste this from the Web page, if it is available there). Optionally, type in some additional text describing the Web page. These will later form the link text and descriptive text for your link list.

6. Repeat these steps for any other URLs you want to include in your Web page. When you finish, you should have a list of URLs in your text editor or word processor, along with titles for the links and, optionally, text describing each link.

7. When you have enough URLs for your Web page (a half-dozen or so should do), just save your file in the Web Page Examples folder (or anywhere else, as long as you remember where you put it) so you can pull it up and use it later. Give it a name you can remember.

Using Your Bookmarks to Get URLs

Your bookmarks or favorites list can be an excellent source for URLs that you might want to include in your Web pages. The following is a quick rundown on how to do this in Navigator or Internet Explorer.

Using Internet Explorer's Favorites

1. Run your text editor or word processor. You'll be pasting the URLs you gather into a text file that you'll save for later. (Note: If you already created a file of links in the previous section, you can just re-open that file here.)

2. Run Internet Explorer (no need to log on to the Internet). Choose Open Favorites from the Favorites menu. In the Favorites tree list, the URLs that correspond to the different Favorites are displayed on the right. Just click the icon to the left of a category folder to expand it and see more URLs.

3. To copy the URL for any listed link, just highlight the URL and then press Command-C. Hop over to your text editor or word processor, and press Command-V to paste the URL into the file where you're storing the URLs you're gathering.

4. Following the URL, type in the title of the Web page you are linking to (you can copy and paste this from the Web page, if it is available there). Optionally, type in some additional text describing the Web page. These will later form the link text and descriptive text for your link list.

5. Hop back and forth between your text or word processing file and Internet Explorer's Favorites list, copying and pasting as many URLs as you want to gather. Type a title and description for each URL.

6. Save (or resave) the file in the Web Page Examples folder.

Using Navigator's Bookmarks

1. Run your text editor or word processor. You'll be pasting the URLs you gather into a text file that you'll save for later. (If you already created a file of links in the previous section, you can just re-open that file here.)

2. Run Navigator (no need to log on to the Internet). Choose Open Page from the File menu and open Bookmarks.html. To find this file, look in Macintosh HD:System Folder:Preferences:Netscape Users:*Your Name*:Bookmarks.html. If you can't find it, just use the Finder to find it (choose Find from the Finder's File menu).

3. With Bookmarks.html open in Navigator, scroll through the file, and look for any links you may want to use. When you find one, click and hold the mouse button on the link, and choose **Copy this Link Location**.

4. Hop back over to your text editor or word processor, click where you want to insert the link, and press Command+V (or select Edit and Paste from the menu bar) to paste in the bookmark's URL. Following the URL, type in a title for the URL (you may want to hop back over to Navigator and check out what is listed for the bookmark). You can also add some descriptive text.

5. Repeat Steps 3 and 4 for any other links you want to copy from Bookmarks.html. When finished, just Save (or resave) the file in the Web Page Examples folder.

NOTE

These days, I don't know of anyone who doesn't want all the links they can get. It is a good idea, however, to let someone know that you've linked to their page, along with any compliments you want to offer (that you think their page is informative, well-designed, or just plain great—most Web authors are gluttons for appreciation). And then ask if they'd like to link back to you—getting reciprocal links is an excellent way to build up your own Web traffic. I also always try to give full credit for any Web page I link to, including the title of the full Web site if I'm linking to a subpage, plus the name of the author, or the name of the organization/company responsible for creating the site. And if someone requests that you don't link to their page, remove their link.

TASK #6: Grab Some URLs

Gather as many URLs as you want (a half-dozen or so is a good number to start out with). Also be sure to include the link text you want to use, as well as any descriptive text you want to follow the link. When you're finished, save your file into which you've pasted your URLs in the Web Page Examples folder. Give it a name that'll tell you what it is (My Links, for instance). You'll use it in the next step when you create your mock-up text file.

Creating Your Mock-Up Text File

In this step, you create a text file that'll include a mock-up of your Web page. I'll refer to this file as your *mock-up text file*. Your mock-up text file should include everything you want in your Web page—any text you have written (such as your title and introductory paragraph), file names of any graphics you want to use, any URLs you want to include in your page, and an address section including your name, company name (if applicable), e-mail address, and any other contact information you wish to provide. A good part of this you may already have created or gathered while doing the previous tasks.

Some of it may still need to be determined, such as the file name for a graphic you have yet to scan or create. Some of it may still be only on that yellow legal pad, needing to be typed in. The basic idea here is to pull everything together in one file, in the rough order and precedence in which you want it to appear in your Web page. Use your outline (created in Task #2) and the example Web page you chose (in Task #3) as guides for how to organize your mock-up text file.

Feel free to use your favorite word processor for this, or you can work directly in your text editor if you want. The idea is to put in just about everything *except* the HTML codes: Your title, level-one heading, introductory paragraph, any image file names, the URLs you want to use, and so on. You want to arrange these "materials" in the rough order in which you want them to appear in your Web page. (This afternoon, in creating your first Web page, either you'll add the HTML to your text or you'll add your text to one of the three Web page examples described earlier; right now, however, don't worry about the code—just focus on the content and organization of your Web page.)

As you gather your materials, you may find that your outline, or even your objective, has changed. A creative process is a fluid one; sometimes, not until you're pulling all the pieces together do you realize what you really want. Don't worry if you don't yet have a fully completed draft; it's enough to have everything put roughly into place, even if some items are in the form of a "To be determined" or a "Need to create logo graphic."

TASK #7: Create Your Mock-Up Text File

Open a new file in your text editor or word processor. Follow the previous directions to create your mock-up text file. If you want to see an example mock-up text file that you can use as a model in creating your own mock-up text file, open the file, Example Mock-Up File, from the Web Page Examples folder.

If you are using the second Web page example, you'll also need any subheadings and subsection text you want to use. Also, you may want to include separate link lists in some or all of your subsections—you'll want to break out the URLs you gathered and arrange them under the subsections where you want them to appear. If you are using the third Web page example (meaning this is at least your *second* Web page, I hope!), you should create a mock-up text file for each page you are creating (for your main page and for each of your subpages).

When finished gathering everything into your mock-up text file, go ahead and save it in the Web Page Examples folder on your Desktop. Give it whatever name you want, just so you remember what it is—for instance, you might save it as My Mock-Up File.

Drawing a Map (Optional)

You only need to work through this section if you're creating a multi-page Web site. (You could create a map for a single Web page, but in most cases it won't be complex enough to be worthwhile.) An outline defines the static structure of your document but does little to highlight and define any dynamic interrelations within your document. This is fine for paper, which doesn't handle interrelations very well anyway. However, the advantage of a hypertext document is that it is dynamic, allowing many different ways to approach and peruse the information you provide. Your map may closely mirror your outline, or it may sharply diverge from it, opening up links between sections that might otherwise remain separate from each other.

This map can be a simple chart like an organization chart, using boxes and lines. It can be a flowchart or a storyboard. Whatever approach you choose to take, it's important that you capture in it the dynamic relationships within and between different parts of your document.

TIP

The Drawing module included in the AppleWorks suite can be an excellent tool for drawing maps. Other programs that work great for drawing maps and diagrams are Freehand, Illustrator, and Corel Draw. Using any of these drawing programs, you can easily draw shapes, lines, and curves, as well as add colors or shades, to illustrate your site's structure and dynamic relationships.

The map of one multi-page site can take many different forms. The important thing is to be able to visualize the layout and relationships in your site. This can also be a great help in conceptualizing the kind of site that will present the information you want to provide. As the first example, you might map your site in the form of an organization chart, as shown in Figure 5-5. If you're a technical type, you might want to do a flowchart. Another kind of map can be described metaphorically as a train. A train map might be a good approach for something that uses sequential chapters. In this type of map, your Web pages are like a string of boxcars, as shown in Figure 5-6. Another approach is to have your home page be the hub of a

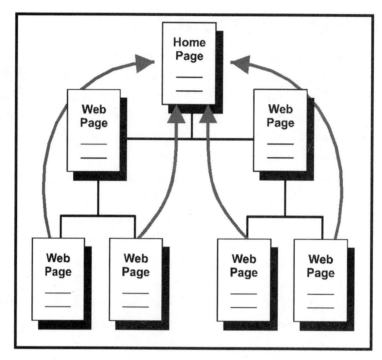

Figure 5-5

A Web site map can look like an organization chart.

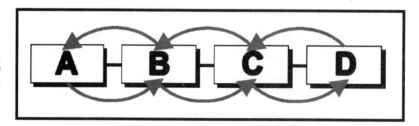

Figure 5-6

A Web site map can be organized like a train.

wheel, with the subpages along the rim, as shown in Figure 5-7. If you want to create a more complex site, you might want to create a more elaborate map, resembling a tree—with a trunk, branches, and sub-branches, like the one pictured in Figure 5-8.

In planning your first Web page, there probably is no need to try to draw up a map; maps are most useful for creating more elaborate, multi-page Web sites. Still, even if you're only creating a single page, you might want

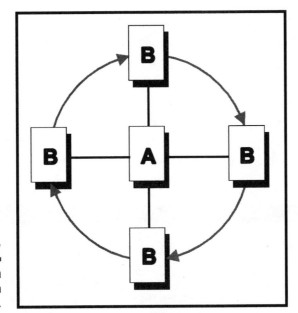

Figure 5-7

A Web site map can take the form of a hub and wheel.

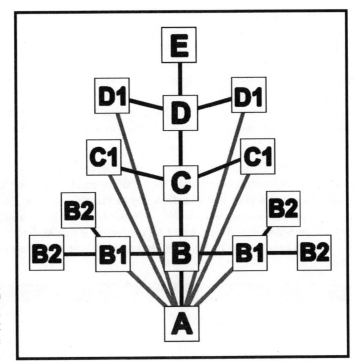

Figure 5-8

A more complex Web site map might be laid out in the form of a tree.

to try to visualize the kinds of dynamic interrelationships you can activate through links. For instance, if you're creating a Web page using subsections (as in the second example) in addition to the table of contents linking to the different subsections, you can include a loop-back link at the end of each subsection to return the reader to the table of contents. Additionally, at the bottom of the page you might provide a link back to the top of the page. You can also include in-context links within the paragraph sections that will jump to different subsections.

TASK #8: Draw a Map (Optional)

You can prepare your map the old-fashioned way, with pen and paper; if you want to use a drawing program, or even a CAD program, that can be a good way to go, as well. Don't just settle on the first map you think up. Try to picture two or three possible maps, and don't just stick to the examples shown here—you want a map that really suits the site you want to create. Visualize, in other words. Use different color pens (or drawing lines) to help distinguish the different relationships between your pages: one color to map out any hierarchical (top-down) or static relationships, and another color to map out any dynamic relationships between pages that are not explicit in your hierarchical plan. Alternatively, use another color pen to draw in any loop-back links, or any cross-links, you want to include. The idea is to be able to see how your Web site will be structured, both statically and dynamically. Remember, you can link from any point within a page to any point within any other page in your site.

Be prepared to reorganize! Seeing the dynamic interactions within your Web site almost always leads to at least one forehead slap ("Of course!")—so don't be afraid to redo your outline to match your visualization. Try to simplify, making sure that everything that is important in your site is only a hop, skip, and jump away. Don't bury that price list ten levels deep! And don't be surprised if you end up redefining your objective—in many ways, you don't really know what you are doing until you can visualize it.

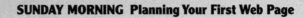

Wrapping Up

Before moving on to this afternoon's session, you should have defined an objective, done an outline, and gathered and organized your materials. The latter includes writing some text for your Web page, as well as possibly creating a banner graphic and gathering any URLs you want to use. The end product of this process should be a mock-up text file, which contains the text you want to include in your Web page, references to the file names of any graphics you want to use, and any URLs inserted in the positions where you want them to appear. The first time through, your mock-up should fairly closely match one of the Web page examples shown earlier; the actual content, however, is entirely subject to your discretion. You'll use this mock-up this afternoon as the raw material for the Web page you create.

Is it lunchtime? Or pretty close? Take a break and fix yourself a sandwich, some soup, something nourishing. While you're at it, let your significant others know you're still breathing (since they may not have seen you since Friday evening!). But don't take too long. I'll see you back in a half-hour or so for the Sunday Afternoon session, when you'll finally create your first Web page.

Creating Your First Web Page

- ✿ Choosing your approach: template or guide?
- ✿ Creating the top section of your page
- ✿ Creating the middle section of your page
- ✿ Creating the bottom section of your page
- ✿ Adding some color and pizazz to your page

I know you want to jump right in and see your work on a Web page—and you should be ready by now, assuming you completed the Basic HTML Tutorial on Saturday morning and the Web page planning session this morning. If you missed those sessions, you should return and pick them up before creating your first Web page. In this morning's planning session, you should have:

⚙ Chosen one of the Web page examples to use as a model for planning and creating your first Web page. First time through, you should have chosen one of the first two Web page examples, either a Web page with a link list or a Web page with a menu and subsections. If you haven't decided yet which Web page example you'll use as a model for creating your first Web page, you should return to this morning's session and review the "Selecting an Example Web Page" section.

⚙ Created a mock-up text file, basing at least its rough structure on the Web page example you selected. This can be fairly simple, if you want, just including a title, an introductory paragraph, and any contact info (name, e-mail address, and so on) that you want to include in your address block. It can be more complex, containing any other text you want to include (such as subheadings and subsections), file names of images you want to display (such as for a banner graphic), and a list of URLs, link text, and link descriptions (for any link lists you want to include). If you haven't created a

mock-up text file yet, you should return to this morning's session and review the "Creating Your Mock-Up Text File" section.

Getting Started

In this afternoon's session, you'll combine your mock-up text file with the Web page examples you chose to use as your model. You can either copy tags from the Web page example to your mock-up text file, or copy text from your mock-up text file to the Web page example you've chosen.

Creating a Folder for Your Web Pages

You should dedicate a folder to hold your Web page, and any other Web pages you may create in the future. Starting out, you should just save all your files (HTML files and image files, for instance) in the same folder. Later, when you get more sophisticated with HTML, you may want to create separate subfolders for different Web publishing projects, or you may want to break out different types of files into different subfolders (images, backgrounds, sounds, and so on). Just make a copy of the Web Page Examples folder on your Desktop, renaming it as the My Pages folder:

1. Hold down the Option key, then click and drag the Web Page Examples folder to make a copy of it on the Desktop.

2. Click on the new folder's name (Web Page Examples copy) to highlight it, and then enter a new name for the folder. If you're going to use a text editor, rather than PageMill, to create your first Web page, type **My Pages** as the new folder name; if you're going to use PageMill to create your first Web page, type **My PageMill Site** as the new folder name.

NOTE   If more than one person will be doing the tutorials and creating a Web page on the same computer, you may want to give this folder a more "personal" name, such as **Mary's Pages** or **Bill's PageMill Site**.

Using a Text Editor

In this session, the primary focus will be on using a text editor (if you're using PageMill, see the following section). To get started using a text editor to create your first Web page, you need to open in your text editor both the mock-up text file you created this morning and the example Web page file you selected to use as your model. Go ahead now and open both of these files in your text editor.

1. You'll find the example Web pages in the folder you copied and renamed to hold your Web pages: Desktop:My Pages (or Joe's Pages, for example, if you've personalized the folder for your Web pages). Open the example Web page you've selected to use as a model. First time through, open either basic-1.html (a Web page with a link list) or basic-2.html (a Web page with subsections); plan on using basic-3.html to create a multi-page Web site only after you've finished creating your first Web page using one of the other two.

2. Open your mock-up text file in your text editor. Your mock-up text file should also be in the folder you copied and renamed to hold your Web pages: Desktop:My Pages (or Beth's Pages, for example, if you personalized it).

3. Resize and move the windows for your two files, so that both are visible and easily accessible (see Figure 6-1).

Using PageMill

To get started using PageMill to create your first Web page, do the following:

1. Run Adobe PageMill 3.0. To create a new PageMill Web site, choose New from the File menu, and then choose New Site. (Setting up a "Web site" in PageMill will ensure that any external files you choose to drag and drop into a page will be included in your site when you publish it to the Web.)

2. In the Name box, type a name for your site. For instance, type **My PageMill Site** (or John's PageMill Site to personalize it).

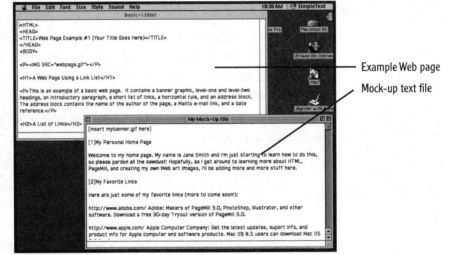

Example Web page

Mock-up text file

Figure 6-1

The first Web page example (basic-1.html) and the mock-up text file are resized and positioned in the text editor so both are easily accessible.

3. Click on the Local Site Location button. Click on the My PageMill Site folder (or whichever folder you named in step 2) to highlight it, and then click on the Choose button. Click on the Create button to create your new site.

NOTE Unlike when you created the PageMill site for the Saturday Evening session, PageMill doesn't create a blank index.html file in this case. That's because there are already HTML files in the folder for the site. You'll save your own index.html file a little further on.

4. Specify a folder where GIF files converted from imported PICT images and other "externals" will be stored. This should still be the same as you specified in the Saturday Evening session. To make sure, choose Preferences from the Edit menu and then scroll down to and click the Site icon. If **images** isn't already typed in the Site Resources Folder Name box, type it and click OK.

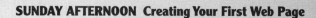

5. To ensure that converted images are placed in the site, even if the site isn't loaded, choose Preferences from the Edit menu and then click the Resources icon. Under Resource Folder, click the folder button, and then open the local root folder for your site (the My PageMill Site folder, for instance). Click the New button, and type the same folder name that you specified in the previous step. Click the Create button, the Choose button, and OK.

6. Open the Web page example you chose to use as a model. In the list of files included in your site's folder, double-click either basic-1.html (for a Web page using a link list) or basic-2.html (for a Web page using subsections).

7. Run your text editor and open your mock-up text file, which should be in the folder for your PageMill site (My PageMill Site, for instance).

8. Reposition and resize your PageMill window, holding your example Web page, and your text editor window, holding your mock-up text file, so they are both visible and accessible (see Figure 6-2).

Figure 6-2

The first Web page example (basic-1.html) and the mock-up text file are resized and positioned so both are easily accessible.

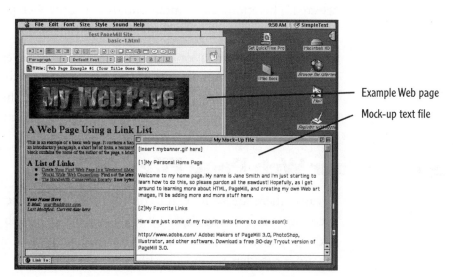

Example Web page

Mock-up text file

Choosing Your Approach

There are two different approaches you can use for creating your first Web page:

- ✿ You can copy and paste (or drag and drop) your title, introductory and other text, link URLs, text, and descriptions, and so on, from your mock-up text file to the Web page example you've selected. Doing it this way involves using the example Web page you've selected as a template.

- ✿ You can do it the other way around, using the Web page example file you've selected as a guide for adding the HTML tags and codes (or for applying format styles and so on in PageMill) to your mock-up text file. Doing it this way involves using the example Web page you've selected as a guide.

If the example Web page you've chosen to use as a model and the organization and content of your mock-up text file are fairly close to each other, you should probably stick to copying and pasting your text and other elements from your mock-up text file to the example Web page you've selected. This approach is tantamount to using the Web page example you've selected as a template.

However, if there are a lot of differences between the example Web page you've chosen and your mock-up text file, you may want to try using the second approach, using the example Web page you've chosen as a guide for adding the HTML tags and codes to your mock-up text file.

Saving Your Web Page File

Because there are some extra considerations that have to be taken into account if you're using PageMill to create your first Web page, this section is divided into two parts, the first for readers using a text editor and the second for readers using PageMill.

Text Editor Users: Saving Your Web Page File

Depending on the approach you've chosen (template or guide), you'll need to save one or the other of the files you've opened in your text editor as your Web page file:

✿ If you're using the example Web page you've selected (basic-1.html, basic-2.html, or basic-3.html) as a template, resave it as **index.html** in your Web page folder (My Pages, for instance).

✿ If you're using the example Web page you've selected as a guide for adding the HTML tags and codes to your mock-up text file, resave your mock-up text file (My Mock-Up File, for instance) as **index.html** in your Web page folder (My Pages, for instance).

PageMill Users: Saving Your Web Page File

Depending on the approach you've chosen (template or guide), the steps in PageMill that you need to follow to save your Web page file will vary.

Using Your Example Web Page As a Template

If you're using the example Web page you've selected (basic-1.html, basic-2.html, or basic-3.html) as a template, do the following to save your Web page file:

1. With the PageMill window containing your example Web page active in the foreground, choose Save Page As from the File menu on the menu bar.

2. Type **index.html** in the Name box, and then click Save.

Using Your Example Web Page As a Guide

If you're using the example Web page you've selected (basic-1.html, basic-2.html, or basic-3.html) as a guide for applying format styles and so on to your mock-up text file, do the following to save your Web page file:

◆ ◆

CAUTION Make sure that all paragraphs in your mock-up text file are separated by *two* hard returns. Single hard returns between paragraphs will be converted to line breaks when you drag and drop your mock-up text from your text editor's window to a PageMill window.

◆ ◆

1. Bring the blank PageMill window (created when you started PageMill) to the foreground: choose the Window menu on the menu bar and click untitled.html at the bottom of the menu.

2. Click your text editor's window (containing your mock-up text file) to activate it in the foreground. Click and drag to highlight all of the text in the file (or press Command-A).

3. Click on the selected text, and drag and drop it into your blank PageMill window.

4. Click your PageMill window (untitled.html) to activate it in the foreground. Choose Save Page As from the File menu on the menu bar.

5. Type **index.html** in the Name box, and then click Save.

● ●

NOTE If you want to see what the actual HTML codes in PageMill look like, select a window containing basic-1.html, basic-2.html, basic-3.html, or basic-3a.html, and choose Source Mode from the View menu (or press Command-H). Repeat to toggle Source Mode off. Note that PageMill may alter or add some HTML codes, so don't be surprised if the codes shown in PageMill's Source Mode don't exactly match what are shown later.

● ●

A Web Page Using a Link List (BASIC-1.HTML)

If your Web page is fairly simple (doesn't include subsections), you should use this Web page example as a template or guide. To see what this should look like in your browser, see Figure 5-1 from the previous session.

```
<HTML>

<HEAD>

<TITLE>Web Page Example #1 (Your Title Goes Here)</TITLE>

</HEAD>

<BODY>

<P><IMG SRC="webpage.gif"></P>

<H1>A Web Page Using a Link List</H1>

<P>This is an example of a basic Web page. It contains a
banner graphic, level-one and level-two headings, an intro-
ductory para-graph, a short list of links, a horizontal
rule, and an address block. The address block contains the
name of the author of the page, a Mailto e-mail link, and a
date reference.</P>

<H2>A List of Links</H2>

<UL>

<LI><A HREF="http://www.callihan.com/create_imac/">Create
Your First iMac/Mac Web Page In a Weekend</A>: HTML is for
everyone!

<LI><A HREF="http://www.w3.org/">World Wide Web Consortium
</A>: Find out the latest about the Web and HTML.

<LI><A HREF="http://www.infohiway.com/faster/homebcs.htm">The
Bandwidth Conservation Society</A>: Save bytes—don't be a
bandwidth hog.

</UL>

<HR>

<ADDRESS>

<STRONG>Your Name Here</STRONG><BR>
```

```
E-mail: <A HREF="mailto:your@address.com">your@address.com
</A><BR>

Last Modified: Current date here

</ADDRESS>

</BODY>

</HTML>
```

A WEB PAGE USING SUBSECTIONS (BASIC-2.HTML)

**If your Web page is more complicated, with a number of subsections under sub-
headings (level-two headings), you should use this Web page example as a template
or guide. To see what this should look like in your browser, see Figure 5-2 from the
previous session.**

```
<HTML>

<HEAD>

<TITLE>Web Page Example #2 (Your Title Goes Here)</TITLE>

</HEAD>

<BODY>

<P><IMG SRC="webpage.gif"></P>

<H1>A Web Page Using Subsections</H1>

<P>This is an example of a Web page using subsections. It is
similar to the first Web page example, except that the list
of links jumps to subsections within the same page, instead
of to other pages out on the Web.</P>

<UL>

<LI><A HREF="#sub1">First Subsection</A>: This link jumps to
the first subsection.

<LI><A HREF="#sub2">Second Subsection</A>: This link jumps
to the second subsection.

</UL>
```

```
<H2><A NAME="sub1">First Subsection</A></H2>

<P>This is the text for the first subsection. This is the text
for the first subsection. This is the text for the first sub-
section. This is the text for the first subsection. This is
the text for the first subsection. This is the text for the
first subsection.</P>

<H2><A NAME="sub2">Second Subsection</A></H2>

<P>This is the text for the second subsection. This is the
text for the second subsection. This is the text for the
second subsection. This is the text for the second sub-
section. This is the text for the second subsection. This
is the text for the second subsection. This is the text for
the second subsection.</P>.

<HR>

<ADDRESS><STRONG>Your Name Here</STRONG><BR>

E-mail: <A HREF="mailto:your@address.com">your@address.com
</A><BR>

Last Modified: Current date here

</ADDRESS>

</BODY>

</HTML>
```

A WEB SITE USING SUBPAGES (BASIC-3.HTML)

This is the third Web page example, the one that uses local links to subpages of your main page. It can be used to get you started creating your own multi-page Web site. (I recommend that you save using this example until you've first tried out one or both of the other example Web pages.) To see what this should look like in your browser, see Figure 5-3 from the previous session.

```
<HTML>

<HEAD>
```

```
<TITLE>Web Page Example #3 (Your Title Goes Here)</TITLE>

</HEAD>

<BODY>

<P><IMG SRC="webpage.gif"></P>

<H1>A Web Site Using Subpages</H1>

<P>This is an example of Web site using subpages. It is
similar to the first two Web page examples, except instead
of a link list that jumps to other pages out on the Web or
that jumps to subsections within the same page, it has a
link list that jumps to subpages that are part of the same
Web site.</P>

<H2>Table of Contents</H2>

<UL>

<LI><A HREF="basic-3a.htm">First Subpage</A>: This links to
the first subpage.

<LI><A HREF="basic-3b.htm">Second Subpage</A>: This links to
the second subpage.

</UL>

<HR>

<ADDRESS><STRONG>Your Name Here</STRONG><BR>

E-mail: <AHREF="mailto:yourname@yourdomain.com">yourname@
your domain.com</A><BR>

Last Modified: Current date here

</ADDRESS>

</BODY>

</HTML>
```

Subpage Example (basic-3a.html)

Here are the codes for the subpage, basic-3a.html. (This page is virtually identical to basic-3b.html, which is also available with the example Web page files.) To see what this should look like in your browser, see Figure 5-4 from the previous session.

```
<HTML>

<HEAD>

<TITLE>Web Page Example #3a (Your Title Goes Here)</TITLE>

</HEAD>

<BODY>

<H1>First Subpage</H1>

<P>This is the text for the first subpage. This is the text
for the first subpage. This is the text for the first
subpage. This is the text for the first subpage. This is the
text for the first subpage. This is the text for the first
subpage. This is the text for the first subpage.</P>

<P>Return to <A HREF="basic-3.htm">Home Page</A>.</P>

<HR>

<ADDRESS><STRONG>Your Name Here</STRONG><BR>

E-mail: <A HREF="mailto:your@address.com">your@address.com</A>

</ADDRESS>

</BODY>

</HTML>
```

Starting Your Page

You're now ready to start constructing your first Web page; you should have both the example Web page and your mock-up text file open in your text editor or in PageMill. If you skipped creating a banner graphic this

morning, feel free to use the sample banner graphic from the example Web pages; also, if you skipped gathering a list of URLs, go ahead and use the sample list of links included in the first Web page example. Use these as placeholders, in other words, until you can come back later and create your own customized banner graphic, as well as gather your own list of links.

Finding Your Way

This session is a bit of a maze, in that there are so many different options that have to be accounted for. Here's a quick rundown to help you find your way through this session:

- ⚙ The Web page creation process is split up into three different sections, covering creating the top, middle, and bottom sections of your page. All readers will do the same top and bottom sections, but the actual middle section you do will depend on the specific Web page example you've selected to use as a template or guide. You only need to do the section that applies to the specific Web page example you've selected.

- ⚙ Since you may not have completed the Intermediate HTML Tutorial (Saturday Afternoon), any examples taken from that tutorial are "Extra Options." Feel free to skip any options you haven't covered yet.

- ⚙ Since the steps for executing the examples will be quite a bit different for PageMill users, a special subsection is included at the end of each section with specific instructions and directions that you can read if you are using PageMill.

Inserting Startup HTML Tags

This section is only required if you are creating your Web page from scratch in your text editor (while using the Web page example you've selected as a guide, rather than as a template). All other readers should skip ahead at this

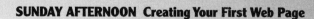

point to the next section, "Creating the Top Section (All Three Example Web Pages)."

If you're not using PageMill and are using the example Web page you've selected as a guide (rather than as a template), you should insert the startup HTML tags into your mock-up text file now. Here are the codes you need to add:

<HTML>

<HEAD>

<TITLE>_Your title goes here_**</TITLE>**

</HEAD>

<BODY>

Insert the following at the bottom of your text file:

</BODY>

</HTML>

NOTE

The following input examples assume that you're using one of the example Web pages as a template rather than as a guide. If you use the Web page example file as a guide in directly tagging your text file, you need to interpret what is shown, realizing that instead of inserting the text into the template, you must insert the HTML codes from the example Web page into your mock-up text file.

CAUTION

Many of the features this session presents as "extra options" require the use of an HTML 3.2-compliant Web browser. If you want to make use of any extra options that use HTML 4.0 features, you should use Netscape Navigator 4.0 or higher or Microsoft Internet Explorer 4.0 or higher.

Creating the Top Section (All Three Example Web Pages)

The following section applies to all three of the example Web pages. It covers creating a title, a banner graphic, a level-one heading, and an introductory paragraph. The following is the top section of the first Web page example, the HTML codes of which are identical to those for the other Web page examples, although the text in the title, level-one heading, and introductory paragraph may be different:

```
<HTML>

<HEAD>

<TITLE>Web Page Example #1 (Your Title Goes Here)
</TITLE>

</HEAD>

<BODY>

<P><IMG SRC="webpage.gif"></P>

<H1>A Web Page Using a Link List</H1>


<P>This is an example of a basic Web page. It contains
a banner graphic, level-one and level-two headings,
an introductory paragraph, a short list of links, a
horizontal rule, and an address block. The address
block contains the name of the author of the page, a
Mailto e-mail link, and a date reference.</P>
```

Creating Your Title

Your title is very important; think of it as your welcome mat. If you are not sure that you have come up with exactly the right title, feel free to just put in a provisional title for now. Including a short description with your title (no more than 40 to 50 characters) is also a good idea—be sure to include a few keywords (even a key phrase) in the description. Delete the sample

text ("Web Page Example #1 (Your Title Goes Here)") from within the TITLE tag, then insert the text for your title inside the TITLE tag:

```
<HTML>
<HEAD>
<TITLE>Insert your title</TITLE>
</HEAD>
```

PageMill Users: Creating Your Title

In the window for whichever page you've saved as index.html, just delete the current contents of the Title box and enter a title for your Web page.

Inserting a Banner Graphic

When planning your first Web page this morning, you had the option of creating your own personalized banner graphic; if you have created your own banner graphic, or have another graphic you want to use (a graphic of your company logo, for instance), you can insert it now. If you have your own banner graphic, it should be saved as a GIF or JPEG image (don't forget to include the file extensions, .gif or .jpg, when you save the image). Stick to typing the file name in all lowercase, and replace any spaces with underscores ("_"). You should save it in the same folder where you're saving your Web page files.

NOTE   The example Web pages all include a sample banner graphic, webpage.gif, that you can use as a placeholder, if you want, until you get to creating your own personalized banner graphic. For the examples shown in the figure illustrations, I'll use a different banner graphic, dummy.gif, which is also included with the example files in the folder for your Web pages. Feel free to use it, rather than webpage.gif, if you want to get some practice inserting an inline image here.

If you have created a personalized banner graphic, replace "webpage.gif" in the example templates with the name of the GIF file you want to use. Figure 6-3 shows what this might look like in a Web browser.

```
<BODY>

<P><IMG SRC="The file name of your banner graphic goes
here"></P>
```

NOTE Since you may insert your own banner graphic and your own mock-up text, the figure illustrations can only approximate what your Web page will look like. To see what your Web page is really going to look like, save your HTML file and hop over to your browser to take a look. You should do so for each example, if only to double-check and debug errors. If your screen doesn't match feature for feature with the figure in the book, and you can't find an error, it may be that your Web browser doesn't support the particular feature you're trying to use. The latest versions of both Netscape Navigator and Internet Explorer should support all the tags and features that this session presents (except where otherwise noted), but other browsers may not.

PageMill Users: Inserting a Banner Graphic

If you've saved the example Web page as index.html, feel free to use webpage.gif as a placeholder until you get to creating your own personalized

Banner graphic

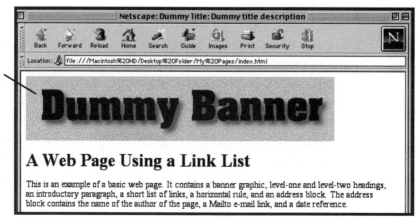

Figure 6-3

A banner graphic is a good way to make your Web page more visually appealing.

banner graphic. If you have created your own banner graphic or have another image you want to use, or want to try using the alternative example banner graphic (dummy.gif), just do the following:

1. If replacing the banner graphic (webpage.gif) included in the example Web page, click on the image and hit the Delete key.

2. With the cursor located at the top of index.html, choose Object from the Insert menu, and then choose Image. Double-click the folder for your site to open it, and then on your banner graphic to insert it. (You can double-click dummy.gif to insert the banner graphic that's shown in the figure illustrations.)

Creating a Level-One Heading

The level-one heading functions as the title that is displayed at the top of your page. This is different from the "title" you included earlier, which is displayed not in your page, but only on the browser's title bar (or when your page is listed in an Internet search). Your level-one heading can be the same as your title, or it can be different.

It is best to have only one level-one heading on your page. You probably have already thought of one for your page during this morning's planning session. If not, just put in a provisional heading—you can always change it later. Try to keep it to fewer than 30 characters. (Figure 6-4 shows how this might appear in a Web browser.) Insert your level-one heading as follows:

```
<BODY>
<P><IMG SRC="The name of your banner graphic"></P>
<H1>Your Level-One Heading goes here</H1>
</BODY>
```

PageMill Users: Creating a Level-One Heading

If you're applying format styles to your mock-up text file, just do the following:

Level-one heading

Figure 6-4

Here is an example of a level-one heading.

1. Click on the text paragraph you're using for your level-one heading.

2. Choose Largest Heading from the Change Format menu on the toolbar.

If you're copying and pasting your text from your mock-up text file to your example Web page, just do the following:

1. Click and drag to highlight the text in your mock-up text file that you want to copy, and then press Command-C to copy it.

2. Click and drag to highlight the corresponding text (for the level-one heading) in index.html, and press Command-V to paste in the new text.

NOTE

In the figure illustrations, I've increased the default font size in Netscape Navigator to 14 points. You were instructed on how to do this in the Saturday Morning session: just choose Preferences from the Edit menu on Navigator's menu bar, choose Fonts, and then change both font sizes to 14. If you're using Internet Explorer to preview your work, you can click the Larger icon on the toolbar to increase the size of the default font (you have to do this each time you run Internet Explorer). Note that because the Macintosh version of Internet Explorer bumps up the size of any headings in your page by one notch, all the illustrations in this session use Netscape Navigator, which will more faithfully represent what most viewers are likely to see on your page.

Creating Your Introductory Paragraph

During this morning's planning session, you may have created an introductory paragraph for your Web page. Again, having an introductory paragraph, although not essential, is a good idea, as it helps viewers decide whether they want to linger; it also helps search engines to index your page, so Web surfers can more easily find it. (Figure 6-5 shows what an introductory paragraph might look like in a Web page.) If you have created an introductory paragraph, insert it as follows:

```
<BODY>
<P><IMG SRC="The file name of your banner graphic"></P>
<H1>Your Level-One Heading</H1>
<P>Your introductory paragraph text goes here</P>
```

PageMill Users: Creating Your Introductory Paragraph

All of the text in your mock-up text file is automatically set in the "Paragraph" format style, so there's no need to apply a format style to the introductory paragraph. If you're copying and pasting text from your mock-up text file to your example Web page, do the same thing as you did with the level-one

Introductory paragraph

Figure 6-5

It's a good idea to start your Web page with an introductory paragraph.

heading: copy the introductory paragraph from your mock-up text file, then highlight the corresponding introductory paragraph in your example Web page, and press Command-V to paste in the new text.

NOTE   As you go through the process of creating your first Web page, be sure to run your browser and hop over to it frequently to check out the results of your work. PageMill users can easily preview their page by choosing Switch To from the View Menu. This is not the same as clicking the Toggle Preview Mode icon in the upper-right corner of the PageMill window to switch to Preview mode. PageMill's Preview mode will only give you a rough approximation of what your page might look like in a Web browser.

Extra Option: Setting the Width and Height Dimensions of Your Banner Graphic

NOTE   Many of these extra options use features that were covered in the Intermediate HTML Tutorial (Saturday Afternoon). If you haven't done that tutorial, you might want to skip ahead to the discussion of creating a middle section that relates to the Web page example you are using, and later come back and experiment with some of the suggested extra options.

It is a good idea to set the WIDTH and HEIGHT attributes for any inline images other than small bullet icons; that way, surrounding text will appear on the screen without waiting for your image to finish downloading. To set these dimensions, you need to know the actual dimensions of your image. If you are using webpage.gif, the sample banner graphic provided with the example Web pages, you should set WIDTH="400" and HEIGHT="100" in the IMG tag. If you are using dummy.gif, the dummy banner graphic displayed in the figure illustrations, you should set WIDTH="500" and HEIGHT="100" in the IMG tag, as shown here:

```
<P><IMG SRC="dummy.gif" WIDTH="500" HEIGHT="100"></P>
```

> **NOTE** PageMill automatically sets the width and height dimensions for any inline images you insert, so there is no need to do this manually.

Extra Option: Centering Your Banner Graphic and Level-One Heading

Most current Web browsers support centering of headings and paragraphs. The most commonly supported centering method involves setting the ALIGN attribute in a heading or paragraph tag. To center your banner graphic and your level-one heading, insert an ALIGN="center" attribute value in the P and H1 tags. (You could also center-align your introductory paragraph by inserting ALIGN="center" inside its paragraph tag.) Figure 6-6 shows what this would look like in a Web browser that supports horizontally aligning paragraphs and headings.

```
<P ALIGN="center"><IMG SRC="The file name of your
banner graphic"></P>

<H1 ALIGN="center">Your Level-One Heading</H1>
```

Centered

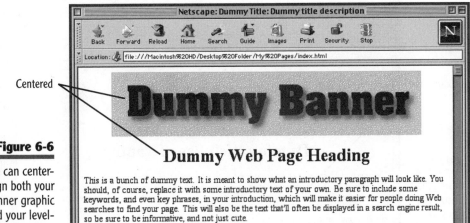

Figure 6-6

You can center-align both your banner graphic and your level-one heading.

PageMill Users: Centering Your Banner Graphic and Level-One Heading

To center your banner graphic, click on it and then on the Center Align Text icon on the toolbar. Do the same to center your level-one heading.

Extra Option: Increasing the Base Font Size

Bumping up the default base font one size can be a great way to make your page more readable. Add a blank line, just below the <BODY> code, and then add a BASEFONT tag to reset the base font size to "4" ("3" is the default size). The BASEFONT tag is a standalone tag in effect until you insert another BASEFONT tag resetting the base font to a different size. Figure 6-7 shows what this would look like in a Web browser that supports resetting the base font size.

```
<BODY>

<BASEFONT SIZE="4">

<P ALIGN="center"><IMG SRC="The file name of your
banner graphic"></P>

<H1 ALIGN="center">Your Level-One Heading</H1>
```

Larger base font

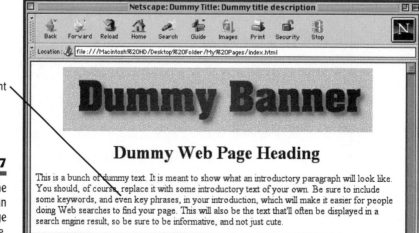

Figure 6-7

Increasing the base font size can help make a page more readable.

PageMill Users: Increasing the Base Font Size

Increasing the base font size in PageMill is easy. Just click on any text in your page, then in the Inspector, change the Base Font value from 3 to 4. (PageMill automatically inserts the BASEFONT code for you at the start of your page; if you want to insert additional BASEFONT codes at other points within your page, so you can vary your base font size, you can type them in yourself in Source Mode.)

Extra Option: Adding a Custom Horizontal Rule

An additional touch you can add to your Web page is to insert a horizontal rule between your level-one heading and your introductory paragraph. Center-alignment is the default alignment for horizontal rules, so if you want to set a percentage width for a horizontal rule, you should do it here in conjunction with a center-aligned level-one heading. (Figure 6-8 shows how this looks in a browser that supports changing the size and width of a horizontal rule.) To insert a ten-pixel unshaded horizontal rule that extends across 66 percent of the browser window below a center-aligned level-one heading, you would do this:

Custom horizontal rule

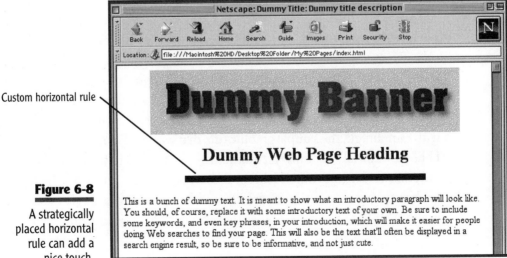

Figure 6-8

A strategically placed horizontal rule can add a nice touch.

```
<P ALIGN="center"><IMG SRC="The file name of your
banner graphic"></P>

<H1 ALIGN="center">Your Level-One Heading</H1>

<HR SIZE="10" WIDTH="66%" NOSHADE>
```

NOTE
You also can set the width of your horizontal rule in actual pixels by leaving off the percent sign (%) at the end of the WIDTH attribute value.

PageMill Users: Adding a Custom Horizontal Rule

To insert a horizontal rule, first click at the start of your introductory paragraph (or wherever else you'd like to insert the rule), and hit the Return key to add a blank line. Next, click on the blank line, and then choose Horizontal Rule from the Insert menu. To change the width to 66 percent, click on the horizontal rule, and then in the Inspector, type **66** in the Width box (while leaving Percent selected). Also in the Inspector, type **10** in the Size box to set the height of the rule to ten pixels. To create an unshaded rule, check the No Shade check box. To center the horizontal rule, click on the Center Align Text icon on the toolbar.

Extra Option: Adding a Graphic Rule

For an even nicer touch, you can use a graphic rule rather than a horizontal rule. By setting the HEIGHT and WIDTH attributes in the IMG tag, along with placing it in a center-aligned paragraph, you can get an effect similar to what you could achieve using the horizontal rule, and you also get to add some extra color to your page. If you want, you can experiment with rain_lin.gif, the sample graphic rule that was used in the "Intermediate HTML Tutorial" (Saturday Afternoon)—just copy it from the HTML Tutorials folder (on your Desktop, if that's where you put it) to the folder you're using in this session to create your first Web page. It's also included in the Web Page Examples folder that you used for this morning's session.

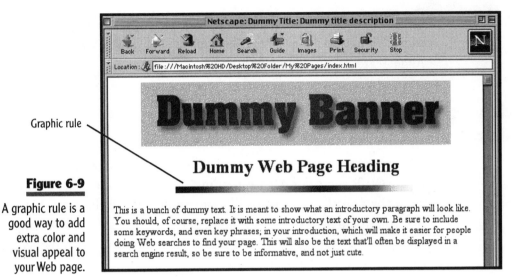

Graphic rule →

Figure 6-9

A graphic rule is a good way to add extra color and visual appeal to your Web page.

For instance, you might substitute rain_lin.gif for the horizontal rule that was used in the previous exercise (see Figure 6-9):

```
<P ALIGN="center"><IMG SRC="The name of your banner
graphic"></P>
```

```
<H1 ALIGN="center">Your Level-One Heading</H1>
```

```
<P ALIGN="center"><IMG SRC="rain_lin.gif" WIDTH="66%"
HEIGHT="10"></P>
```

PageMill Users: Adding a Graphic Rule

To add the example graphical rule, first delete the horizontal rule (if you added it). Choose Object from the Insert menu, and then choose Image. Double-click on the My PageMill Site folder (or on whichever folder you're using to create your first Web page in PageMill) to open it, and then on rain_lin.gif to insert it. Click on the graphic rule to select it, and then edit the settings in the Inspector. To change the width and height, first uncheck the Scale to Height check box and the Scale to Width check box. Type **66** in the Width box and select Percent (instead of Pixels). Type **10** in the Height box (leave Pixels selected). The paragraph containing the graphic

rule may still be centered (from the horizontal rule example); if not, to center it, click on the graphic rule to select it, and then click on the Center Align Text icon on the toolbar.

Extra Option: Changing the Typeface, Color, and Size of Your Heading Fonts

One way to give your page a snazzier look is to change the typeface (as in Figure 6-10) and color of each heading, and at the same time to bump up its size by a notch, to make it still more prominent (see Figure 6-11). Note that you would need to tag each heading individually. Here's an example of using the FACE attribute to set the level-one heading to a monospace font, changing its font color (by name, in this case, rather than with a hexadecimal RGB color code), and changing its font size to the largest displayable size:

```
<H1 ALIGN="center"><FONT FACE="Courier New, Courier"
COLOR="blue" SIZE="7">Your Level-One Heading</FONT>
</H1>
```

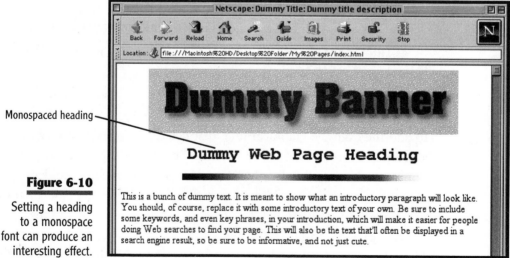

Monospaced heading

Figure 6-10

Setting a heading to a monospace font can produce an interesting effect.

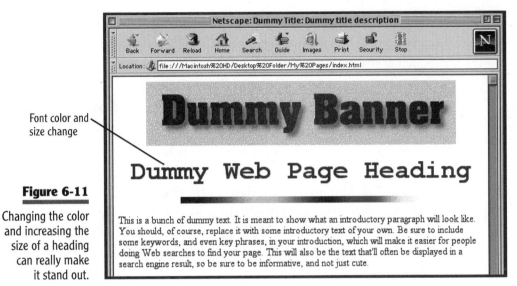

Font color and size change

Figure 6-11

Changing the color and increasing the size of a heading can really make it stand out.

CAUTION

Even though PostScript fonts are native to the Macintosh system, they aren't necessarily native to other systems. Windows users must purchase Adobe Type Manager as a separate product if they want to be able to display smoothly rendered PostScript fonts on their systems. If they don't have Adobe Type Manager installed, and most of them won't, they will see a very poor quality bitmap version of your PostScript font.

For this reason, in a list of typefaces for the FONT's FACE attribute, you should always list one or more True-Type fonts in front of any PostScript fonts you may also want to list. If you want to list the Courier typeface, always insert the New Courier typeface first; if you want to insert Helvetica, always insert Arial first; if you want to insert Times, always insert Times New Roman first.

You can, of course, assign typefaces other than monospace using the FACE attribute of the FONT tag. To set a sans serif font, list "Arial, Verdana, Helvetica" as the typefaces. When choosing fonts to include in a list of typefaces, the first typeface you specify will be displayed if it is present on a system; if not, the next typeface will be displayed, and so on. If none of the

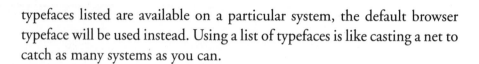

typefaces listed are available on a particular system, the default browser typeface will be used instead. Using a list of typefaces is like casting a net to catch as many systems as you can.

PageMill Users: Changing the Typeface, Color, and Size

To specify Courier New as the typeface for your level-one heading (Largest Heading), first click and drag to highlight it, and then choose Courier New from the Set Font menu. If you want to specify alternative typefaces in PageMill, to increase the chances that you'll match a typeface on a viewer's system, you need to edit the source code for your page in PageMill: choose Source Mode from the View menu, and then edit the FONT tag's FACE attribute. For instance, edit it so it looks like this: `FACE="Arial, Verdana, Helvetica"`.

To change the color of your level-one heading, click and drag to highlight your heading (if it isn't already selected). Click the Set Color icon on the toolbar. Click the blue color rectangle to change the color of your level-one heading to blue.

To increase by one notch the relative font size of your level-one heading, click and drag to highlight your heading, and then click once on the up arrow button on the left side of the Relative Font Size control on the toolbar. You could also make this change by choosing Size from the Style menu and then clicking +1.

Using a Drop Cap Image

There is no tag for creating a drop cap, but you can create a graphic of the first letter of your paragraph and then insert it in place of that letter. Set left-alignment in the IMG tag, and following text wraps around the graphic. I've included a sample drop cap graphic, drop-t.gif (which is 52 pixels wide by 55 pixels high), with the example Web page files; it can be used to insert a drop cap "T" at the start of the introductory paragraph. (See Figure 6-12 to see what this looks like in a Web browser that supports wrapping text around a left-aligned image.)

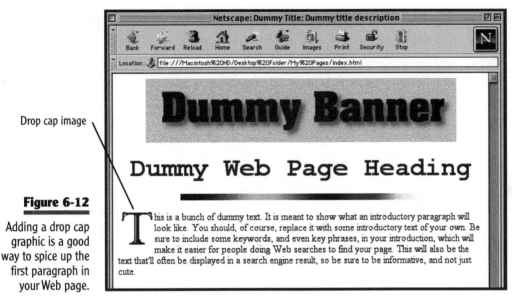

Drop cap image

Figure 6-12

Adding a drop cap
graphic is a good
way to spice up the
first paragraph in
your Web page.

```
<P><IMG SRC="drop-t.gif" ALIGN="left">This is your
introductory paragraph text...
```

PageMill Users: Using a Drop Cap Image

To insert the sample drop cap image, first click at the start of your introductory paragraph and then choose Object from the Insert menu, and then choose Image. Double-click on the My PageMill Site folder and then on drop-t.gif. Click on the drop cap image to select it, and then on Format, Align Object, and Left. If you want to add any vertical or horizontal space around your drop cap image, you can add VSPACE or HSPACE attributes (for instance, HSPACE="4") to the drop cap's IMG tag in Source Mode.

Take a Break?

You can see how this is starting to work, and you may want to rush right on to the guts of the page. But it might be a good idea to stop and stretch, touch your toes, and get your energy level up for the next section. Scratch your cat. Let your dog slobber on you. Water your plants. See you in a few minutes!

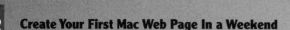

Middle Section (First Example Web Page)

If you have selected the first example Web page (a Web page with a list of external links) as your guide or template for creating your Web page, you should proceed with this section—skip to the next section if you're using the second example Web page (a Web page with subsections). The middle section of the Web page example file you've chosen, basic-1.html, includes a subheading and a list of external links:

```
<H2>A List of Links</H2>

<UL>

<LI><A HREF="http://www.callihan.com/create_imac/
">Create Your First iMac/Mac Web Page In a Weekend</A>:
HTML is for everyone!

<LI><A HREF="http://www.w3.org/">World Wide Web
Consortium</A>: Find out the latest about the Web
and HTML.

<LI><A HREF="http://www.infohiway.com/faster/
homebcs.htm">The Bandwidth Conservation Society</A>:
Save bytes--don't be a bandwidth hog.

</UL>
```

Adding a Subheading

The example includes a level-two heading (H2). Right now, the text simply indicates that a list of links follows the heading. You can exclude this or you can insert the specific subheading that you want (see Figure 6-13). If you're creating a Web page focused on stamp collecting, then the subheading here might read "Philatelist Links," or something like that. Insert a level-two heading like this:

```
<H2>Your Level-Two Heading goes here</H2>
```

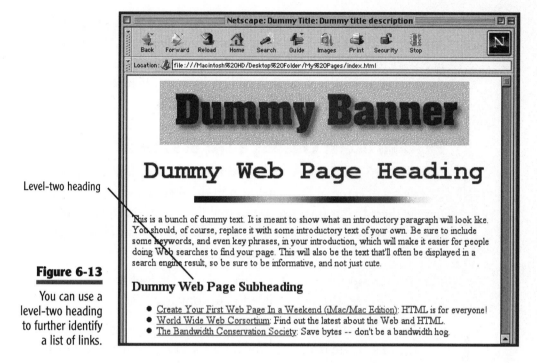

Level-two heading

Figure 6-13

You can use a
level-two heading
to further identify
a list of links.

Creating a List of External Links

The example template uses a list of hypertext links to other pages on the
Web. You may want to include explanations for some links, but eliminate
them from others that you feel are self-explanatory; feel free to eliminate
descriptions, or even links, from the example. The following shows how to
create a link list with descriptions. (If you only want to create a list here,
eliminate the links and link text; if you want to create a link list without
descriptions, eliminate the link descriptions.)

```
<UL>

<LI><A HREF="Insert the URL of your first link">Insert
the link text</A>: Insert the link description.

<LI><A HREF="Insert the URL of your second link">Insert
the link text</A>: Insert the link description.

</UL>
```

Most link lists include more than two items. To add items to your link list, just duplicate either of the item examples shown here, as many times as necessary to create your full link list. Insert the specific URL, link text, and descriptive text for each additional link list item. Figure 6-14 shows what the example link list looks like in a Web browser.

PageMill Users: Creating a List of External Links

If you haven't yet gathered your own list of external links, you can use the sample list of external links included in the first example Web page. If you have gathered your own list of external links, you can replace the sample links, or you can just add your links to the sample list. Here's how to edit one of the sample links, replacing it with your own:

1. In your mock-up text file, click and drag to highlight the URL you want to use. Press Command-C to copy it.

2. In the example Web page, click and drag to highlight the link text of the link you're replacing. You'll see the current URL for the link displayed in the Link To box at the bottom of the PageMill window.

Sample link list

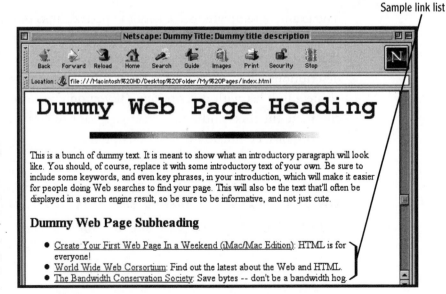

Figure 6-14

A link list, preferably with descriptions, is a good way to connect your visitors to your favorite destinations on the Web.

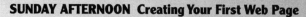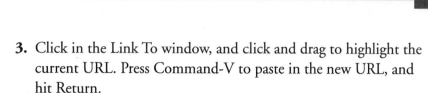

3. Click in the Link To window, and click and drag to highlight the current URL. Press Command-V to paste in the new URL, and hit Return.

4. Replace the old link text with your new link text. You'll need to type this in to keep the link active— if you try to paste it in, it'll go in as straight text, instead of as link text.

5. Copy and paste in any descriptive text, or just type it in.

If you're doing it the other way around, applying format styles, images, and links to your mock-up text file, here's a quick rundown on how to turn a list of URLs, text for links, and descriptive text into a list of hypertext links. Just follow these steps for each link:

NOTE   The following steps assume that the components that make up your links have been typed in your mock-up text file in this order: first the URL, second the text to be displayed as the link, and third any descriptive text for the link. They also assume that the components for your links have been arranged in separate paragraphs (with a paragraph break, rather than just a line break, at the end of each link).

1. In PageMill, click and drag to highlight all of the paragraphs you'll be including in your link list. From the Change Format pop-up window on the toolbar, select Bullet List.

2. Click and drag to highlight the URL for the first link, including the following space if there is one (for instance, "http://www.adobe. com/"). Press Command-X to cut it.

3. Click and drag to highlight the text you want to use for the link. Click in the Link To box at the bottom of the PageMill window, and press Command-V to paste in the URL. If there's a space at the end of the URL, hit the Delete key to get rid of it. Hit Return.

Extra Option: Changing the Size, Color, and Font of Your Level-Two Heading

If you did the extra options for the top section, you've already done this for your level-one heading. This time, however, include a list of font faces, and select a color other than blue. Also, bump the size up one notch, from 5, the default size for the H2 tag. (See Figure 6-15.) Here's an example:

```
<H2><FONT FACE="Verdana, Arial, Helvetica" COLOR=
"green" SIZE="6">Your Level-Two Heading</FONT></H2>
<UL>
```

Middle Section (Second Example Web Page)

If you have selected the second example Web page (a Web page using subsections) as your guide or template for creating your Web page, you should proceed with this section. The example Web page file you've chosen, basic-2.html, includes the following list of internal links, which acts as a menu that can jump to the following subsections:

Font face, color, and size change

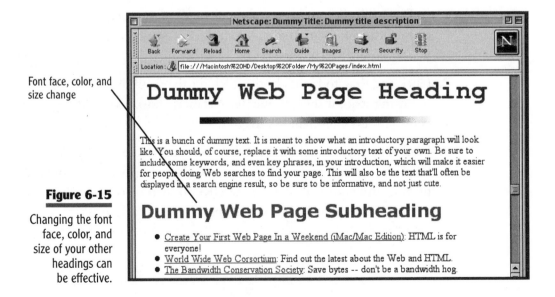

Figure 6-15

Changing the font face, color, and size of your other headings can be effective.

```
<UL>

<LI><A HREF="#sub1">First Subsection</A>: This link
jumps to the first subsection.

<LI><A HREF="#sub2">Second Subsection</A>: This link
jumps to the second subsection.

</UL>

<H2><A NAME="sub1"></A>First Subsection</H2>

<P>This is the text for the first subsection. This is
the text for the first subsection. This is the text for
the first subsection. This is the text for the first
subsection. This is the text for the first subsection.
This is the text for the first subsection. This is the
text for the first subsection.</P>

<H2><A NAME="sub2"></A>Second Subsection</H2>

<P>This is the text for the second subsection. This is
the text for the second subsection. This is the text
for the second subsection. This is the text for the
second subsection. This is the text for the second
subsection. This is the text for the second subsection.
This is the text for the second subsection.</P>
```

Creating Your Menu

This Web page example uses a link list as a menu, with the links jumping to target anchors set at the start of each subsection. Although the example includes a description for each link, you can feel free to eliminate the descriptions, or to include descriptions only where you feel they are necessary. Use the following HTML code list as a guide in creating a link list to serve as a menu to the following subsections:

```
<UL>

<LI><A HREF="#sub1">Insert the link text</A>: Insert
the link description.

<LI><A HREF="#sub2">Insert the link text</A>: Insert
the link description.

</UL>
```

Although the example contains only two items, you should include as many link list items as you have subsections to which you want to link. Just duplicate either of the list items for as many additional links as you need to add, then edit them to add new anchor names, link text, and link descriptions. Note also that the "sub1" and "sub2" anchor names correspond to the same anchor names used to create the "target" links in the subheadings for the subsections. When creating additional list items in your menu, you should be sure that each hypertext anchor has a unique anchor name ("sub3," "sub4," and so on).

PageMill Users: Creating a Menu

If you're using the example Web page as a template, you just need to edit the example menu to add your link text and descriptive text. To add additional list items in your menu, just copy and paste one of the list items to create additional list items—make sure that you click and drag to highlight the link text and specify a unique anchor name (#sub3, #sub4, and so on) in the Link To box. If you're doing it the other way around (using the example Web page as a guide), here's what you need to do:

1. In your mock-up text file in PageMill (index.html), if you haven't already included them, add the lines for your menu ("First Subsection," "Second Subsection," and so on), along with any descriptive text you want to include. Click and drag to highlight all of these lines, and then choose Bullet List from the Change Format menu on the toolbar.

2. Click and drag to highlight the text you want to use for the first link in your menu. Click in the Link To box at the bottom of the PageMill window. Type a unique anchor name for the link (**#part1**, for instance). Click Return.

3. Repeat Step 2 for each of the other list items in your menu, being careful to type a unique anchor name for each link in the Link To box (**#part2**, **#part3**, and so on).

NOTE

See the "PageMill Users" subsection in the following section for instructions on how to add the target anchors to your page's subsections.

Creating the Subsections

Next, you need to create the subheadings and subsections that correspond to the list items in your menu (see Figure 6-16).

```
<H2><A NAME="sub1"></A>Insert first subheading</H2>
<P>Insert text for the first subsection...
<H2><A NAME="sub2"></A>Insert second subheading</H2>
<P>Insert text for the second subsection...
```

To create additional subsections, just duplicate the second subsection example as many times as you need. Make sure, however, that each subheading has a unique anchor name. Have each correspond to the anchor name used in your menu ("sub3," "sub4," and so on).

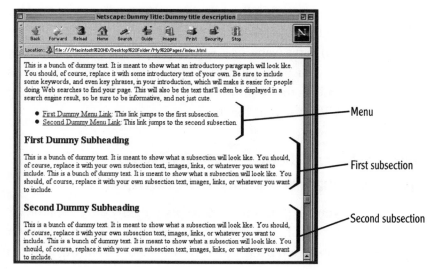

Figure 6-16

A menu of links can jump to as many subsections as you want to include in a Web page.

PageMill Users: Creating the Subsections

If you're using your example Web page as a template, copy the text for the first two subsection headings from your mock-up text file, pasting them in place of the example subsection headings in the example Web page. Do the same for the body of each subsection. If you have more than two subsections in your mock-up text file, just copy and paste the second subsection (heading and body) in the example Web page you're using to add additional subsections. Because copying and pasting the second subsection will duplicate the anchor name inserted at the start of the subsection heading, you'll need to edit the anchor (located at the start of the subsection heading) for each additional subsection you add to specify a unique anchor name. Click on the anchor for each additional subsection you add, and in the Inspector, type a unique anchor name (**part3, part4**, and so on) in the Name box. (The anchor names you use must match the corresponding anchor names used as URLs in the menu you created previously, minus the leading # character.)

If you're using the example Web page as a guide for formatting your mock-up text file in PageMill, you'll need to add the target anchors at the start of each subsection heading. Just click at the start of a subheading, and then choose Anchor from the Insert menu. Click on the anchor that was inserted and, in the Inspector, type a unique anchor name (**part1, part2**, and so on) in the Name box. Repeat this process for each subsection you're including in your page—just make sure anchor names for your subsections match (minus the "#") the corresponding anchor names you specified as the link URLs for your menu.

Extra Option: Using a Definition List to Format Your Subsections

You can give your subsections a slightly different look by using a definition list (DL), also called a glossary list. Using a definition list indents your subsection paragraph text, instead of displaying it flush to the left margin.

(Alternatively, you could nest your paragraph text within BLOCKQUOTE tags to get a similar look.) Just insert your subheading on the definition term (DT) line, and use definition data (DD) tags for any following paragraph tags, like this:

```
<DL>
<DT><H2><A NAME="sub1"></A>Your first subheading</H2>
<DD><P>The text for the first subsection...
<DT><H2><A NAME="sub2"></A>Your second subheading</H2>
<DD><P>The text for the second subsection...
</DL>
```

To include additional subsections, just duplicate either of the preceding subsection examples, and then plug in the relevant text. You can include additional indented paragraphs in each subsection by beginning each paragraph with a DT tag rather than a P tag. Figure 6-17 shows what a Web page using definition list subsections might look like in a Web browser.

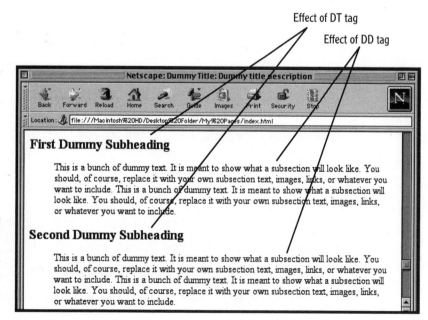

Figure 6-17

You can use a definition list to give your subheadings and subsections a different look.

PageMill Users: Using a Definition List to Format Your Subsections

The easiest way to do this in PageMill is to insert the DL, DT, and DD tags directly in Source Mode; choose Source Mode from the View menu, and then follow the example in the previous section to add the Definition List tags to your page's source code. After adding the Definition List tags, you'll notice that the formatting (Larger Heading) for your subheadings has disappeared, and two "?" icons now bracket them. This just means that PageMill doesn't recognize nesting an H2 tag (Larger Heading format) inside a DT tag. It'll display just fine in a browser, however—choose Switch To from the View menu and click on your browser to hop over and check it out.

Extra Option: Adding Loop-Back Links

If you're using more than just a few subsections, or if your subsections are fairly long, you may want to include loop-back links that let viewers jump back to your menu list, without having to scroll all the way back up to the top of your page, after they finish reading a subsection. Add the following codes to create loop-back links that'll jump back to your menu (see Figure 6-18 for how this'll look in a browser):

```
<UL><A HREF="top"></A>

<LI><A HREF="#sub1">The link text</A>: The link
description.

<LI><A HREF="#sub2">The link text</A>: The link
description.

</UL>

<DL>

<DT><H2><A NAME="sub1"></A>Your first subheading</H2>

<DD><P>The text for the first subsection...

<P>Return to <A HREF="#top">Top</A>.</P>

<DT><H2><A NAME="sub2"></A>Your second subheading</H2>
```

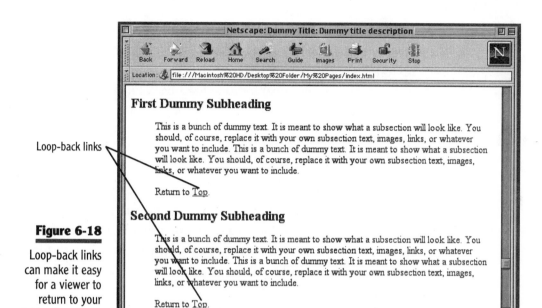

Loop-back links

Figure 6-18

Loop-back links
can make it easy
for a viewer to
return to your
table of contents.

```
<DD><P>The text for the second subsection...
<P>Return to <A HREF="#top">Top</A>.</P>
</DL>
```

PageMill Users: Adding Loop-Back Links

You add a loop-back link exactly the same way you created the other links
and anchors for your menu of links. Just do the following:

1. First insert a target anchor at the top of your menu. Choose
    Anchor from the Insert menu, click on the anchor icon, and then
    enter a name (**top**, for instance) for the anchor in the Name box
    in the Inspector.

2. Click at the end of the first subsection text, and hit the Return key
    to add a line. Type **Return to Top.** Click and drag to highlight the
    word "Top," click in the Link To box at the bottom of the PageMill
    window, and type the name of the target anchor preceded by a #
    character (**#top,** for instance).

3. Repeat Step 2 for each additional subsection for which you want to create a loop-back link. Because each loop-back link is jumping back up to the same target anchor, you should use the same target anchor name (**#top**, for instance) for each loop-back link.

Changing the Size, Color, and Font of Your Subsection Headings

If you did the extra options for the top section, you've already done this for your level-one heading. This time, however, for any subheadings (H2 tags), include a list of typefaces and select a color other than blue. Also, bump the size up one notch, from 5, the default size for the H2 tag. Repeat for each of your subsection subheadings. (See Figure 6-19 to see what this looks like in a Web browser.) Here's an example:

```
<DT><H2><A NAME="sub1"></A><FONT FACE="Verdana, Arial,
Helvetica" COLOR="green" SIZE="6">Your Level-Two
Heading</FONT></H2>
```

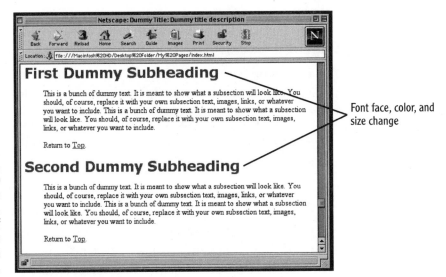

Figure 6-19

Changing the font face, color, and size of your subsection subheadings can be effective.

Middle Section (Third Example Web Page)

If you have selected the third example Web page (a Web page with subpages) as your guide or template for creating your Web page, you should proceed with this section. The middle section of the Web page example file you've chosen, basic-3.html, includes a table of contents that links to two example subpages (basic-3a.html and basic-3b.html). This is the middle section of the third Web page example.

```
<H2>Table of Contents</H2>

<UL>

<LI><A HREF="basic-3a.html">First Subpage</A>: This
links to the first subpage.

<LI><A HREF="basic-3b.html">Second Subpage</A>: This
links to the second subpage.

</UL>
```

Creating a Table of Contents

Edit the table of contents of the third example Web page, inserting the file name, link text, and descriptive text for each subpage you are linking to (see Figure 6-20).

NOTE

The file names for the subpages in the example are basic-3a.html and basic-3b.html. You need to substitute the actual names you want to use for your subpages, either variants of your main page's name or names that are more descriptive of the subpages. The only absolute requirement here is that the file name you include in the link menu below match the actual file name of the subpage to which you want to link.

```
<UL>

<LI><A HREF="Insert the file name of your first subpage">
Insert the link text</A>: Insert the link description.
```

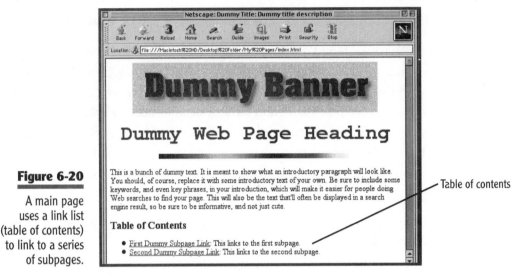

Figure 6-20

A main page uses a link list (table of contents) to link to a series of subpages.

Table of contents

```
<LI><A HREF="Insert the file name of the second
subpage">Insert the link text</A>: Insert the link
description.

</UL>
```

NOTE If the file for your subpage is in the same folder as your main page, you only need to insert its file name. Otherwise, if your subpage is in the same folder structure (in the same Web site), I highly recommend that you insert a relative URL, rather than an absolute URL. To find out about using relative URLs, see "Using Relative URLs" in the Saturday Afternoon session. Until you get more experience working with HTML, I strongly recommend that you store all related files (including subpages, graphics, and icons) in the same folder as your Web page. After you get a better feel for how HTML works, you'll most likely want to start organizing different Web page projects in their own subfolders, while still sharing common files, as well as separating out images into their own subfolders—and you'll want to use relative URLs to link files across folders. But for now, as long as you just put everything in the same folder, you don't have to worry about that.

Creating Your Subpages

I've provided two example subpages, basic-3a.html and basic-3b.html; other than their file names, they are almost identical. The following is the first example subpage, basic-3a.html, that is linked to from the example home page:

```
<HTML>

<HEAD>

<TITLE>Web Page Example #3a (Your Title Goes Here
</TITLE>

</HEAD>

<BODY>

<H1>First Subpage</H1>

<P>This is the text for the first subpage. This is the
text for the first subpage. This is the text for the
first subpage. This is the text for the first subpage.
This is the text for the first subpage. This is the
text for the first subpage. This is the text for the
first subpage.</P>

<P>Return to <A HREF="basic-3.html">Home Page</A>.</P>

<HR>

<ADDRESS><STRONG>Your Name Here</STRONG><BR>

E-mail: <A HREF="mailto:your@address.com">your@
address.com</A>

</ADDRESS>

</BODY>

</HTML>
```

Save a separate copy of the subpage example file for each subpage you want to create. You'll probably want to give them names that are more descriptive (about.html, prices.html, contact.html, and so on) and more closely fit the actual subpages you want to create. The only requirement is that the file names match what you use in your table of contents in the linking page, or vice versa. Go ahead and edit your subpage, inserting a title, level-one

heading, introductory paragraph, and loop-back link to your main page (see Figure 6-21).

```
<HEAD>
<TITLE>Insert a title for your subpage</TITLE>
</HEAD>
<BODY>
<H1>Insert your subpage level-one heading</H1>
<P>Insert an introductory paragraph...
<P><A HREF="Insert the file name of your main
page">Return to Home Page.</A>
```

A subpage doesn't have to be this simple, of course. It can be a complete Web page, including a list of external links, as in the first Web page example, or a table of contents linking to internal subsections, as in the second Web page example. It could even link to subpages of its own! In creating your subpages, feel free to use any of the example Web pages as models, although I would try using the first two examples first, before trying to create a site that links to subpages that link, in turn, to further subpages.

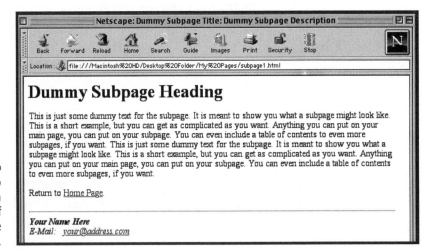

Figure 6-21

A subpage is a Web page linked from the home page of a multi-page Web site.

Adding a Logo Graphic to Your Subpage

For your main page, you added a banner graphic. For your subpages, one option is to add a smaller graphic, either a resized version of your banner graphic or a logo graphic. A logo graphic, as its name implies, may be a company logo—but by this term, I generally refer to any smaller graphic utilized at the top of your page that doesn't extend all or most of the way across the browser window (like a "banner" graphic does). A neat trick to use with a logo graphic is to left-align it, so that your level-one heading wraps around the logo (see Figure 6-22). This example also uses a couple of effectively placed BR tags, one to move the heading down a line and the other, using a `CLEAR="left"` attribute, to make sure that the following text doesn't also wrap:

```
<H1><IMG SRC="logo.gif" ALIGN="left" HSPACE="10"><BR>
Your subpage level-one heading<BR CLEAR="left"></H1>

<P>The introductory or other text for your subpage...
```

PageMill Users: Adding a Logo Graphic

To insert logo.gif, just click at the start of the level-one heading (Largest Heading), and choose Object from the Insert menu, and then choose Image. After inserting logo.gif, click on the image to select it. Choose Align from

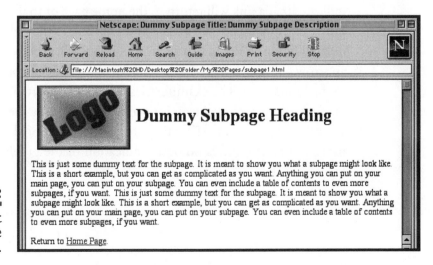

Figure 6-22

A logo graphic can be effective on a subpage.

the Format menu, and then choose Align, and Left. To add the HSPACE attribute and the two BR tags shown in the previous code example, select Source Mode from the View menu, and then insert these attributes manually (see the previous code example). When finished, choose Source Mode again from the View menu to return to Edit Mode.

NOTE

The subpage example includes a loop-back link at the bottom of the page. This is a navigational device that lets the viewer get from the subpage to the home page. Including a loop-back link on subpages is important because you don't know how somebody is going to end up at a subpage—they don't have to go through your home page to get to it, but can jump in from anywhere as long as they have its URL. If someone comes to your subpage via a search engine, pressing the Web browser Back button returns them to the search engine list, not to your home page.

Extra Option: Using a Navigational Icon

Navigational icons are a way to visually indicate a link without having to spell it out. Generally, an arrow or hand pointing up indicates that a link will return to the home page. (An image of a house is also often used to indicate a link back to a home page.) An arrow or hand pointing to the left indicates that a link will return to the home page or to the previous page in a sequence of pages; an arrow or hand pointing to the right indicates that a link will jump to the next page in a sequence. The following example uses an arrow pointing left as a navigational icon to indicate that the link returns to the home page. The example uses the ALT attribute in the IMG tag to identify the navigational icon for people who can't see the image itself. You should always use an ALT attribute with navigational icons, because a navigational icon offers no other indication of the graphic's purpose (see Figure 6-23):

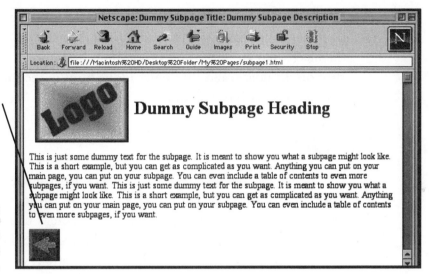

Navigational icon

Figure 6-23

You can use a navigational icon as a loop-back link.

```
<P><A HREF="The file name of your main page"><IMG
SRC="arr-left.gif" HEIGHT="50" WIDTH="50" ALT="Home"
BORDER="0"></A></P>

<HR>

<ADDRESS><STRONG>Your Name Here</STRONG><BR>
```

TIP

If you're creating a series of subpages that visitors should view in sequence, you can use a right-pointing arrow or hand to indicate a link to the next subpage in the series. In that context, a left-pointing arrow would indicate a link back to the previous page, and an up-pointing arrow could then indicate a link to the home page. Besides the left-pointing arrow you've already seen (arr-left.gif), a right-pointing arrow (arr-right.gif) and an up-pointing arrow (arr-up.gif) are included with the example Web page files.

PageMill Users: Use a Navigational Icon

PageMill automatically inserts images with their borders turned off, so there's nothing extra you have to do to get rid of the border. PageMill also automatically inserts the WIDTH and HEIGHT values for you.

To add the alternative text to the image, click on the image, and then in the Inspector, type **Home** (for instance) in the Alternative Label box. To turn the image into an image link that'll jump back to your home page, just click on the image, and then enter **index.html** in the Link To box at the bottom of PageMill's window.

Take a Break?

Hey, designing your own Web page can get pretty intense! If you feel you need another break, get up and take a step back from the screen. If this session has snuck past the dinner hour, grab a quick bite, throw some TV dinners in the microwave for the kids, fill the dog's dish. I'll see you back in ten minutes or so, when you'll complete the bottom section of your Web page, and add the final dazzling touches!

Bottom Section (All Three Example Web Pages)

The bottom section of the example Web pages contains the address block, and is the same for all three examples (including the subpages for the third).

```
<HR>

<ADDRESS>

<STRONG>Your Name Here</STRONG><BR>

E-mail: <A HREF="mailto:your@address.com">your@address.
com</A><BR>

Last Modified: Current date here

</ADDRESS>

</BODY>

</HTML>
```

Creating Your Address Block

Edit the address block, inserting your own name, your e-mail address, and the current date (see Figure 6-24).

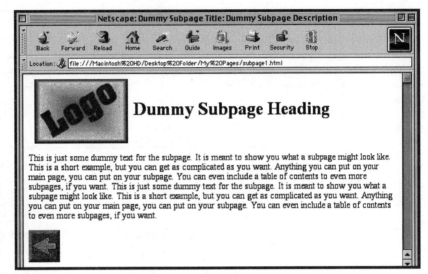

Figure 6-24

Every Web page should have an address block telling a visitor how to contact you.

```
<ADDRESS>

<STRONG>Insert your name here</STRONG><BR>

E-mail: <A HREF="mailto:Insert your e-mail
address">Insert your e-mail address again</A><BR>

Last Modified: Insert the current date

</ADDRESS>
```

Extra Option: Centering Your Address Block

You don't have to use a left-flush address block. You can center it for Web browsers that can read the <CENTER> and </CENTER> tags (see Figure 6-25). For instance:

```
<ADDRESS>

<CENTER><STRONG>Your name</STRONG><BR>

E-mail: <A HREF="mailto:Your e-mail address">Your
e-mail address again</A><BR>

Last Modified: The current date</CENTER>

</ADDRESS>
```

Figure 6-25

Address blocks are often centered to make them stand out.

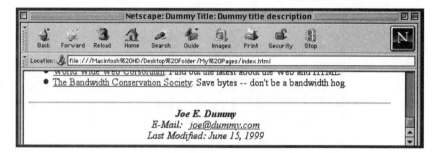

NOTE You also could insert a center-aligned paragraph at the start of the address block, but this has the effect of moving the address text further down from the horizontal rule.

Extra Option: Using a Customized Horizontal Rule or a Graphic Rule

You don't have to stick with using an ordinary horizontal rule as a divider between your page and your address block. For a more emphatic divider, you could use a customized horizontal rule or a graphic rule (see Figure 6-26). If you did the extra options for the top section, you should already have some practice doing both of these. Here's a quick example of using a graphic rule as a divider:

Figure 6-26

You can use a graphic rule, instead of a horizontal rule, to set off your address block.

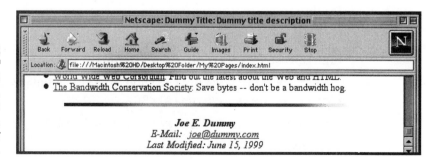

```
<P><IMG SRC="rain_lin.gif" WIDTH="80%" HEIGHT="5"></P>
<ADDRESS>
<CENTER><STRONG>Your name</STRONG><BR>
E-mail: <A HREF="mailto:Your e-mail address">Your
e-mail address again</A><BR>
Last Modified: The current date</CENTER>
</ADDRESS>
```

If you're creating a home page with subpages, you should create an address block for each page. On each of your pages, you should include information on how viewers of your page can contact you, if only to inform you when "link rot" has begun to set in. If you have an e-mail address, you should include it or some other means (such as a guestbook link) by which a visitor to your page can contact you. If you're creating your page for a business, you could also include your address, phone number, fax number, and so on.

When the page you're creating isn't the home page for your site, it is a good idea to include the URL of your home page in your address block. You could also include a loop-back link just above your address block that a viewer could use to hop back to your home page, or to the parent page of the current page. Remember, you don't know how somebody is going to get to a particular page—they don't have to go through your home page to get to one of your subpages. Some search engines use robot agents (sometimes called *worms* or *spiders*) to scan and index the Web. These agents can pick up your subpages even when you didn't list them—and direct people to the depths of your site who have no idea where it is or what else might be on it.

Extra Options for the Whole Page

This section contains a series of extra options that you can use to adjust the overall look and feel of your Web page. This section applies to all three example Web pages. The options include creating an icon link list, changing the background and text colors, setting font sizes and colors, and using a background image.

Extra Option: Creating an Icon Link List

Using an icon link list, instead of a plain unordered link list, is a good way to add color and visual appeal to your Web page. Because an icon link list doesn't use an unordered list, you need to first delete the UL start and end tags, and all the LI tags, so that the text for your link list looks like this:

NOTE In the following, URL refers to the first basic Web page example, anchor name refers to the second basic Web page example, and subpage file name refers to the third basic Web page example.

```
<A HREF="The URL, anchor name, or subpage file name
for your first link">The link text</A>: The link
description.

<A HREF="The URL, anchor name, or subpage file name
for your second link">The link text</A>: The link
description.
```

Now, to create an icon link list, you need to add three bits of code: a paragraph tag at the start of the list, a graphic icon bullet at the start of each list line, and a BR tag with the CLEAR="left" attribute value set. (Figure 6-27 shows how an icon link list might look applied to the first basic Web page example.) To do this, edit the text for your link list like this:

```
<P><IMG SRC="icon.gif" ALIGN="left" HSPACE="6" VSPACE=
"3">

<A HREF="The URL of your first link">The link text</A>:
The link description.<BR CLEAR="left">

<IMG SRC="icon.gif" ALIGN="left" HSPACE="6" VSPACE="3">

<A HREF="The URL of your second link">The link text
</A>: The link description.<BR CLEAR="left">

<IMG SRC="icon.gif" ALIGN="left" HSPACE="6" VSPACE="3">

<A HREF="The URL of your third link">The link text</A>:
The link description.<BR CLEAR="left">
```

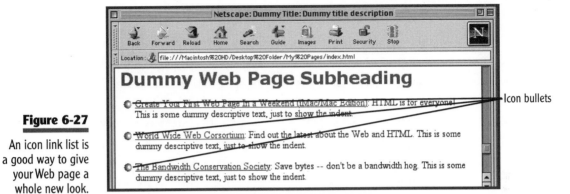

Icon bullets

Figure 6-27

An icon link list is a good way to give your Web page a whole new look.

> **TIP**
>
> For a slightly more advanced method of creating icon link lists, see Appendix C, "Creating Tables." It'll give you more control over the positioning of the bullet icon and allow you to indent as many following lines of text as you wish.

PageMill Users: Creating an Icon Link List

You've already had some practice inserting left-aligned inline images (images with text wrapping around them on the right). You'll need to add the VSPACE and HSPACE attributes, shown in the previous code example, directly in Source Mode. Choose Source Mode from the View menu to edit the actual HTML codes of your page. When done, choose Source Mode again from the View menu to uncheck it, which will turn Edit Mode back on.

The only problem is that if one of your icon link list items has only a single line of text, the following icon link list item will also try to wrap around the previous left-aligned icon. You can switch to Source Mode and manually insert the `<BR CLEAR="left">` tag at the end of each paragraph in your icon link list, as shown in the previous code example; or you can, while still in Edit Mode, just click at the end of each paragraph in your icon link list and choose Margin Break from the Insert menu.

Setting Background, Text, and Link Colors

You can add significant impact to your Web page just by changing the background and text colors. The text colors here include not just the text color, but also the color of links, visited links, and activated links (links where you have pressed but not released the mouse button). To do this, you assign either color names or hexadecimal RGB color codes to BGCOLOR, TEXT, LINK, VLINK, and ALINK attributes in your page's BODY tag. While you're at it, you should also adjust any FONT COLOR attributes you've set, so they'll still look good against the new background color (see Figure 6-28). Here's an example that sets different colors for the background, text, links, visited links, and active links:

```
<HTML>

<HEAD>

<TITLE>Your title</TITLE>

</HEAD>

<BODY BGCOLOR="#003366" TEXT="#FFFFCC" LINK="#99FFFF"
VLINK="#339999" ALINK="#CC0000">

. . .
```

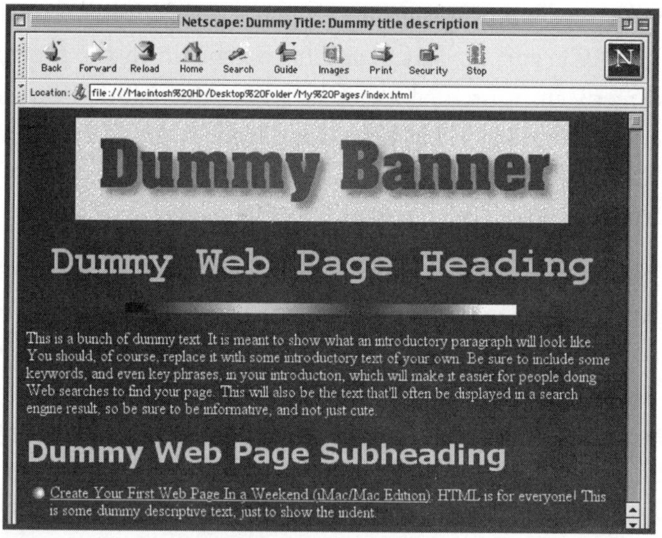

Figure 6-28

To give your Web page a completely different look, assign colors to the background, text, and links.

```
<H1 ALIGN="center"><FONT FACE="Courier New, Courier"
COLOR="#66CCFF" SIZE="7">Your Level-One Heading Here
</FONT></H1>

. . .

<H2><FONT FACE="Verdana, Arial, Helvetica"
COLOR="#FFCC00" SIZE="6">Your Level-Two Heading Here
</FONT></H2>
```

PageMill Users: Set Background, Text, and Link Colors

Setting the background, text, and link colors in PageMill is easy. Click anywhere within the page (but don't select an object, such as an image). In the Inspector, under Colors, you can set the colors for the Body Text, Background, Normal Links, Active Links, and Visited Links. If you want to set your background, text, and link colors using hexadecimal RGB codes, as shown in the previous code example, you can insert them directly into your page's HTML code in Source Mode.

Using a Background Image

You can add a background image to your Web page by using the BACKGROUND attribute in the BODY tag. Insert a BODY tag with 3dgreen.gif (included with the example Web page files) set as a background image (see Figure 6-29).

```
<HTML>

<HEAD>

<TITLE>Your title</TITLE>

</HEAD>

<BODY BACKGROUND="3dgreen.gif" BGCOLOR="#003366"
TEXT="#ffff00" LINK="#99ffff" VLINK="#339999"
ALINK="#cc0000">
```

When using a background image, you may also want to set the text and link colors so that they are coordinated with the colors in your background image. Especially when using a dark background image, you'll want to

Figure 6-29

For a dramatic effect, use a background image.

make sure the colors for your text and links are still easily readable. When using hex color codes, it is a good idea to stick to using those that are included in the browser-safe palette rather than using the standard 16-color names. For more information on selecting browser-safe hex color codes, see "Working with Fonts," in the Saturday Afternoon session. Also, when using a dark background image, you should set a dark background color too—otherwise you might end up with light (or even white) text against a white background in a browser with the display of graphics turned off.

PageMill Users: Using a Background Image

Using a background image in your Web page is pretty easy in PageMill. Just click on any text in your page, and then in the Inspector, click on the small icon at the lower left of the window. Open your site's folder, and double-click on 3dgreen.gif (or any other background image you want to use) to insert it. If you don't like how your current text and links colors look against a background image, just choose new colors for them in the Inspector until you get a combination you like.

> ### GETTING MORE BACKGROUNDS
>
> If you're wondering where you can find additional background images to try out for your page, there are two additional background images in the Web Page Examples folder: backgrnd.gif and mottle.gif. Since you copied that folder to create the folder you're using for this session, you can simply replace 3dgreen.gif with either backgrnd.gif or mottle.gif to see what they'll look like.
>
> If you have an iMac, you can find additional background images on the Adobe PageMill 3.0 CD-ROM. Just mount and open the CD-ROM, and then double-click on Web Pages and Content, WebMorsels, and index.html. Click the top banner ("WebMorsels Catalog"), scroll down and click the Tiles link (under "WebMorsels Image Index"), and then click on whichever category you want to check out. To save a background image (or "tile," according to Adobe) to your Web site folder, just hold the mouse button on the image, and in Navigator choose Save this image as (in Internet Explorer choose Download Image to Disk). Open the folder you're using in this session to save your Web page (My Pages or My PageMill Site, for instance, if you're using PageMill), and then click Save to save the image.
>
> FIND IT ON ▶   You can also find many background images included in the Clip Art
> **THE CD**   section of this book's CD-ROM. Also, be sure to check the Web site
> FIND IT ON ▶   for this book, www.callihan.com create_imac/, for background
> **THE WEB**   images and other Web art images that you can download.

Using a Transparent Banner Graphic

You can give your Web page a three-dimensional look by using a transparent GIF image for your banner graphic. With its background color set to be transparent, the image will appear to float on top of the background. An example banner graphic with its background color set to transparent, dummy_tr.gif, is included, so that you can see exactly what this looks like (see Figure 6-30).

```
<BODY BACKGROUND="3dgreen.gif" BGCOLOR="#003366"
TEXT="#ffff00" LINK="#99ffff" VLINK="#339999"
ALINK="#cc0000">

<BASEFONT SIZE="4">

<P ALIGN="center"><IMG SRC="dummy_tr.gif"></P>
```

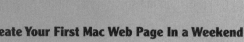

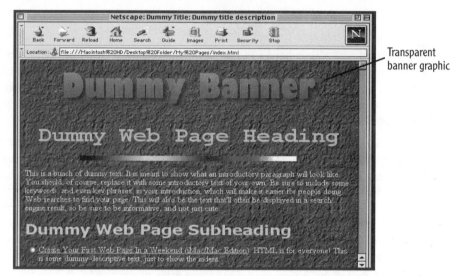

Figure 6-30

A transparent banner graphic can give your page a 3-D look.

Transparent banner graphic

PageMill Users: Using a Transparent Banner Graphic

Just click on your current banner graphic and hit the Delete key to get rid of it. Choose Object from the Insert menu, and then choose Image. Double-click on your site's folder to open it, and then on dummy_tr.gif to insert it.

Wrapping Up

You should now have created your first Web page. Hooray! You may have stuck to creating a very basic Web page, which uses only tags and features from the Basic HTML Tutorial. Or you may have incorporated a number of the suggested extra options to jazz it up, most of which are based on tags and features from the "Intermediate HTML Tutorial." You may also have used one of the example banner graphics, or the example link list provided as placeholders until you get the time to create your own. A Web page tends to be a work in progress—never, ever finished, in other words. And one page tends to lead to another, and to another, and so on.

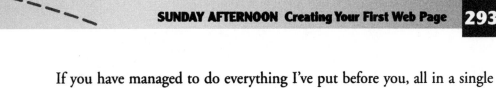

If you have managed to do everything I've put before you, all in a single weekend, that's fantastic; even if you've stuck to doing the Basic HTML Tutorial, skipped all the extra options when creating your first Web page, and used the sample banner and links, you've still accomplished a lot!

If you've still got time and energy left this weekend, try out the bonus session this evening, "Creating Your Own Web Images," to learn how to use the AppleWorks Painting and Drawing modules to create personalized Web images. So take a break and fix a good dinner (or a midnight snack!), and I'll see you back in half an hour, when you'll start learning how to create your own Web images.

Creating Your Own Web Images (Bonus Session)

- ✿ Creating banners and buttons
- ✿ Creating text objects and drop shadows
- ✿ Applying color, pattern, texture, and gradient fills
- ✿ Using clip art

It's Sunday evening! If you're on schedule, you planned your first Web page this morning and created it this afternoon. You may have taken the time to create a quick-and-dirty banner graphic for your page, or you may have already had a graphic you wanted to use, such as your company logo or a scanned photo of yourself; however, I deliberately put off having you get into creating your own Web images in any depth until after you had created your first Web page. Depending on how much energy you have left over, feel free to do all or just some of this session, or save it for next weekend.

There are many software tools available for creating Web images; these include some relatively expensive programs, such as Adobe Photoshop or MetaCreations Painter, which are favored by many professional Web designers. I've chosen in this session to focus on using the AppleWorks 5 Painting and Drawing modules to create Web images. If you have an iMac, AppleWorks 5 is already installed on your computer; for other Macintosh OS users, a trial version of the suite is

FIND IT ON ▶
THE WEB

available for download at **www.apple.com/appleworks/**. AppleWorks 5 is the same program as ClarisWorks 5, if you already have the latter program installed on your computer (the trial version that can be downloaded is, in fact, still called ClarisWorks 5).

AppleWorks does have a few limitations when it comes to creating Web images; you can compensate for these by using AppleWorks in combination with freeware and inexpensive shareware image editing utilities that are available on this book's CD-ROM or on the Web.

Creating a Banner Graphic

For this example, you'll use the AppleWorks Painting module to create a banner graphic. You'll learn how to add text, create drop shadow effects, and apply a variety of fill effects; you'll also learn how to save your banner graphic as a JPEG or GIF image, so it can be used in a Web page.

NOTE •

For this example you'll be squeezing a lot of effects into a single image to learn the most in the shortest period of time. Whether you want to use all of the effects covered here in your final product depends entirely on the kind of page you want to create and your own preferences and taste.

• •

Run AppleWorks 5 (on the iMac you can find it already installed in the Applications folder of the Macintosh HD). Double-click the Painting line in the menu list to open the AppleWorks Painting module (see Figure 7-1).

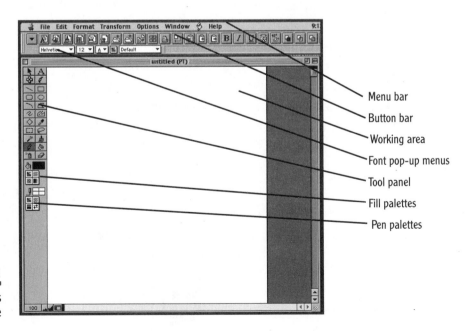

Figure 7-1

The AppleWorks Painting module

Specifying a Size for Your Image

You can work in the default image size (468 pixels across by 648 pixels down) and later resize your image, or you can start out working in the actual size you want for your image. Sometimes you need the extra working area, so you can copy and move text and other image objects. For this example, you'll just create a simple banner image, so go ahead and set the image size now to 500 pixels across by 100 pixels down:

1. On the menu bar, choose Document from the Format menu.

2. Under Size, type **500** in the Pixels Across box and **100** in the Pixels Down box. Click OK (see Figure 7-2).

Creating the Text for Your Banner

You can use any text you want for your banner. Make it any length that you choose, as long as it will fit within the dimensions of the banner image.

1. Click the text tool (the "A" icon) in the tool panel, and then click in the upper left corner of the image.

2. Change the default font (Helvetica) in the Font pop-up menu to any other font you want to use. If you want to match what's shown in the figures, select Gadget as the font, if it is available.

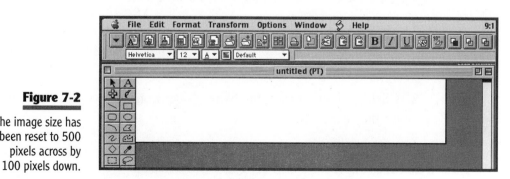

Figure 7-2

The image size has been reset to 500 pixels across by 100 pixels down.

NOTE If Gadget isn't available on your system, feel free to choose any other font available on your system that you'd like to use. Other fonts may be wider or narrower than the font used in the example, so you may need to adjust the point size up or down in the next step, depending on which font you're using.

3. Increase the default font size (12) in the Font Size pop-up menu. For instance, if you want to match what's shown in the figures, choose Other from the Font Size pop-up menu, type **52**, and click OK.

4. Change the default font style to Bold in the Font Style pop-up menu (the default is Plain Text, or "A").

5. Click the Text Color pop-up palette and choose a color for the text. For example, choose the slate blue color, fifth from the left in the eleventh row (sixth row up from the bottom).

6. Type the text for your banner. To match the figures, type **Kristina's Page** (but feel free to substitute your own name or other alternative text here).

NOTE If you run out of space typing your banner text, just hit the Delete key to delete the text you've typed, and then change the font size to a smaller size. Alternatively, you could also select a font that takes up less horizontal space (Impact, for instance). Then retype your text to see the new settings.

7. Make a note of your text's font, font size, and font style (Gadget, 52 points, and Bold, for instance). You'll need to use them again a bit later.

8. Click the Pointer tool (the "Arrow" icon) on the tool panel (to turn off the Text tool).

Centering Your Banner Text

To center your text in the image area, do the following:

1. First, click the Options menu to check if Autogrid is turned on or off. If the option reads, "Turn Autogrid Off," click it (if not, just leave it as it is). This will allow you to more minutely position your text, without having to jump from one autogrid juncture to another.

2. Click the Selection tool (the "dashed rectangle" icon, eighth icon down on the left column of the tool panel). Click and drag to select the text (hold the mouse button down above and to the left of the text and then drag it down and to the right, until the dashed rect-angle entirely boxes the text). Then click the mouse on the text and drag it so it is roughly centered in the image area (see Figure 7-3).

Creating a Drop Shadow Effect

A drop shadow effect is a great way to give your banner a snazzy 3-D look, setting your banner graphic apart. Many image editors have filters or plug-ins that make creating drop shadow effects a snap; it is not that easy with the AppleWorks Painting module, but here is the trick: First, apply successive blending effects to blend your initial text into the background. Then, retype your text, superimposed over, but slightly above and to the left of, your blended text; use the same font, font size, and font style, but select a different color.

Selection tool

Figure 7-3

The text has been selected and centered in the image area.

Applying the Blend Effects

1. On the menu bar, choose Select All from the Edit menu.

2. Choose Blend from the Transform menu. Repeat this around seven times (see Figure 7-4).

Superimposing Your New Text

Now, this gets a little tricky, in that you can only estimate the position for your superimposed text. You may need to reposition and retype it several times in order to place it exactly where you want it.

1. Click the Text tool again (the "A" icon on the tool panel).

2. Click above and to the left of your blended text. Reselect the same font settings you used before (Gadget, 52, and Bold, for instance). Select a different color, such as light green (fourth from the left in the tenth row).

3. Retype the same text you typed previously for your blended text. If you can immediately see that the text isn't positioned where you want it relative to the blended text, just click the Delete key to back up and delete the letters you've typed, and then click the mouse in a different place to reposition the starting point for your text. You'll need to reselect the font settings (font, font size, font style, and font color) you selected in the previous step. (You may have to do this a few times before you get the text positioned where you want it.)

Figure 7-4

The banner text has been blended into the background.

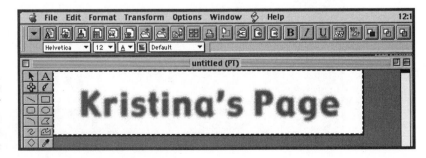

4. When you've typed your text and are happy with where it is positioned, click the Pointer tool (the "Arrow" icon) on the tool panel to see the result.

5. If your superimposition is still not as close as you'd like it to be (see Figure 7-5 for an example of what to aim for), just choose Undo from the Edit menu. Go back to Step 1 above, and keep trying until you get your new text superimposed exactly as you want it over your blended text.

Saving Your Banner Image

This is a good place to save your image. That way, if you don't like something you do later to the image, and can't undo it, you can always return to your saved version.

1. Choose Save As from the File menu.

2. If you have not already created a folder for your AppleWorks images (**My Images**, for instance), click the New button, type a folder name, and click Create.

3. Leave AppleWorks selected as the file type, type a file name for your banner image (**My Banner**, for instance), and then click the Save button.

Figure 7-5

The new banner text has been superimposed over the blended text.

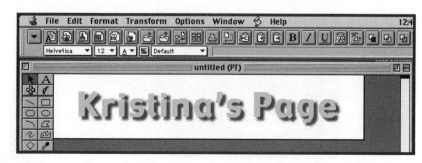

Trying Different Fill Options

There are two different palette areas, for fill palettes and pen palettes, located at the bottom of the tool panel. In the upper palette area are four icons through which you can apply fills to areas in your image; these fill palette icons are organized in a square, with the upper-left icon opening the color palette, the upper-right one opening the pattern palette, the lower-left one opening the texture palette, and the lower-right one opening the gradient palette. The lower palette area, for the pen palettes, allows you to change the characteristics of lines that you draw in your image or that appear as outlines around objects.

Applying a Color Fill to the First Letter of Your Banner Text

1. In the fill palettes square, click the upper-left icon to open the color palette (see Figure 7-6).

2. Click any color you want to use to fill the first letter in your banner text. For instance, click the bright red color, fourth from the left in the third row. You'll notice that the color of the fill swatch (just to the right of the "paint bucket") has changed to the color you selected.

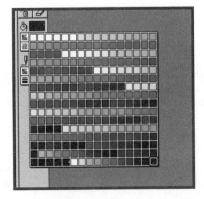

Figure 7-6

The fill color palette is opened.

3. Click on the Fill tool (the "paint bucket" icon) in the tool panel, and then click in the first letter of your banner text (see Figure 7-7). (If you accidentally miss the letter and spill paint, so to speak, all over the image's background, just choose Undo Paint from the Edit menu or press Command-Z and try again.)

Applying a Pattern Fill

The patterns in the fill pattern palette, although they're displayed in black and white, are applied in whatever color you've selected in the fill color palette. Select a different color from the fill color palette, select a pattern from the fill pattern palette, and then apply the combination to the second letter of your banner text:

1. In the fill palettes square, click the upper-left icon to open the color palette. Click a different color (try the sky blue color, first color in the thirteenth row).

2. In the fill palettes square, click the upper-right icon to open the pattern palette (see Figure 7-8).

3. Click any pattern you want to use to fill the second letter in your banner text. For instance, click the second pattern in the third row. You'll notice that the fill swatch is now displaying the pattern you just selected, in the color you previously selected.

Figure 7-7

A bright red fill color is applied to the first letter of the banner text.

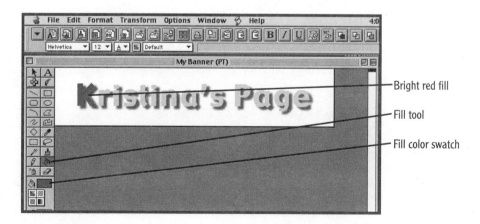

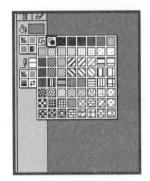

Figure 7-8

The pattern palette is opened.

4. With the Fill tool (the "paint bucket" icon) still selected, click in the second letter of your banner text. See Figure 7-9.

Applying a Texture Fill

The fill texture palette allows you to choose from a selection of textures to apply to an area in your image. Select a texture, and apply it to the third letter of your banner text:

1. In the fill palettes square, click the lower-left icon to open the texture palette (see Figure 7-10).

2. Click a texture to use to fill the third letter in your banner text. For instance, click the second texture in the second row. You'll notice that the fill swatch is now displaying the texture you selected.

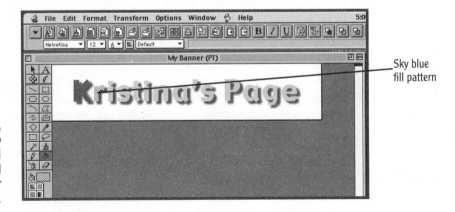

Sky blue fill pattern

Figure 7-9

A sky blue fill pattern is applied to the second letter of the banner text.

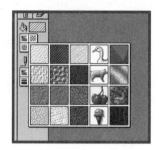

Figure 7-10

The texture palette
is opened.

3. With the Fill tool still selected, click in the third letter of your banner text (see Figure 7-11).

 TIP

With the "i" and "j" letters, you have to fill the body of the letter and the dot separately. A nice touch can be to apply different fills to the letter and the dot.

Applying a Gradient Fill

A gradient fill is a combination of up to four colors blended together. This type of fill gets its name from the color gradients between colors. Apply a gradient fill to the fourth letter of your banner text:

1. In the fill palettes square, click the lower-right icon to open the gradient palette (see Figure 7-12).

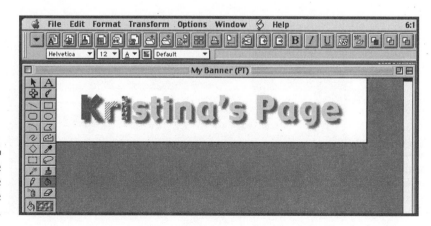

Figure 7-11

A gold texture
is applied to the
third letter of the
banner text.

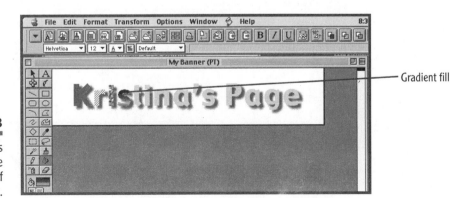

Figure 7-12

The fill gradient palette is opened.

2. Click one of the colored gradient fills to fill the fourth letter in your banner text. For instance, click the fifth gradient in the third row. You'll notice that the fill swatch is now displaying the gradient you selected.

3. With the Fill tool still selected, click in the fourth letter of your banner text (see Figure 7-13).

Editing a Gradient Fill

You're not stuck with using the default gradient fills displayed in the gradient palette—you can create your own. Follow these steps for an example of creating your own gradient fill:

1. Choose Gradients from the Options menu to open the Gradient Editor.

2. In the Gradient palette, to avoid replacing one of the color gradients (in case you want to use it later), click one of the black and white gradients. For instance, click on the fourth gradient in the second row (see Figure 7-14).

Figure 7-13

A gradient fill is applied to the fourth letter of the banner text.

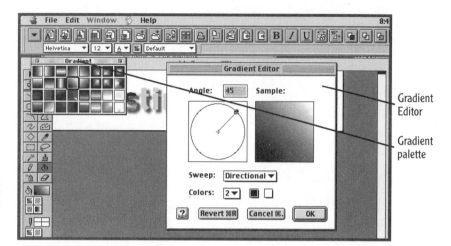

Gradient Editor

Gradient palette

Figure 7-14

You can edit any of the gradient fills in the Gradient Editor.

In the Gradient Editor, you can change the sweep, focus, and angle of a gradient. Refer to these definitions as you get some practice making these changes with the gradient that is currently open:

- The **sweep** of a gradient can define a Directional, Circular, or Shape Burst gradient fill.

- The **focus** of a gradient fill is determined by the position of the hollow circle. For instance, in a Directional gradient, you drag the hollow focus circle along the angle radius, to specify where the center of the gradient pattern will be positioned.

- The **angle** of a gradient fill is determined by the position of the solid circle. In a Directional or Circular gradient, you can specify the angle degree either by dragging the solid circle in a circular motion, or by typing a number in the Angle box.

Follow these steps to edit the gradient in the Gradient Editor:

1. For this example, leave Directional selected as the Sweep.

2. Click on the hollow circle at the end of the angle radius, and drag it so it is positioned about midway on the angle radius.

3. Click on the solid circle, and drag it clockwise around the circle, until the Angle value reads 315 (or just type that number in the Angle box).

4. From the Colors pop-up menu, select 4 as the number of colors; then click on each of the four color squares, and select a color (see Figure 7-15). Feel free to experiment with different color combinations until you get a combination you like.

5. Click OK to exit the Gradient Editor.

6. Click the lower-right icon in the fill palettes square, and select the gradient fill you just created. With the Fill tool still selected, click in the fifth letter of your banner text (see Figure 7-16).

Filling the Rest of the Letters in Your Text Banner

You can also create new patterns in the Pattern Editor and new textures in the Texture Editor. To access the Pattern Editor, choose Patterns from the Options menu; to access the Textures Editor, choose Textures from the Options menu. Apply whichever color, pattern, texture, and gradient fills you want to the rest of the letters in your text banner. Figure 7-17 shows a text banner with fills applied to all of the text letters.

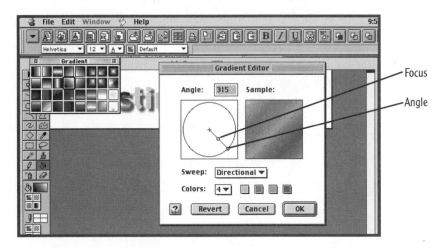

Figure 7-15

A new gradient fill has been created in the Gradient Editor.

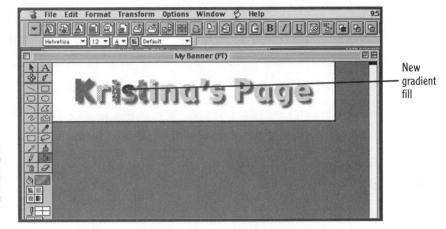

New gradient fill

Figure 7-16

The new gradient fill is applied to the fifth letter of the banner text.

Figure 7-17

Different fills have been applied to all of the letters in the text banner.

Saving Your Graphic As a Web Image

In order to use your banner graphic in a Web page, you need to save it as either a JPEG or a GIF image. JPEG images can display colors from a palette of up to 16.7 million colors, and are a good choice for displaying photographic images or images that contain blend or gradient effects. GIF images can display colors only from a palette of up to 256 colors, but have the advantage of being able to be made transparent. (AppleWorks automatically converts a white background in a GIF image to transparent.) To save your banner graphic as a JPEG or GIF image in AppleWorks, just do the following:

1. Choose Save As from the File menu.

2. In the Save As dialog box, open the folder where you want to save your image.

3. From the Save As menu, select either JPEG or GIF.

4. In the file name box, type the name of your image. You're saving this image for use on the Web, so follow the appropriate conventions. Type the file name in all lowercase letters, use underscores ("_") rather than spaces, and add an extension. For instance, you might type **mybanner.jpg** or **mybanner.gif** as the file name.

5. Click the Save button to save the graphic.

Figure 7-18 shows how a JPEG image looks when displayed in a Web browser against a background image; Figure 7-19 shows how a GIF image looks. If your image and the HTML file where you want to display it are in the same folder, and you know the image's width and height in pixels, you can just insert HTML code in the following form into your HTML file to insert your inline image:

```
<IMG SRC="mybanner.jpg" WIDTH="500" HEIGHT="100">
```

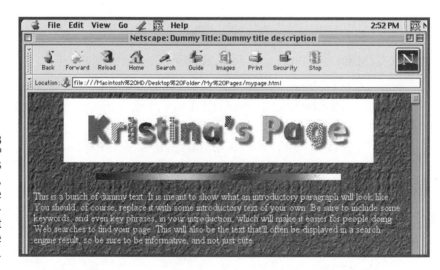

Figure 7-18

Since JPEG images aren't transparent, you can see the image's background against the Web page background image.

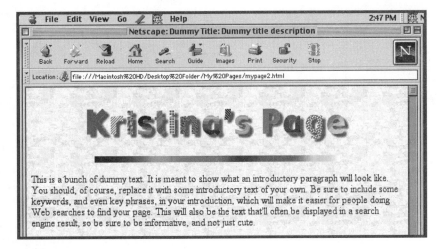

Figure 7-19

When saving GIF images with blank backgrounds, AppleWorks automatically sets the background to be transparent.

Stick to saving your banner image and any other images you want to include in your page in the same folder where you've saved your Web page. That way, you only need to include the image's file name as the URL to display it in your Web page as an inline image. Later, when you want to start organizing your Web pages into separate folders, you may also want to create a separate folder in your Web site just for images. That way, the same image can be shared by different Web pages, even if the Web pages are in different folders. (See "Using Relative URLs" in the Saturday Morning session for more information as to how to do this.)

Displaying Transparent GIF Images Against Non-White Backgrounds

The problem with a transparent GIF saved in AppleWorks is that it'll only work when displayed against a background image that also has white (or near white) as its primary color (as shown in Figure 7-19). If you try to display the same image against a non-white background color or a background image in which the primary color is not white or near white, you'll see what may be called a "cookie-cutter" or "halo" effect (see Figure 7-20).

Figure 7-20

A drop shadow is outlined by a white "halo" effect when a transparent GIF is displayed against a non-white background.

The problem is that the drop shadow effect blends to white, the color of the image background in the AppleWorks Painting module. Only the pure white color is made transparent—all the other "blended" shades of color remain non-transparent. Here's a rundown on what you need to do if you want to display a drop shadow effect transparently against a non-white background:

1. When starting your image in the AppleWorks Painting module, apply a color fill to the background of your image that matches as closely as possible the background color or the primary color in the background image you want to display it against. The match doesn't have to be exact, but the closer you can get it the better.

TIP

To match your image background to the primary (or close to primary) color in a background image, open a blank Painting document in AppleWorks, insert the background image (File->Insert), and click the Eye Dropper tool inside the background image (repeat this until the color shade you want is shown in the fill swatch). Reselect the background image and delete it from your image. Reset the size dimensions of your image (Format->Document). Click the Fill tool, and click in your image to fill the background with the color you picked up with the Eye Dropper.

2. Create the remainder of your image, adding text, creating drop shadows (blends), and so on, against your image's colored background. When finished, save your image as a GIF image.

3. Open your GIF image in a software program that allows you to select the color in the image that you want to be transparent. Select the background color, and resave the image as a transparent GIF (see Figure 7-21).

HANDY UTILITIES

A handy freeware utility, Transparency, is available on the Web that makes setting non-white GIF backgrounds to be transparent a snap. You just open the image in Transparency, click on the color you want to be transparent, and then resave the image. You can download Transparency at http://Syracuse.allmacintosh. com/imgeditmac.html. A similar shareware program, Vanishing Cream, is also available on the Web. Just go to www.zdnet.com/mac/download.html, type "Vanishing Cream" in the search box, and click Search (Vanishing Cream costs $10 to register).

These utilities allow you to specify a single color (and tone) as transparent. Some commercial image editing programs, such as Adobe Photoshop, allow you to specify a range of tones within a color to be transparent. This can give you more control in the process, especially if you're using a drop shadow or other blend effect against the color you want to set as transparent.

Take a Break?

It's been a long weekend and a busy day! If the clock is sneaking up on the midnight hour, feel free to call it an evening. You've already learned everything you need to know to create a super-duper banner graphic for

Figure 7-21

If you match the background colors, you can float a transparent GIF image on top of a background image.

your Web page. You can come back next weekend, if you like, and do the rest of this session.

Or feel free to continue on. Just take a breather. If you need a picker-upper, grab a cola or brew some tea. I'll see you back here in ten minutes or so, when you'll learn how to overcome some of AppleWorks' image editing limitations, create a Web button, and use some of AppleWorks' clip art.

Overcoming AppleWorks' Limitations

While AppleWorks does a good job of creating many different types of images, it lacks a few capabilities that can help enhance your Web images. Here are some of the limitations of AppleWorks:

- Does not allow you to select the compression setting for JPEG images, but applies its default compression setting to all saved JPEG images.

- Does not allow you to save a non-white background in a GIF image as transparent.

- Does not allow you to set the transparency level for GIF images, fine-tuning which areas are changed to transparent, so that images are limited to having a single color (and tone) made transparent.

- Does not allow you to save a GIF image with a customized color palette, creating a color palette for the image composed only of colors included in the image, while the standard palette for GIF images may include many colors not actually included in the image.

You don't have to spend hundreds of dollars to purchase a professional image editor, such as Photoshop or Painter. While there is otherwise no one program that will do all of these things for you, there are several different graphic editors and utilities available on the Web, either for free or for a small registration fee, that together can provide you with many of these capabilities:

✿ GraphicConverter (**www.lemkesoft.de/**), included on this book's CD-ROM, is a shareware utility (costing $35 to register) that allows you to specify a compression level from 1 to 100 for a JPEG image. Just open a true-color or high-color image (PICT or JPEG) and choose Compression Settings from the Picture menu, and then choose Still Image. With Photo - JPEG selected, move the button on the Quality slider to select the compression level. You may need to experiment to find out what gives you the best result for a given image. The goal is the smallest possible file size that lets you retain a maximum of image quality.

NOTE

JPEG images use what's called a "lossy" compression scheme to reduce the size of an image. This is done by selectively subtracting pixels from the image, with more pixels subtracted the higher the compression level is set. Once you compress a JPEG image, you can't uncompress it (the subtracted pixels are gone forever). For this reason, you should always save your original image, or at least a JPEG version with the compression level set to 1.

✿ GraphicConverter also allows you to save a GIF image with a customized color palette. Open a true-color or high-color image (PICT or JPEG, for instance) and select Pictures, Colors, and 256 Colors. A customized color palette, containing only colors in the image, is automatically created.

✿ GIFConverter (**www.kamit.com/gifconverter/**) is a shareware utility (costing $30 to register) whose image manipulation capabilities include allowing you to save a GIF image with a customized color palette. Just open a true-color or high-color image (a PICT or JPEG image, for instance), choose Reduce Number of Colors from the Image menu, and then enter the number of colors (256 or lower) to which you want to reduce the image palette.

Creating a Web Button

In this example, you'll use the AppleWorks Drawing module in conjunction with the AppleWorks Painting module to create a "Home" button that can be used in a Web page.

Running the AppleWorks Drawing Module

Start out working with AppleWorks' Drawing module:

1. If you've exited AppleWorks, launch it, and then double-click Drawing in the menu list.

2. If AppleWorks is still open, select it in the Application menu to bring it to the foreground if necessary, and then choose New from the File menu. Double-click Drawing in the menu list.

You'll notice that the user interface of the Drawing module is very similar to that of the Painting module—the main difference is simply that there are no paint tools in the tool panel, but only drawing tools. You can, though, do some things in this module that you can't do in the Painting module; that's why you'll use both for this example.

You'll draw two "button" shapes, one interposed over the other (to give a relief or "shadow" effect). You'll also create two versions of the same text for your button, one interposed over the other, and then you'll interpose both over your button shapes. Lastly, you'll save your drawing and then insert it into a Painting document to add some finishing touches.

By default, the display of the rulers is turned off. You'll do some positioning of objects relative to each other. Turn the display of the rulers on: Choose Rulers from the Format menu. Make sure that Graphics is set as the Ruler Type and that Inches is set as the Units. Click OK.

Setting the Fill and Pen Characteristics

You'll draw your button shape using the Rounded Rectangle tool on the tool panel. In the Painting module you can first draw a shape and then apply a fill to it, as you did with the text in your banner graphic. In the Drawing module, you can do it two different ways: you can first define the fill and pen characteristics and then draw a shape with those characteristics, or you can select a shape and define fill and pen characteristics for that shape. For this example, you'll define the fill and pen characteristics first:

1. In the fill palettes square, click the lower-right icon to open the gradients palette. Click the seventh gradient in the fourth row.

2. In the pen palettes square, click the upper-left icon to open the colors palette. Select a color that won't contrast too much with the colors of the gradient fill you selected above (otherwise the shape may have too visible of an outline). Try the third color down in the third column.

Drawing Your Button Shape

To draw your button shape, just do the following:

1. Click on the Rounded Rectangle tool in the tool panel (the fourth button down in the left column).

2. Using the rulers as a guide, draw a shape that is one inch high by two inches wide: click and hold the mouse button on one of the junctions in the grid, pull the mouse down one grid segment and to the right two grid segments, and then release the mouse button (see Figure 7-22).

Creating Your Second Button Shape

Your second button shape is actually going to end up behind your first button shape (serving as a relief or "shadow"), although you'll initially interpose it on top of your first button shape. You can either define the fill

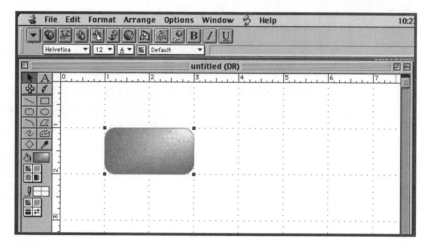

Figure 7-22

A one-inch by
two-inch button
shape with a
gradient fill
is drawn.

and pen characteristics and then draw the shape, or do it the other way around. So that the position of the second button shape will show up better, in this example you'll define the fill and pen characteristics first.

Editing the Gradient Fill

Edit the gradient fill you used in the first button shape, but substitute different colors:

1. Choose Gradients from the Options menu. The gradient you selected for your first button shape should be open in the Gradient Editor.

2. Click the first color square (the "orange" square), and click the fourth color down in the first column (a darker red color).

3. Click the second color square (the "yellow" square), and click the seventh color down in the first column (the pink color, third up from the bottom). Click OK.

Defining the Fill and Pen Characteristics

Now, you need to define the fill and pen characteristics for the second button shape:

1. Click outside the first button shape to deselect it.

2. Click the gradient icon (lower-right icon) in the fill palettes square and click the gradient you just edited (seventh from the right in the fourth row).

3. Click the colors icon (upper-left icon) in the pen palettes square and click a color that won't contrast too much with the colors used in your gradient fill (try the fourth color down in the first column).

Drawing the Second Button Shape

You're going to draw the second button shape so it is offset by one eighth of an inch (one segment on the rulers), both to the right of and down from the top-left corner of the first button shape:

1. Click on the Rounded Rectangle tool in the tool panel (the fourth button down in the left column).

2. Position the mouse pointer so it is one eighth of an inch to the right of and one eighth of an inch down from the top-left corner of the first button shape's grid space. (In the rulers, a dotted line shows the current position of the pointer.)

3. Draw a shape that is one inch high by two inches wide: click and hold the mouse button, pull the mouse pointer down one inch and to the right one inch (so the mouse pointer is positioned one eighth of an inch to the right of and down from the lower-right corner of the first button shape's grid space), and then release the mouse button (see Figure 7-23).

TIP

Another way to do this is to copy the first shape and change the fill and pen characteristics in the copy. Then just click and drag it to position it over the first shape.

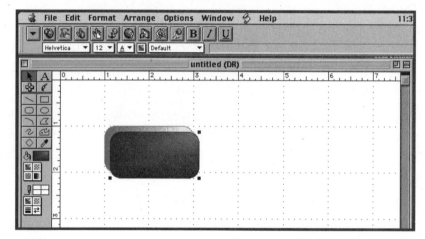

Figure 7-23

A second
button shape is
superimposed
over the first
button shape.

Moving the Second Button Shape Behind the First

Because the Drawing module uses "objects" to create an image, rather than pixels, you can easily rearrange how different objects overlap each other. To move the second button shape behind the first button shape, just choose Move To Back (or Move Backward) from the Arrange menu. The second button shape should now be moved behind the first button shape (see Figure 7-24).

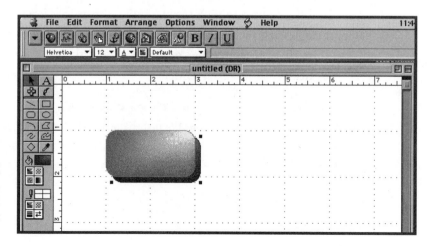

Figure 7-24

The second button
shape is moved
behind the first
button shape.

Creating the Text for Your Button

Now add some text to your button. For this example, as with the button shapes, you'll actually create two text objects, superimposing one over the other, in order to create a relief (or "shadow") effect.

Creating the First Text Object

You can use any text you want (as long as it fits in the button). Create your first text object:

1. First turn the Autogrid off: choose Turn Autogrid Off from the Options menu. This will allow you to more precisely position your text.

2. Click the Text tool (the "A" icon) on the tool panel, and then click anywhere in the image area.

3. Change the default typeface from Helvetica (the default) to any of the "display" fonts (Impact, or any font that looks good to you if you don't have Impact available). Click the font size pop-up window, select Other, type **42** as the font size, and click OK.

4. From the text style pop-up menu, select Bold. From the text color pop-up menu, select a color for your text. Select a color that'll contrast with your first button shape, the first color in the second row, for instance. (You'll be using this color for the "shadow" text.)

5. Type your text.

6. Click the Pointer tool on the tool panel and click and drag your text object to position it over the top button shape. Position your text object just a little off-center (down and to the right) relative to the top button shape, as shown in Figure 7-25.

Creating the Second Text Object

Repeat the steps you just followed to create the second text object, selecting a different color for the text. If you want, just copy and paste your first text object to create a second text object, and then change the color for the text

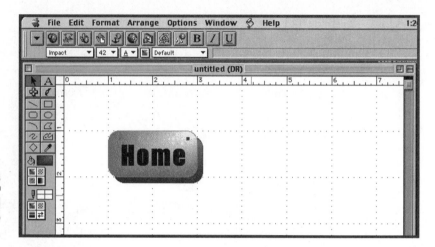

Figure 7-25

The text is dragged on top of the top button shape.

in the Text Color menu on the toolbar. Drag it over the first text object. Drop it so that it overlaps the first text shape, but slightly up and to the left. Figure 7-26 shows the result.

TIP

As long as your text object is selected, you can reselect the typeface, font size, font style, and text color. The changes will automatically be reflected in your text object. (Note that you can't change the color of the text by changing the color in the fill colors palette—doing this would instead fill the whole box of the text object with the selected color.)

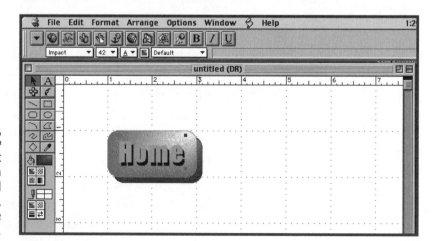

Figure 7-26

The second text object has been superimposed over the first, slightly above and to the left.

Saving Your Drawing

For a final touch, you'll apply a gradient fill to your button's text. However, that's something you can't do in the Drawing module—you'll need to save your image and reopen it in the Painting module. Go ahead and save your drawing now:

1. Deselect any selected object in your drawing by clicking in the blank section of the work area.

2. Choose Save As from the File menu. In the dialog box, open the My Images folder (or whichever folder you're using to save your images created in Appleworks).

3. With AppleWorks selected as the file type, type **My Button** as the file name, and then click the Save button.

4. Go ahead and close the window containing your My Button image.

Insert "My Button" in a Painting Document

Next, open a new Painting document and insert your "My Button" drawing:

1. From the AppleWorks menu bar, choose New from the File menu. Double-click Painting in the menu list.

2. Choose Insert from the File menu. Double-click My Button.

3. Click on the inserted image, and drag it to the upper-left part of the document, so that it is positioned snug up against the left and top edges of the document. Increase the Zoom factor to 200, to make sure you've got it positioned exactly where you want it. (See Figure 7-27 to see the positioning, as well as a call-out to the button that increases the Zoom factor.)

Applying a Fill to the Text

In the Drawing module, you could only change the color of your text, but you couldn't apply any fills to your text. In the Painting module, you can apply color, pattern, texture, or gradient fills to your text. For this example,

Figure 7-27

The inserted
image has been
positioned at the
top-left corner of
the document, and
the Zoom factor
has been increased
to 200.

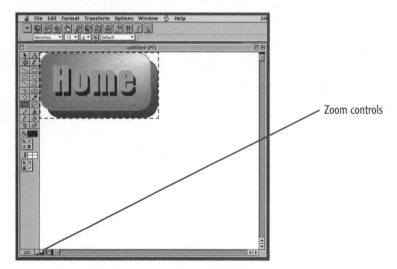

Zoom controls

you'll apply the same gradient fill that you used for the two button shapes,
but you should change the colors so they form a good contrast with the
other colors:

1. Choose Gradients from the Options menu. In the Gradient palette
   window, click the same gradient fill you've used before (seventh
   gradient in the fourth row).

2. In the Gradient Editor, click the first color square (the "orange"
   color), and select a different color. For instance, select the navy blue
   color (sixth color in the third row up from the bottom).

3. Click the second color square (the "yellow" color) and select a
   different color. For instance, select a light blue color (try the second
   color in the fourth row from the bottom). Click OK.

4. Click the gradients palette (lower-right icon) in the fill palettes
   square, and select the gradient fill you just edited.

5. Click the Fill tool (the "Paint Bucket" icon) in the tool panel.
   Position the Fill pointer over the first letter, and click to fill the
   letter. Click the Fill pointer in each of the other letters, to also fill
   them with the gradient. (See Figure 7-28.)

Figure 7-28

A gradient fill is
applied to the text.

If the color you filled over in your text is a lot lighter than the darker color
for the gradient, you've probably noticed that the gradient fill didn't fill all
of the letters, especially the ones with curves (for instance, "o" and "e").
You could avoid this problem simply by using a darker blue color for your
text to begin with; I wanted you to be able to check this out for yourself,
however. To fix this, you can simply go back to the Drawing module, set a
darker blue color for the text, and resave your drawing; then, just reimport
it into your Painting document, and follow the steps above for applying
the gradient fill to the text. The second way to fix it is to touch up your
image, to get rid of the lighter areas around the edges of the letters.

Touching Up Your Image

1. Increase the Zoom factor to at least 800, and use the scroll bar to
   position the first two letters of the text in the document window
   (see Figure 7-29).

2. Click the colors icon (upper-left icon) in the fill palettes square, and
   click a darker blue color to do the touch-up with. Click the Fill
   pointer in the pixel squares you want to touch up. Feel free to re-
   pick the color as you go, selecting a darker or lighter blue color, to
   match the areas you're trying to touch up. (If you accidentally fill the
   wrong area, just choose Undo Paint from the Edit menu.) Use the
   scroll bar to scroll through the text.

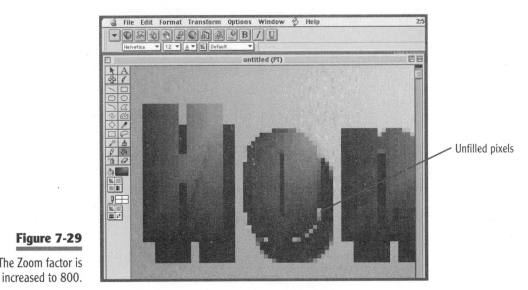

Figure 7-29

The Zoom factor is increased to 800.

Unfilled pixels

3. When done, just decrease the Zoom factor back to 400, to see all of your text (see Figure 7-30). Increase the Zoom factor again, if you see any more areas you need to fix up. When satisfied, reduce it to 200 or 100.

Figure 7-30

The text has been cleaned up, and the Zoom factor is decreased to 400.

Resizing the Document to Fit the Button

You'll want to resize the document to fit the button—otherwise, there'll be a bunch of white space to the right of and below your button. Just choose Document from the Format menu. Try setting the Pixels Across to **152** and the Pixels Down to **80**. (You may need to adjust the Pixels Across or Pixels Down value up or down by a pixel or so.) Click OK.

Saving Your Graphic As a Web Image

The first thing to watch out for: don't save over your AppleWorks drawing file (My Button). If you want to save this image as an AppleWorks file, give it a different name than the Drawing file. That way, you can always go back to the Drawing file and do more with it.

The same considerations apply here as applied when you saved your banner graphic. Because this image includes three separate gradient fills, you'll get your best results saving it as a JPEG image. Because you're saving this image for use on the Web, use all lowercase letters in the file name, don't include any spaces, and add the file extension; for instance, type **mybutton.jpg** as the file name when you save your file.

You may want to save your image as a transparent GIF so the rounded corners of the button display transparently against a background color or image. Although AppleWorks saves the image as a GIF image with the background set to transparent, it will also save it using the stock 256-color system palette. Because you've used a number of gradient fills in this image, the results of saving your image that way will likely provide a pretty ugly result. You should first save your image as a JPEG image (with the compression level set to 1). Next, use GraphicConverter (available on the CD-ROM) to save your image as a GIF image using a customized color palette (so only image colors are included in the color palette); then use Transparency (mentioned earlier) to save your GIF image with the background color set to transparent. Your result will be a thousand times better than just saving your image directly as a GIF image in AppleWorks.

Using the AppleWorks Clip Art

The AppleWorks suite comes with a collection of clip art you can use. For an example of using the clip art, relaunch AppleWorks if you closed it, reopen your My Button drawing in the Drawing module, and delete the text (click each text object to select it, and then hit the Delete key); then replace the text with a clip art image of your choice (an arrow, a house, whatever suits your fancy). To insert a clip art image:

1. Choose Library from the File menu. Choose one of the clip art categories. For instance, choose Arrows.

2. From the Arrows dialog box menu bar, choose By Object from the View menu. Just drag and drop the arrow image you'd like to use from the dialog box into the document window. For instance, scroll down to arrow 014, and drag and drop it into the document window (see Figure 7-31).

3. Close the Arrows window, and then click and drag the "arrow" clip art image. Move it over your button, until you've got it positioned where you want it (see Figure 7-32).

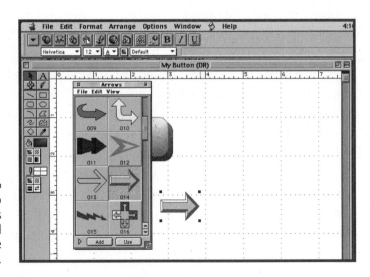

Figure 7-31

An "arrow" clip art image is dragged and dropped into the document window.

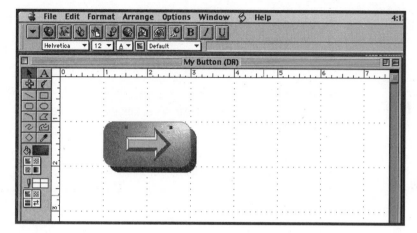

4. To flip the "arrow" image so it is pointing to the left, rather than to the right, choose Flip Horizontally from the Arrange menu. (You can also change the direction in which it points by choosing Rotate from the Arrange menu, typing a number, and clicking OK.)

5. To increase or decrease the size of the clip art image, choose Scale By Percent from the Arrange menu. For instance, to increase both the height and the width by a factor of 110 percent, type **110** in both of the text boxes. Click OK (see Figure 7-33).

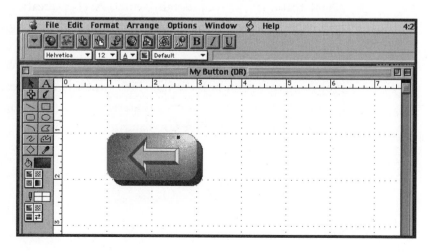

6. Save the file, giving it a name other than My Button (try **My Arrow**, for instance). If you want to save it to use in a Web page, your best bet, as noted before, is to save it as a JPEG file.

NOTE As mentioned previously, because this image uses a gradient fill, if you want to save this image as a transparent GIF, your best bet is to save it first as a JPEG image, and then use other graphics utilities that allow you to save a GIF image using a custom color palette and to set the background color as transparent.

Other Image Editing Resources

There is a wide variety of image editing tools available that can do an excellent job of creating Web images for your pages. The minimum requirement is that an image editor be able to save images as GIF and JPEG files.

Using Professional Image Editors

Many professional Web art designers use Adobe Photoshop, a commercial image editor that costs several hundred dollars. Others swear by MetaCreations' Painter program, which excels at creating more "painterly" images, as its name implies; it too is an "industrial strength" image editing solution. Another excellent choice is Adobe ImageStyler, which can be used by non-professional designers to create fancy images for Web sites. Another interesting program is Electrifier Pro, which is a full-feature multimedia authoring environment. If you're interested in getting the best Web image tools available, here's where you can find out more:

FIND IT ON ▶
THE WEB

- Adobe Photoshop at **www.adobe.com/prodindex/photoshop/main.html**

- Metacreation's Painter at **www.metacreations.com/products/painter/**

- Adobe ImageStyler at **www.adobe.com/prodindex/imagestyler/main.html**

FIND IT ON ▶
THE CD

- Electrifier Pro at **www.larisoftware.com/** (the trial version is available on the CD-ROM)

Other Available Image Editing and Multimedia Tools

I've previously told you about a few utilities available over the Web or on the CD-ROM that can help to overcome some of AppleWorks' image editing limitations. There are many other software tools available, either free or inexpensive, that can assist you in creating or enhancing your own Web images. Here are some you might want to check out:

FIND IT ON ▶
THE WEB

- BME at **www.softlogik.com/Products/freestuff.html**—a freeware image editor.

- NIH Image at **http://Syracuse.allmacintosh.com/imgeditmac.html**—a freeware image editor.

- Painting at **http://sarwat.net/painting/**—a full-feature shareware image editor. ($15 to register.)

- Smoothie at **www.peircesw.com/Smoothie.html**—a shareware anti-aliasing utility that helps smooth out the "jaggies" in your Web images. ($24.95 to register.)

FIND IT ON ▶
THE CD

- CompuPic at **www.photodex.com/**—a versatile image viewer. The demo version is available on the CD-ROM. ($49.95 to register.)

- ShareDraw at **www.peircesw.com/ShareDraw.html**—a shareware drawing program that can create lots of neat effects. Exports PICT or EPS files. ($24.95 to register.)

Wrapping Up

You've barely scratched the surface of the world of creating your own Web images. You may already have a really snazzy banner graphic for your first Web page. If you want to get even fancier, go ahead and create some Web buttons for your page, such as navigation icons. Or branch out and create some graphic rules. If you skipped any of the optional sessions or sections earlier in the book, you may want to go back and try them next; if you've managed to complete *everything* that I've thrown at you this weekend, you're well on your way to becoming a Web publishing whiz!

Feel free to come back and check out the material included in the Appendixes. Look in Appendix A, "Resources," to see where you can find out more about HTML and Web publishing on the Web, download software tools, and download some clip art. Appendix B, "Using Special Characters," includes a chart of the HTML codes for all of the non-keyboard characters you can include in your Web page. In Appendix C, "Creating Tables," I've included a tutorial on creating HTML tables, a must-know if you want to become a true pro! Appendix D, "Putting It Up on the Web," gives you a rundown on how to find a Web host for your pages, and how to transfer your pages up to your Web host's server.

PRIMA TECH has included lots of great freeware, shareware, and demonstration software programs on the CD-ROM that you can use or try out; for details on what's included, see Appendix F, "What's On the CD-ROM?" Finally, see the glossary at the end of this book for a handy compilation of some of the terms that were used in this book or that you're likely to run across in your future Web publishing travels.

APPENDIX A

Resources

The world of HTML and Web publishing includes a great deal more than what can be covered in a single book, especially one that you are completing in just a few days. To really become a Web publishing pro will take much more time than that, so hopefully you've gotten a big leg up this weekend. This appendix is a short roadmap to where on the Web you can find out more about HTML and Web publishing. You'll find here information about where on the Web to find:

- Web Publishing References, Guides, and Tutorials
- Macintosh Web Publishing Software Tools
- Web Graphics Sources

Web Publishing References, Guides, and Tutorials

The World Wide Web Consortium
www.w3.org
This is where to find out all about the latest developments in HTML and other emerging Web standards, including Cascading Style Sheets (CSS), XML and XHTML, DOM, MathML, SMIL, and more. It includes the official specification for HTML 4.0.

Sizzling HTML Jalfrezi
http://vzone.virgin.net/sizzling.jalfrezi/
This is an excellent A to Z HTML reference.

Introduction to HTML by Ian Graham
www.utoronto.ca/webdocs/HTMLdocs/NewHTML/htmlindex.html
It provides plain English explanations of the HTML 4.0 specification.

The HTML Guru! by Chuck Musciano
http://members.aol.com/htmlguru/
It's another excellent source for HTML and Web publishing.

The HTML Writers Guild
www.hwg.org
This is a great central stopping point for all things HTML.

Style Guide for Online Hypertext by Tim Berners-Lee
www.w3.org/Provider/Style/Overview.html
Here are wise words from the inventor of the World Wide Web.

WDVL: Web Developer's Virtual Library
www.stars.com
If you want to get serious about becoming a Web developer, this is the place to start.

WebDeveloper.com
www.webdeveloper.com
This is a great repository of info for the serious Web developer.

Web Developer's Journal
www.WebDevelopersJournal.com
Don't miss the "Wacky HTML" page.

Web Techniques
www.webtechniques.com
This is the online version of Web Techniques magazine. Read the current issue or browse the archives for lots of great articles on Web publishing.

DevEdge Online by Netscape
`http://developer.netscape.com`
This is Netscape's omnibus site for Web developers.

MSDN Online Web Workshop by Microsoft
`http://msdn.microsoft.com/workshop/default.asp`
This is Microsoft's omnibus site for Web developers.

HTML Goodies by Joe Burns
`www.htmlgoodies.com`
This is a great collection of tutorials on just about everything related to Web publishing; you'll find tutorials for creating frames, forms, tables, and much more.

Steve Callihan's Web Links
`www.callihan.com/weblinks/`
This is my Web site of Web publishing links.

Macintosh Web Publishing Software Tools

All Macintosh.com
`www.allmacintosh.com`
This is the Tucows repository of Macintosh Internet and Web publishing software tools.

The Mac Orchard
`www.macorchard.com`
This has links to lots of Mac browsers and FTP software.

Mac's Diner
`www.macsdiner.com`
This is a large Mac shareware and freeware software repository—you'll have to browse to find Web publishing tools.

The AusMac Archive
`www.ausmac.net`
This is an excellent repository of Mac software, including Web publishing tools, located in Australia.

ZDNet Macintosh Software Library
`www.zdnet.com/mac/download.html`
ZDNet's repository of Macintosh software, including graphics, multimedia, and Web publishing tools.

Download-Zone.Com
www.download-zone.com
This is a directory site with links to where you can download Macintosh software tools, including image editors/viewers, image mappers, image animators, FTP applications, and more.

Steve Callihan's Web Tools
www.callihan.com/webtools/
This is my Web site of links to Web publishing software tools, updated to cover both Windows and Macintosh tools.

Web Graphics Sources

DiP: A Guide to Digital Pictures & More
www.algonet.se/~dip/
This is a gold mine of tips and tricks for users of Photoshop, Painter, and Kai's Power Tools.

The Pixel Foundry by Tom Karlo
www.pixelfoundry.com
Here you'll find tips, tricks, and techniques for Photoshop and Kai's Power Tools. It also includes an archive of backgrounds.

Bryan Livingston's CoolText.com: Online Graphics Generator
www.cooltext.com
You can create your own eye-boggling text banner, in seconds, ready to download and insert in your page.

The Bandwidth Conservation Society
www.infohiway.com/faster/index.html
Here's lots of great info on how to optimize your Web images for faster download.

Barry's Clip Art Server
www.barrysclipart.com
This is a big collection of clip art that you can download and use in your Web pages.

Rose's Backgrounds Archive
www.wanderers2.com/rose/backgrounds.html
This has not just backgrounds, but lots of other Web art as well, including icons, arrows, and rules.

The Clip Art Connection by Eric Force
www.ClipArtConnection.com
This site includes tons of Web art images, including alphabets, arrows, buttons, and numbers.

Backgrounds by NCSA
`www.ncsa.uiuc.edu/SDG/Software/mosaic-w/coolstuff/`
`Backgrnd/`
This is a nice collection of backgrounds from NCSA, developers of the Mosaic
Web browser.

The Background Sampler from Netscape
`http://home.netscape.com/assist/net_sites/bg/`
`backgrounds.html`
It's another nice collection of backgrounds.

AOLpress Clip Art Gallery
`www.aolpress.com/gallery/index.html`
Here is an excellent collection of free Web art, including coordinated sets and themes,
as well as sidebar background images.

Create Your First Mac Web Page In a Weekend
`www.callihan.com/create_imac/`
Visit this book's Web site to find additional Web art collections that you can download
and use.

Special Characters

The ISO 8859-1 character set is an 8-bit character set, which allows for 256 code positions. Characters 0 through 31 and 127 are assigned as control characters. 32 through 126 correspond to the US-ASCII characters that you can type in at the keyboard. 128 through 159 are designated as unused in ISO 8859-1, although both the Macintosh and Windows assign characters to many of these positions. 160 through 255 designate extended (or special) characters in ISO 8859-1; they should be displayable in most Web browsers, but 14 of them display different characters on Macintosh and Windows systems.

Reserved Characters

These are the numerical and named characters that are reserved for formatting HTML tags and codes.

Number	Name	Description	Character
"	"	Double quotation	"
&	&	Ampersand	&
<	<	Left angle bracket, less than	<
>	>	Right angle bracket, greater than	>

Left and right angle brackets should be used in an HTML document only to designate the start or end of an HTML tag; use one of the HTML codes above for any other use of the < and > symbols. Double quotations and ampersands generally need only be replaced in an HTML file if they are part of an HTML code that you want to display "as is" (and not to let it be interpreted by a browser).

NOTE   When inserting character codes into an HTML file, other than for the named entity codes for the reserved characters, the copyright symbol, the registered symbol, and the upper-case and lowercase accented characters (such as A-grave and a-grave) used in many foreign languages, you should stick to using the numerical entity codes. Other named entity codes are unlikely to be supported by any but the most recent browsers.

Unused Characters

Both Windows and the Macintosh assign characters to many of the code positions that the ISO 8859-1 character set designates as unused, and 12 of these extra characters are dissimilar on the two systems. *There is no guarantee that any of these characters will display on other platforms.* Generally, it is best to avoid using these characters in an HTML file, with the possible exception of the trademark symbol (™), which is supported in most browsers.

Number	Name	Description	Character
€		Unused	
		Unused	
‚		Single quote (low)	‚
ƒ		Small Latin f	ƒ
„		Double quote (low)	„
…		Ellipsis	…
†		Dagger	(not on Mac)
‡		Double dagger	‡
ˆ		Circumflex	ˆ
‰		Per mile sign	‰
Š		S-caron	(not on Mac)
‹		Left angle quote	‹
Œ		OE ligature	Œ
		Unused	
Ž		Unused	
		Unused	
		Unused	
‘		Left single quote	'
’		Right single quote	'
“		Left double quote	"
”		Right double quote	"
•		Bullet	•

Number	Name	Description	Character
–	–	En dash	–
—	—	Em dash	—
˜		Small tilde	~
™	™	Trademark	™
š		s-caron	(not on Mac)
›		Right angle quote	›
œ		oe ligature	œ
		Unused	
ž		Unused	
Ÿ		Y-umlaut	Ÿ

Special Characters

The following characters, 160 through 255, are all part of the ISO 8859-1 character set. They should generally be available on any operating system that uses the ISO-8859-1 character set, but 14 of the codes display as different characters on the Macintosh.

Number	Name	Description	Character
		Non-breakable space	[ ] (brackets added)
¡	¡	Inverted exclamation	¡
¢	¢	Cent sign	¢
£	£	Pound sign	£
¤	¤	Currency sign	_

Number	Name	Description	Character
¥	¥	Yen sign	¥
¦	¦	Broken vertical bar	(not on Mac)
§	§	Section sign	§
¨	¨	Umlaut	¨
©	©	Copyright	©
ª	ª	Feminine ordinal	ª
«	«	Left guillemet	«
¬	¬	Not sign	¬
­	­	Soft hyphen	−
®	®	Registered	®
¯	&hibar;	Macron	¯
°	°	Degree	°
±	±	Plus/minus sign	±
²	²	Superscripted 2	(not on Mac)
³	³	Superscripted 3	(not on Mac)
´	´	Acute accent	´
µ	µ	Micro sign	µ
¶	¶	Paragraph sign	¶
·	·	Middle dot	·
¸	¸	Cedilla	¸
¹	¹	Superscripted 1	(not on Mac)
º	º	Masculine ordinal	º

Number	Name	Description	Character
»	»	Right guillemet	»
¼	¼	1/4 fraction	(not on Mac)
½	½	1/2 fraction	(not on Mac)
¾	¾	3/4 fraction	(not on Mac)
¿	¿	Inverted question mark	¿
À	À	A-grave	À
Á	Á	A-acu	Á
Â	Â	A-circumflex	Â
Ã	Ã	A-tilde	Ã
Ä	Ä	A-umlaut	Ä
Å	Å	A-ring	Å
Æ	Æ	AE ligature	Æ
Ç	Ç	C-cedilla	Ç
È	È	E-grave	È
É	É	E-acute	É
Ê	Ê	E-circumflex	Ê
Ë	Ë	E-umlaut	Ë
Ì	Ì	I-grave	Ì
Í	Í	I-acute	Í
Î	Î	I-circumflex	Î
Ï	Ï	I-umlaut	Ï
Ð	Ð	Uppercase Eth	(not on Mac)

Number	Name	Description	Character
Ñ	Ñ	N-tilde	Ñ
Ò	Ò	O-grave	Ò
Ó	Ó	O-acute	Ó
Ô	Ô	O-circumflex	Ô
Õ	Õ	O-tilde	Õ
Ö	Ö	O-umlaut	Ö
×	×	Multiplication sign	(not on Mac)
Ø	Ø	O-slash	Ø
Ù	Ù	U-grave	Ù
Ú	Ú	U-acute	Ú
Û	Û	U-circumflex	Û
Ü	Ü	U-umlaut	Ü
Ý	Ý	Y-acute	(not on Mac)
Þ	Þ	Uppercase Thorn	(not on Mac)
ß	ß	Sharp s (German)	ß
à	à	a-grave	à
á	á	a-acute	á
â	â	a-circumflex	â
ã	ã	a-tilde	ã
ä	ä	a-umlaut	ä
å	å	a-ring	å
æ	æ	ae ligature	æ

Number	Name	Description	Character
ç	ç	c-cedilla	ç
è	è	e-grave	è
é	é	e-acute	é
ê	ê	e-circumflex	ê
ë	ë	e-umlaut	ë
ì	ì	i-grave	ì
í	í	i-acute	í
î	î	i-circumflex	î
ï	ï	i-umlaut	ï
ð	ð	Lowercase Eth	(not on Mac)
ñ	ñ	n-tilde	ñ
ò	ò	o-grave	ò
ó	ó	o-acute	ó
ô	ô	o-circumflex	ô
õ	õ	o-tilde	õ
ö	ö	o-umlaut	ö
÷	÷	Division sign	÷
ø	ø	o-slash	ø
ù	ù	u-grave	ù
ú	ú	u-acute	ú
û	û	u-circumflex	û
ü	ü	u-umlaut	ü

Number	Name	Description	Character
ý	ý	y-acute	(not on Mac)
þ	þ	Lowercase Thorn	(not on Mac)
ÿ	ÿ	y-umlaut	ÿ

NOTE

The latest versions of Internet Explorer for the Macintosh actually do display the "not on the Mac" characters listed above, by substituting the "Western (Latin 1)" character set ("Latin 1" is another name for the ISO 8859-1 character set) for the native Macintosh character set. These characters will not be displayed in any version of Netscape Navigator or in earlier versions of Internet Explorer for the Macintosh.

Netscape Navigator 2.0+ and many other Macintosh browsers transpose similar characters (from other positions in the native Mac character set) in place of several of the "not on the Mac" characters. These are the broken vertical bar (displayed as |), superscripts 1, 2, and 3 (displayed as normal digits 1, 2, and 3), and the multiplication sign (displayed as a lowercase x).

APPENDIX C

Creating Tables

HTML tables are the key to many of the more sophisticated, multi-column layouts you've seen on the Web. Although tables were not included in the Saturday Afternoon session, "The Intermediate HTML Tutorial," you shouldn't think they're an "advanced" HTML feature; just invest some time in learning how tables work and what they can do for you, and you'll be able to master the subject quite quickly—assuming that you've already finished the intermediate tutorial.

An HTML 3.2-compliant Web browser is required for this tutorial. If you use Netscape Navigator 2.0 or greater or Microsoft Internet Explorer 3.0 or greater, you should be able to do all the HTML 3.2 sections in this tutorial. (This tutorial includes a section on using HTML 4.0 TBODY, THEAD, and TFOOT tags; these tags are currently supported only by Microsoft Internet Explorer 4.0 or greater, so if you're using a different browser, feel free to skip that section.)

351

Getting Started

This tutorial uses two example graphic files that have already been used in previous tutorials; no other example files are required. If the example graphics files have worked properly in the Basic and Intermediate HTML Tutorials, then you're all ready to use them in this tutorial. (If you haven't copied the example files, return to "Copying the Example Files" at the start of the Saturday Morning session, and do so now before starting to do this tutorial.)

What's Covered

This appendix consists of three sections:

- Creating HTML 3.2 Tables
- Creating Icon Link Lists Using Tables
- Creating HTML 4.0 Tables

The first section, "Creating HTML 3.2 Tables," forms the main part of the Tables tutorial, covering most of what was included in the HTML 3.2 tables specification; the tags and attributes covered should be displayable in all graphical Web browsers that support HTML 3.2. The second section, "Creating Icon Link Lists Using Tables," covers how to create indented icon link lists that have no limit on the number of indented lines—you also have much more control over the vertical positioning of the icon bullet relative to the following link text and link description text. The third section, "Creating HTML 4.0 Tables," is a bonus section that covers some of the new table features included in HTML 4.0, including new HTML 4.0 table tags and a taste of using styles to format tables.

Creating HTML 3.2 Tables

The features covered in this section should be displayable in all Web browsers that support HTML 3.2. To get started with this section of the tutorial, just do the following:

1. Run your text editor.

2. Run the Web browser you'll be using to preview your work. (Just click Cancel if your dialer tries to connect to the Internet, since you'll be working offline.)

3. In your text editor, open the starting template, **startpage.html**, that you saved in the Basic HTML Tutorial. (If you didn't save a starting template, you can just retype the starting codes as shown.)

4. Resave your starting template as **scratch3.html** (in the same folder).

Your new "scratch pad" file should look like the following listing. Feel free to save your file after each example and hop over to your Web browser to see what it looks like:

```
<HTML>
<HEAD>
<TITLE>Your Title: Describe Your Title</TITLE>
</HEAD>
<BODY>
</BODY>
</HTML>
```

TIP ■■■

With the example files you copied from the CD-ROM, you'll find a file, tables.html, that shows all the examples covered in this tutorial as separate tables. Don't bother to copy and paste each example as a separate table, just to be able to save an example file showing each feature. Instead, make all the changes in a single table file, and use tables.html for future reference on how to implement each feature.

■■

Starting Your Table

The TABLE tag needs to bracket your table. All other tags or text to be included in your table should be nested inside the TABLE tag. Enter the following HTML nested in the BODY tag:

```
<BODY>

<P>

<TABLE>

</TABLE>

</P>

</BODY>
```

 NOTE •
Because the TABLE element is not a block element but rather an inline element, you should nest the TABLE tag inside a block element, such as the P tag, to make sure sufficient space is added above and below the table.

• •

Defining Columns and Rows

You can use the TR (Table Row) and TD (Table Data) tags to create a grid of rows and columns. Every table must have at least one row (one TR tag) and one cell (one TD tag). You add TR tags to define your rows by nesting them inside of the TABLE tag; you add TD tags to define the cells in your table by nesting them inside of the TR tags. The number of TD tags you include in your first row determines how many columns your table will have. To create a table that includes two rows and four columns, add the following TR and TD tags to the example:

```
<TABLE>

<TR><TD></TD><TD></TD><TD></TD><TD></TD></TR>

<TR><TD></TD><TD></TD><TD></TD><TD></TD></TR>

</TABLE>
```

So far, you've only created the framework for your table. Right now, your table will still display nothing. You still need to add the content that'll be displayed in your table cells. Insert the following inside your TD tags:

```
<TABLE>
<TR><TD>1A</TD><TD>1B</TD><TD>1C</TD><TD>1D</TD></TR>
<TR><TD>2A</TD><TD>2B</TD><TD>2C</TD><TD>2D</TD></TR>
</TABLE>
```

Now, you've got something you can actually see in your browser, as shown in Figure C-1. Feel free to save your file and hop over to your browser, to see what this looks like in your Web browser.

Adding and Controlling Borders

A table hardly looks like a table without a border, right? Well, sometimes, you don't want your table to look like a table, but for the sake of this tutorial, you do.

NOTE ●
Actually, leaving the borders turned off is the key to many of the more sophisticated multi-column layouts you see on the Web. By leaving the borders turned off, you can use HTML tables behind the scenes to format and precisely position different elements on your page. A visitor only sees the result, but not how you did it, unless they want to take a peek at your source code.
● ●

To turn display of borders on in your table, use the BORDER attribute inside the TABLE tag (see Figure C-2).

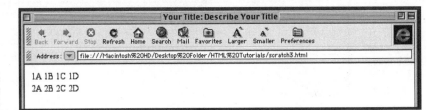

Figure C-1

A table consists of columns and rows.

Figure C-2

You can add borders to a table.

```
<TABLE BORDER="1">

<TR><TD>1A</TD><TD>1B</TD><TD>1C</TD><TD>1D</TD></TR>
```

HTML 3.2 also recognizes the BORDER attribute by itself, which should have exactly the same result as BORDER="1". Increasing the value of the BORDER attribute has a result you might not expect: It increases the thickness of the outer border of the table, displaying it in 3-D relief. However, it doesn't affect the appearance of the interior lines of the table. Increase the BORDER to six pixels (see Figure C-3).

```
<TABLE BORDER="6">

<TR><TD>1A</TD><TD>1B</TD><TD>1C</TD><TD>1D</TD></TR>
```

Setting Spacing and Padding

Your table looks a bit cramped, don't you think? The CELLSPACING attribute adds space between cells, whereas the CELLPADDING attribute adds space within each cell. (In Figure C-4, both the space between the cells and the padding within the cells have been increased.) Add six pixels of spacing and padding, like this:

Figure C-3

Table borders go 3-D when you boost their thickness.

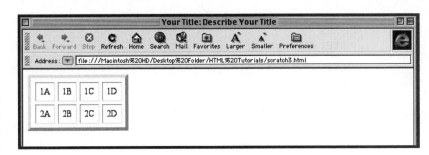

Figure C-4

You can add space between cells and padding within cells.

```
<P><TABLE BORDER="6" CELLSPACING="6" CELLPADDING="6">
<TR><TH>1A</TH><TH>1B</TH><TH>1C</TH><TH>1D</TH></TR>
```

Defining Column Headings

It isn't a table without column headings, right? The TH (Table Heading) tag works the same way as the TD (Table Data) tag, except it defines a particular cell as a heading cell rather than as an ordinary data cell—the content of a heading cell is bolded and centered to distinguish it from that of a regular data cell. To create a row of four column headings at the top of your table, use the TR tag to define a row; then, instead of using TD tags, insert TH tags to define the cells. (As Figure C-5 shows, table headings automatically show up centered and bolded.)

Figure C-5

Table headings are automatically bolded and centered.

```
<P><TABLE BORDER="6" CELLSPACING="6" CELLPADDING="6">
<TR><TH>A</TH><TH>B</TH><TH>C</TH><TH>D</TH></TR>
<TR><TD>1A</TD><TD>1B</TD><TD>1C</TD><TD>1D</TD></TR>
```

Adding a Caption

The CAPTION tag allows you to specify a caption for your table. (As you can see in Figure C-6, by default a caption will appear above the title.)

```
<P><TABLE BORDER="6" CELLSPACING="6" CELLPADDING="6">
<CAPTION>I. Table Example</CAPTION>
```

• •

The Macintosh version of Internet Explorer displays table captions somewhat differently than other browsers (even differently than the Windows version of Internet Explorer), in that it doesn't add any extra space between the text for the table caption and the body of the table. For that reason, you should avoid using the CAPTION tag in tables to get a particular format look, but just stick to using it for actual table captions.

• •

You can display the caption below the table by setting an ALIGN="bottom" attribute value in the CAPTION tag. (HTML 4.0 also specifies that you can use an ALIGN="left" or an ALIGN="right" in the CAPTION tag to align a table caption along the left or right side of a table. No browser actually does this, however—Internet Explorer right-aligns or left-aligns the caption within the caption space, but this isn't exactly what the specification calls for.)

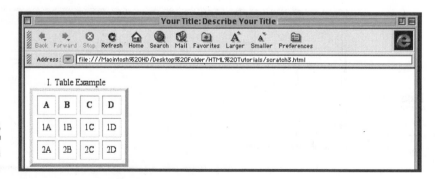

Figure C-6

You can add a caption to a table.

Centering a Table

To center the table, just insert an ALIGN="center" attribute value in the TABLE tag (see Figure C-7).

```
<P><TABLE ALIGN="center" BORDER="6" CELLSPACING="6"
CELLPADDING="6">

<CAPTION>I. Table Example</CAPTION>
```

Alternatively, you can get exactly the same result by putting your table inside a CENTER tag, or by nesting it inside a center-aligned paragraph. To indent your table rather than center it, nest it inside a BLOCKQUOTE tag.

NOTE

A table is not a block element, but rather an inline element that functions on a Web page in a similar fashion to how an inline image created with the IMG tag functions. Just as with an inline image, you can flow text or other elements around a table by inserting an **ALIGN="left"** or **ALIGN="right"** attribute value in the TABLE tag. You can even flow a right-aligned table around a left-aligned table, as shown in Figure C-8. You can also flow text, other elements, or another table between the two tables shown in Figure C-8. This works the same way as the examples included in the Saturday afternoon session for flowing text or an image between two other images.

As with flowing text or images around or between other images, to stop the wrapping of following elements, be sure to insert a <BR CLEAR="all"> tag where you want the wrapping to stop.

Figure C-7

You can center a table by inserting the **ALIGN="center"** attribute value in the TABLE tag.

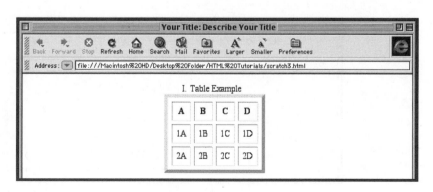

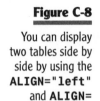

Figure C-8

You can display two tables side by side by using the **ALIGN="left"** and **ALIGN= "right"** attribute values.

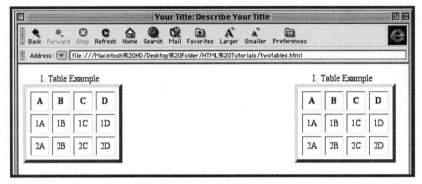

Setting Table Width and Height

You can include WIDTH and HEIGHT attributes to specify the size of your table. You can use either absolute values (number of pixels) or relative values (percentages). If you just tried flowing text or other elements around a table in the previous note, go back to the original table you were working on. Specify a width of 75 percent (see Figure C-9).

```
<TABLE ALIGN="center" BORDER="6" CELLSPACING="6"
CELLPADDING="6" WIDTH="75%">

<CAPTION>I. Table Example</CAPTION>
```

You can also set the HEIGHT attribute in the TABLE tag, although it's generally less useful than setting the WIDTH attribute. You can use this technique to increase the row heights in a table by setting an absolute value (number of pixels) for the height of the table that is greater than the normal height.

Figure C-9

You can set the width of a table to a percentage (here, 75 percent) of a browser window.

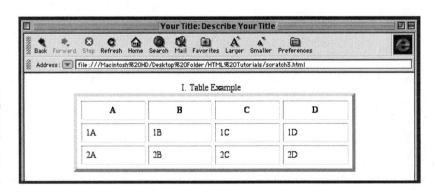

Adding Row Headings

Now you can add some row headings. To create a row heading, just add a TH cell (instead of a TD cell) at the start of a table row. (As Figure C-10 shows, row headings are formatted just like column headings—centered and bolded.)

```
<TABLE ALIGN="center" BORDER="6" CELLSPACING="6"
CELLPADDING="6" WIDTH="75%">

<CAPTION>I. Table Example</CAPTION>

<TR><TH></TH><TH>A</TH><TH>B</TH><TH>C</TH><TH>D</TH>
</TR>

<TR><TH>Row 1:</TH><TD>1A</TD><TD>1B</TD><TD>1C</TD>
<TD>1D</TD></TR>

<TR><TH>Row 2:</TH><TD>2A</TD><TD>2B</TD><TD>2C</TD>
<TD>2D</TD></TR>

</TABLE>
```

Horizontally Aligning Cell Contents

The text in the row headings and the data cells is left-aligned. Use the ALIGN attribute to right align the two rows of the table, like this:

```
<CAPTION>I. Table Example</CAPTION>

<TR><TH></TH><TH>A</TH><TH>B</TH><TH>C</TH><TH>D</TH>
</TR>
```

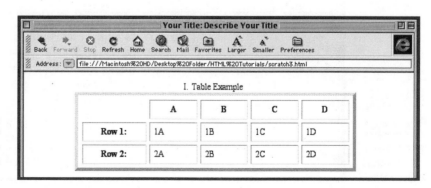

Figure C-10

You can also add row headings to a table.

```
<TR ALIGN="right"><TH>Row 1:</TH><TD>1A</TD><TD>1B</TD>
<TD>1C</TD><TD>1D</TD></TR>
```

```
<TR ALIGN="right"><TH>Row 2:</TH><TD>2A</TD><TD>2B</TD>
<TD>2C</TD><TD>2D</TD></TR>
```

If you check this out in the Macintosh version of Internet Explorer, you'll notice that the contents of the TD cells are right-aligned, but the contents of the TH cells aren't. This is a "browser quirk"—all other browsers capable of handling HTML 3.2 tables right-align any included TD and the TH cells when you set a table row (the TR tag) as right-aligned. To make sure that the TH cells that you're using to create your row headings are also right-aligned in the Macintosh version of Internet Explorer, you need to specifically set them as right-aligned. (Figure C-11 shows the new alignment for the rows and their headings.)

```
<CAPTION>I. Table Example</CAPTION>
```

```
<TR><TH></TH><TH>A</TH><TH>B</TH><TH>C</TH><TH>D</TH>
</TR>
```

```
<TR ALIGN="right"><TH ALIGN="right">Row 1:</TH><TD>1A
</TD><TD>1B</TD><TD>1C</TD><TD>1D</TD></TR>
```

```
<TR ALIGN="right"><TH ALIGN="right">Row 2:</TH><TD>2A
</TD><TD>2B</TD><TD>2C</TD><TD>2D</TD></TR>
```

You can also individually set TD cells to be right-aligned by including an ALIGN="right" attribute in the TD tag. Possible values for the ALIGN

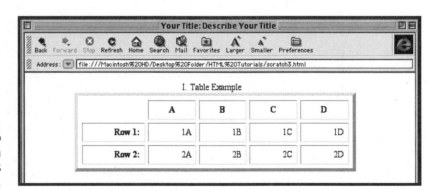

Figure C-11

You can right-align cell contents within a table.

attribute in TR, TD, and TH tags are "left", "center", and "right." Center-alignment is the default for TH cells, and left-alignment is the default for TD cells.

Setting Column Widths

By inserting a WIDTH attribute in the top cell of a column, you can specify the width of the entire column; column widths can be set in either percentages or pixels. The columns of your table are fairly equal in width; only the first column, where the row header cells are, is somewhat wider than the other columns. A browser will expand or contract the columns depending on their contents (the first column is wider because its contents take up more horizontal space). In other words, you can't depend on any column's remaining the same width once you've started to fill it in with real data. The table has five columns, so set each column to an equal width by inserting a WIDTH="20%" attribute in each of the TH tags in the top row of the table:

```
<CAPTION>I. Table Example</CAPTION>

<TR><TH WIDTH="20%"></TH><TH WIDTH="20%">A</TH><TH
WIDTH="20%">B</TH><TH WIDTH="20%">C</TH><TH
WIDTH="20%">D</TH></TR>
```

The percentage for setting equal column widths will depend on the total number of columns. If your table had six columns, you would set each to "16%" (100 divided by 6). Figure C-12 shows what percentage-based column widths look like.

Column widths set in percentages will expand or contract, depending on the width of the browser window. Column widths set in pixels will remain the same width, regardless of the width of the browser window. You can set the first column of a table in pixels and the remaining columns in percentages, the other way around, or in any other combination you want. If you do set all the columns to a fixed width using pixels, you should not set a percentage width in the TABLE tag.

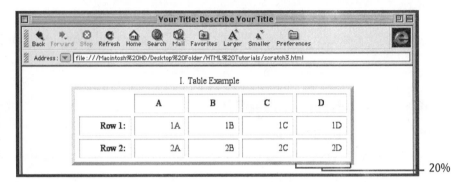

Figure C-12

Each column of
the table has been
set to a width of
20 percent.

— 20%

Inserting an Image

You can insert an image inside a table cell. The following HTML code
inserts a graphic, ONE.GIF, inside the upper-left corner cell. (This graphic
was used in the HTML tutorials, so it should already be available.) As
Figure C-13 shows, a graphic image of the number 1 has been inserted in
the top-left cell.

```
<CAPTION>I. Table Example</CAPTION>

<TR><TH WIDTH="20%"><IMG SRC="one.gif"></TH><TH
WIDTH="20%">A</TH><TH WIDTH="20%">B</TH><TH
WIDTH="20%">C</TH><TH WIDTH="20%">D</TH></TR>
```

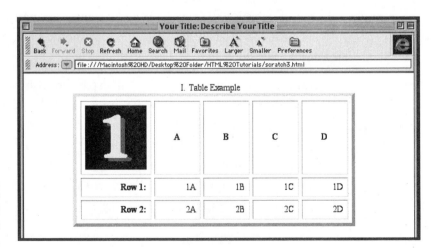

Figure C-13

You can insert
an inline image
inside a table cell.

Vertically Aligning Cell Contents

You can use the VALIGN attribute set to "top," "middle," or "bottom" to set the vertical alignment of a table row (TR), table heading (TH), or table data (TD) cell. Middle alignment is the default. (As Figure C-14 shows, the top row of the table is bottom-aligned.) Set the top row to bottom alignment:

```
<CAPTION>I. Table Example</CAPTION>

<TR VALIGN="bottom"><TH WIDTH="20%"><IMG
SRC="one.gif"></TH><TH WIDTH="20%">A</TH><TH
WIDTH="20%">B</TH><TH WIDTH="20%">C</TH><TH
WIDTH="20%">D</TH></TR>
```

Spanning Columns

The COLSPAN attribute lets you create cells that span across columns. Add a row to your table that includes two cells that span across two columns each. (Figure C-15 shows the result of inserting a new row that includes three cells: a blank cell in the first column and then two following cells spanning two columns each.)

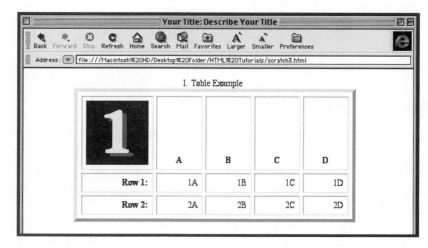

Figure C-14

You can vertically align cell contents.

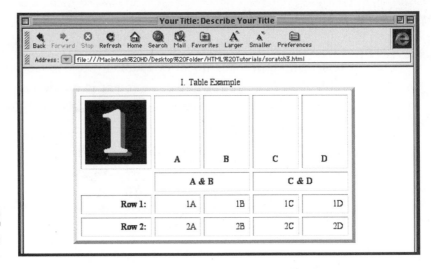

Figure C-15

Table cells can span columns.

```
<TR VALIGN="bottom"><TH WIDTH="20%"><IMG
SRC="one.gif"></TH><TH WIDTH="20%">A</TH><TH
WIDTH="20%">B</TH><TH WIDTH="20%">C</TH><TH
WIDTH="20%">D</TH></TR>
```

```
<TR><TH></TH><TH COLSPAN="2">A & B</TH><TH
COLSPAN="2">C & D</TH></TR>
```

```
<TR ALIGN="right"><TH ALIGN="right">Row 1:</TH><TD>1A
</TD><TD>1B</TD><TD>1C</TD><TD>1D</TD></TR>
```

To span additional columns, specify the number with the COLSPAN attribute. Just make sure you don't exceed the total number of columns in the table. For instance, this example amounts to three cells spanning five columns (1 + 2 + 2).

Spanning Rows

You can also create cells that span rows. To create a cell that spans rows, use the ROWSPAN attribute to specify the number of rows to span. This gets a little tricky: The cells to be spanned need to be removed from any following rows. (See Figure C-16.) In the following example, the cell you need to delete has a line running through it:

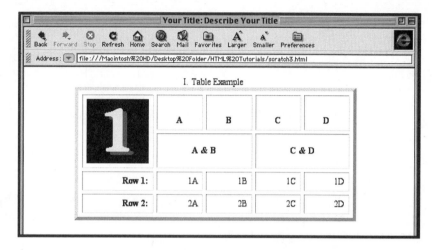

Figure C-16

Table cells can also span rows.

```
<CAPTION>I. Table Example</CAPTION>

<TR VALIGN="bottom"><TH ROWSPAN="2" WIDTH="20%"><IMG
SRC="one.gif"></TH><TH WIDTH="20%">A</TH><TH
WIDTH="20%">B</TH><TH WIDTH="20%">C</TH><TH
WIDTH="20%">D</TH></TR>

<TR><TH></TH><TH COLSPAN="2">A & B</TH><TH
COLSPAN="2">C & D</TH></TR>
```

Setting Row Heights

The top row and the second row in your table are the same height. Just as you can set the width of your table's columns, you can also set the height of the first cell in a row, to determine the height of the whole row. There is a limitation, however. In the table you're creating, the cell including an inline image that spans the first two rows determines the combined height of the two rows; the limitation is that you can increase the height of either row, but you can't directly decrease the height of either row beyond what it would otherwise be. Thus, in this case, to decrease the height of the second row, you have to increase the height of the first row, or vice versa.

```
<CAPTION>I. Table Example</CAPTION>

<TR VALIGN="bottom"><TH ROWSPAN="2" WIDTH="20%"><IMG
SRC="one.gif"></TH><TH HEIGHT="75" WIDTH="20%">A</
TH><TH WIDTH="20%">B</TH><TH WIDTH="20%">C</TH><TH
WIDTH="20%">D</TH></TR>

<TR><TH COLSPAN="2">A & B</TH><TH COLSPAN="2">C & D
</TH></TR>
```

You'll notice in the previous code example that the HEIGHT attribute was actually inserted into the second table cell in the row. That's because the first table cell is spanning two rows and is no longer the first cell in that row. Figure C-17 shows what this looks like in a Web browser.

Changing Font Sizes and Colors

You can change the font size and color of the contents of a table cell by inserting a FONT tag bracketing the text you want to be affected. Set the font size to "7" and the color to "blue" for one of the cells (see Figure C-18).

```
<CAPTION>I. Table Example</CAPTION>

<TR VALIGN="bottom"><TH ROWSPAN="2" WIDTH="20%"><IMG
SRC="one.gif"></TH><TH HEIGHT="75" WIDTH="20%"><FONT
SIZE="7" COLOR="blue">A</FONT></TH><TH WIDTH="20%">B
</TH><TH WIDTH="20%">C</TH><TH WIDTH="20%">D</TH></TR>
```

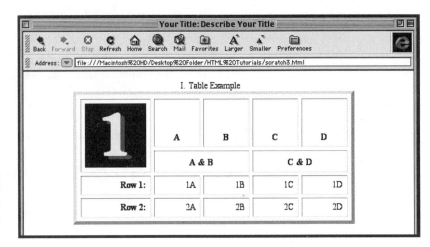

Figure C-17

The height of the first row is increased to 75 pixels.

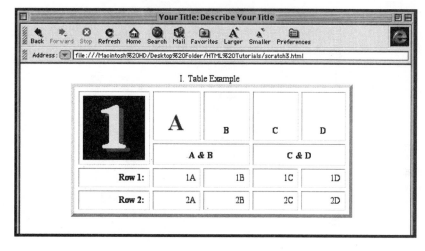

Figure C-18

You can assign
different font sizes
and colors to text
inside a table cell.

Assigning Background Colors

You can assign a background color to an entire table, a row within a table, or a single cell. A table can be made more readable by assigning different background colors to row heading cells and row cells.

Assigning a Background Color in the TABLE Tag

Unfortunately, Navigator and Internet Explorer do not handle assigning a background color to an entire table in the same fashion. Navigator displays the background color only in the table's cells, not in the borders between the cells; Internet Explorer fills in the borders with the background color. Earlier versions of Internet Explorer also fill in a table caption with the background color.

If you want to ensure your table is displayed at least similarly in both of these browsers, you should avoid setting a background color in the TABLE tag altogether. To see what it does, use the BGCOLOR attribute to set a background color in the TABLE tag (you can delete it later). Internet Explorer, as shown in Figure C-19, displays a background color inserted in the TABLE tag behind the whole table; Navigator, as shown in Figure C-20, displays a background color inserted in the TABLE tag only inside the table's cells.

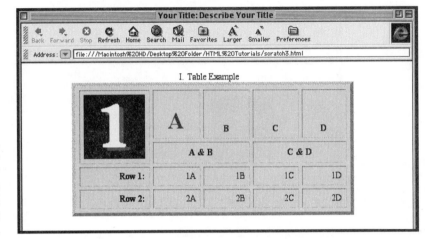

Figure C-19

Internet Explorer displays a background color behind the whole table.

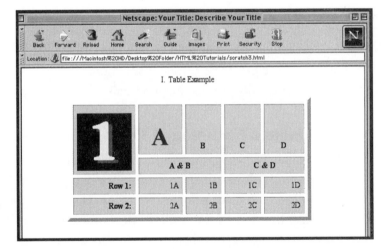

Figure C-20

Navigator displays a background color only within the table's cells.

```
<TABLE BGCOLOR="aqua" ALIGN="center" BORDER="6"
CELLSPACING="6" CELLPADDING="6" WIDTH="75%">

<CAPTION>I. Table Example</CAPTION>
```

Assigning a Background Color in the TR, TH, and TD Tags

If you want your table to look the same in both browsers, you should set background colors only in the TR, TH, and TD tags. You can assign background colors to individual table rows (TR tags), as well as to individual table heading (TH) and table data (TD) cells. The following code will assign lime to the top row, red to the top-left TH cell (the one with the image in it), olive to the second row, and yellow to the bottom two rows (notice that BGCOLOR="aqua" should be deleted).

```
<TABLE BGCOLOR="aqua" ALIGN="center" BORDER="6"
CELLSPACING="6" CELLPADDING="6" WIDTH="75%">

<CAPTION>I. Table Example</CAPTION>

<TR BGCOLOR="lime" VALIGN="bottom"><TH BGCOLOR="red"
ROWSPAN="2" WIDTH="20%"><IMG SRC="one.gif"></TH><TH
HEIGHT="75" WIDTH="20%"><FONT SIZE="7" COLOR="blue">A
</FONT></TH><TH WIDTH="20%">B</TH><TH WIDTH="20%">C
</TH><TH WIDTH="20%">D</TH></TR>

<TR BGCOLOR="olive"><TH COLSPAN="2">A & B</TH><TH
COLSPAN="2">C & D</TH></TR>

<TR BGCOLOR="yellow" ALIGN="right"><TH
ALIGN="right">Row 1:</TH><TD>1A</TD><TD>1b</TD><TD>1C
</TD><TD>1D</TD></TR>

<TR BGCOLOR="yellow" ALIGN="right"><TH
ALIGN="right">Row 2:</TH><TD>2A</TD><TD>2B</TD><TD>2C
</TD><TD>2D</TD></TR>
```

As shown in Figure C-21, different background colors appear behind one of the table cells, as well as the top, second, and last two table rows. You'll need to hop over to your Web browser, though, to really see what this looks like.

Figure C-21

You can set different background colors for rows or individual cells.

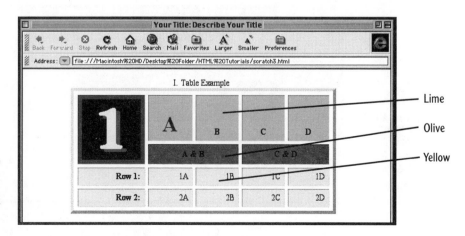

Removing Borders and Cell Spacing

You might think that you can get rid of the spacing and borders just by removing the BORDER and CELLSPACING attributes in the TABLE tag. Not so. To get rid of them completely, you have to set the attribute values to zero (see Figure C-22).

```
<TABLE ALIGN="center" BORDER="0" CELLSPACING="0"
CELLPADDING="6" WIDTH="75%">

<CAPTION>I. Table Example</CAPTION>
```

Using Background Images

You can also use background images in tables via the BACKGROUND attribute. However, this gets just a bit tricky, because Navigator and Internet Explorer don't work exactly the same way:

❖ Just as was the case with a background color, Internet Explorer displays a background image set in the TABLE tag behind the entire table, including behind the cell spacing. Navigator puts it only behind the individual cells.

❖ Internet Explorer does not recognize background images specified in the TR tag, but Navigator does. To specify a background image for a table row that will show up in both browsers, you need to specify it for each individual cell (TH or TD) in the row.

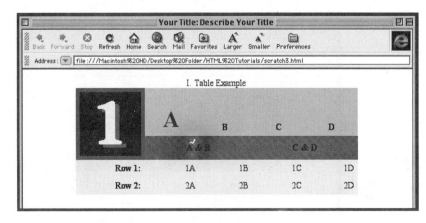

Figure C-22

You have to set BORDER and CELLSPACING to zero to completely get rid of them

⚙ In Navigator, a background image specified in the TABLE tag takes precedence over any background colors set in the rows, heading cells, or data cells, but in Internet Explorer, it's the other way around. Therefore, if you want to specify a background image in the TABLE tag that will display identically in both browsers, get rid of any BGCOLOR attributes elsewhere in the table.

The BACKGROUND attribute for the table tags is actually not a standard HTML attribute (in either HTML 3.2 or 4.0), unlike the BGCOLOR attribute—most likely because of the wide variance between how the two main browsers interpret it. Background images in tables can give a very nice effect, so I wouldn't necessarily avoid using this attribute just because it hasn't got the official stamp of approval yet. To check out what a BACKGROUND attribute set in the TABLE tag looks like, specify a background image in the TABLE tag, reset the BORDER and CELLSPACING attributes as shown, and delete any BGCOLOR attributes. (Figures C-23 and C-24 show what the result looks like in Internet Explorer and Navigator respectively.)

```
<TABLE BACKGROUND="backgrnd.gif" ALIGN="center"
BORDER="6" CELLSPACING="6" CELLPADDING="6" WIDTH="75%">

<CAPTION>I. Table Example</CAPTION>
```

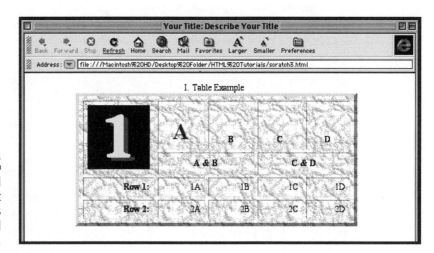

Figure C-23

A background image in Internet Explorer is displayed behind the whole table.

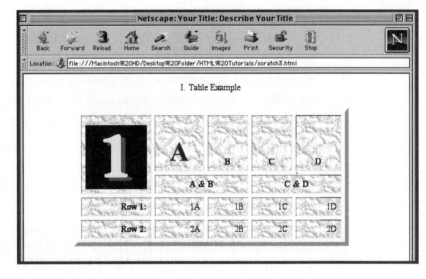

Figure C-24

A background image in Navigator is displayed only behind the table cells.

```
<TR BGCOLOR="lime" VALIGN="bottom"><TH BGCOLOR="red"
ROWSPAN="2" WIDTH="20%"><IMG SRC="one.gif"></TH><TH
HEIGHT="75" WIDTH="20%"><FONT SIZE="7" COLOR="blue">A
</FONT></TH><TH WIDTH="20%">B</TH><TH WIDTH="20%">C
</TH><TH WIDTH="20%">D</TH></TR>

<TR BGCOLOR="olive"><TH COLSPAN="2">A & B</TH><TH
COLSPAN="2">C & D</TH></TR>

<TR BGCOLOR="yellow" ALIGN="right"><TH
ALIGN="right">Row 1:</TH><TD>1A</TD><TD>lB</TD><TD>1C
</TD><TD>1D</TD></TR>

<TR BGCOLOR="yellow" ALIGN="right"><TH
ALIGN="right">Row 2:</TH><TD>2A</TD><TD>2B</TD><TD>2C
</TD><TD>2D</TD></TR>
```

Saving Your Work

Save the HTML file you just created (as scratch3.html, if that's what you named it at the start of this section). You'll use it again in the "Creating HTML 4.0 Tables" section at the end of this appendix. A file called tables.html has been included with the sample files in the HTML Tutorials folder that you copied from the CD-ROM; it includes all the previous examples, broken out into separate tables, so you can have a reference for each of the features covered here. Feel free to pull it into your text editor, or to check it out in your browser.

Creating Icon Link Lists Using Tables

In the Intermediate HTML Tutorial, I showed you how to create indented icon link lists using left-aligned bullet images. That method works fairly well, except it is limited to indenting only two lines of text, and you don't have very much control over the vertical positioning of your icon bullets relative to the following text. In the following exercise, you'll see how to create an indented icon link list using tables. That this method is perhaps a bit more difficult to implement than using left-aligned bullet images is compensated for by the lack of any limitation on the number of indented lines; you also have a lot more control over how your icon bullets are positioned relative to the following text. To get started with this section of the tutorial, just do the following:

1. If they aren't already open, run your text editor and your Web browser.

2. Open your starting template, **startpage.html**, in your text editor. Resave your starting template as **scratch4.html** (in the same folder). Your new "scratch pad" file should look like the following listing (you can type the codes in, if you didn't create a starting template).

```
<HTML>
<HEAD>
<TITLE>Your Title: Describe Your Title</TITLE>
</HEAD>
<BODY>
</BODY>
</HTML>
```

Adding the Links, Link Text, and Descriptive Text

Before you can create an icon link list, using tables or otherwise, you need something to make it out of. Go ahead and type the following example links, link text, and descriptive text into your HTML file:

```
<BODY>

<A HREF="http://pages.nyu.edu/~tqm3413/yoyo/">Tomer's
Page of Exotic Yo-Yo</A>. Dedicated to the "little-
known, original, unusual, difficult, or otherwise
interesting tricks." This is more text just to show
that you can indent as much text as you wish. This is
more text just to show that you can indent as much text
as you wish.

<A HREF="http://www.socool.com/socool/yo-yo.html">Just
Say YO!!!</A> Features the Web's first Yo-Yo animation.
This is more text just to show that you can indent as
much text as you wish. This is more text just to show
that you can indent as much text as you wish.

<A HREF="http://www.pd.net/yoyo/">American Yo-Yo
Association</A> Read past issues of the AYYA News-
letter. This is more text just to show that you can
indent as much text as you wish. This is more text just
to show that you can indent as much text as you wish.

</BODY>
```

Adding the Icon Bullets and the Table Tags

Now, go ahead and add the icon bullets and the table tags. Note that explanations of the different tags and attributes follow the example code (see Figure C-25).

```
<BODY>

<TABLE WIDTH=100%>
```

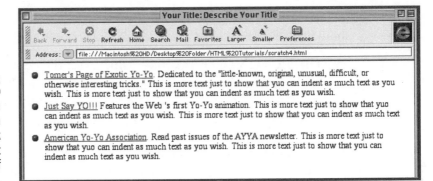

Figure C-25

Using tables, you can create an indented icon link list with no limit on the number of indented lines.

```
<TR VALIGN="top"><TD WIDTH="20"><IMG SRC="redball.gif"
VSPACE="2"> </TD><TD><P><A HREF="http://pages.nyu.edu/
~tqm3413/yoyo/">Tomer's Page of Exotic Yo-Yo</A>.
Dedicated to the "little-known, original, unusual,
difficult, or otherwise interesting tricks." This is
more text just to show that you can indent as much text
as you wish. This is more text just to show that you
can indent as much text as you wish.</P></TD></TR>
```

```
<TR VALIGN="top"><TD><IMG SRC="redball.gif" VSPACE="2">
</TD><TD><P><A HREF="http://www.socool.com/socool/yo-
yo.html">Just Say YO!!!</A> Features the Web's first
Yo-Yo animation. This is more text just to show that
you can indent as much text as you wish. This is more
text just to show that you can indent as much text as
you wish.</P></TD></TR>
```

```
<TR VALIGN="top"><TD><IMG SRC="redball.gif" VSPACE="2">
</TD><TD><P><A HREF="http://www.pd.net/yoyo/">American
Yo-Yo Association</A> Read past issues of the AYYA
Newsletter. This is more text just to show that you can
indent as much text as you wish. This is more text just
to show that you can indent as much text as you wish.
</P></TD></TR>
```

```
</TABLE>
```

```
</BODY>
```

In this example of creating an indented icon link list using tables, you should pay especially close attention to a number of things:

- The TR tags include **VALIGN="top"** to set the vertical alignment. Without this, the icon bullet images would be middle-aligned, which is not what you want. You could also set this attribute value in the TD tag containing the icon bullet graphic.

- A WIDTH attribute value of 20 pixels is set in the first cell of the top row to specify the width of the first column. This width can be increased or decreased to suit your taste.

- A P tag is inserted in the first cell of each row, with a space also inserted at the end of the same cell. This makes allowance for older Web browsers, which don't support displaying tables. The P tag will cause a non-supporting browser to display the table row as a separate line, and the space will be inserted between the icon graphic and the following text. Note that adding the P tag and inserting the space will not affect the display of the table in a tables-capable Web browser.

- The IMG tags for the icon bullet graphics include a VSPACE (vertical space) attribute of 3 pixels. Rarely will an icon bullet line up evenly with a following line of text. You can add or subtract pixels in the VSPACE attribute in the IMG tag to adjust the position of the icon bullet relative to following text.

Double-Indenting and Centering Your Icon Link List

Right now, the table for the icon link list is set to a width of 100 percent of the browser window. If you want to double-indent and center your icon link list, you just need to edit the TABLE tag and insert a WIDTH percentage value, and center-align the table (see Figure C-26).

```
<BODY>

<TABLE WIDTH=85% ALIGN="center">
```

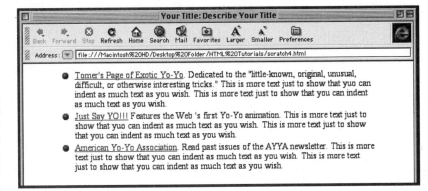

Figure C-26

You can easily
double-indent
and center an icon
link list created
using tables.

Changing the Spacing in Your Table

You can also adjust the spacing in your table by using inserting a CELLSPACING or CELLPADDING attribute in the TABLE tag (see Figure C-27).

```
<BODY>

<TABLE WIDTH=85% ALIGN="center" CELLSPACING="15">
```

Save your file, but don't save it over the file you created in the first section of this tutorial (you're going to need it for the next section). I've also included a file in the HTML Tutorials folder, tables2.html, that shows what your result should like like.

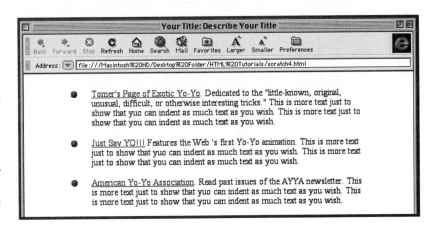

Figure C-27

You can adjust the
spacing within an
icon link list table
by setting the
CELLSPACING or
CELLPADDING
attribute in the
TABLE tag.

Creating HTML 4.0 Tables

HTML 4.0 introduced a number of new table tags, including the TBODY, THEAD, TFOOT, COLGROUP, and COL tags. Currently, the TBODY, THEAD, and TFOOT tags are supported only by Internet Explorer 4.0+; the COLGROUP and COL tags are not yet supported on Mac OS platforms at all, but currently only by Internet Explorer 5.0 for Windows. These tags, like the SPAN tag, come to life only when characteristics are assigned to them in a style sheet. You'll see how to apply TBODY, THEAD, and TFOOT tags to your table, as well as how to use regular styles to get virtually the same result in Navigator.

NOTE The HTML 4.0 table features depend on the use of a style sheet to have any significant effect. The following examples contain sample style sheets that illustrate how the HTML 4.0 table features work. You should be able to edit the sample style sheets (changing font sizes, colors, and background colors) for any element that you want to define a style for, as well as use them as a basis for creating new styles.

 FIND IT ON THE WEB

If you want to find out more about using styles, read Eric Meyer's excellent introduction to the subject, "Creating Your First Style Sheet," at **http://webreview.com/wr/pub/ 97/10/10/style/index.html**. Then see the W3C's page on Cascading Style Sheets at **www.w3.org/Style/CSS/**. See also Web Review's Cascading Style Sheets Guide for compatibility charts, showing which style features work in which Web browsers, at **http:/ /webreview.com/wr/pub/guides/style/style.html**.

1. If they aren't already open, run your text editor and your Web browser.

2. In your text editor, open the "scratch pad" file you saved at the end of the first section of this tutorial (scratch3.html, if that's what you named it).

3. Save your file, giving it a new name (**scratch5.html**, for instance).

4. Add a sample style sheet to your HTML file.

```
<HTML>

<HEAD>

<TITLE>Your Title: Describe Your Title</TITLE>
```

<STYLE TYPE="test/css">

<!--

TBODY {font-family: monospace; font-style: bold; font-size: 125%; color: navy; background-color: aqua}

THEAD {font-family: sans-serif; font-style: bold; font-size: 150%; color: yellow; background-color: maroon}

TFOOT {font-family: sans-serif; font-style: italic; color: white; background-color: #ff6600}

-->

</STYLE>

```
</HEAD>

<BODY>
```

Whenever you define a TBODY tag in an HTML file's style sheet, its formatting characteristics will automatically be applied to all of the cells of your table, as shown in Figure C-28.

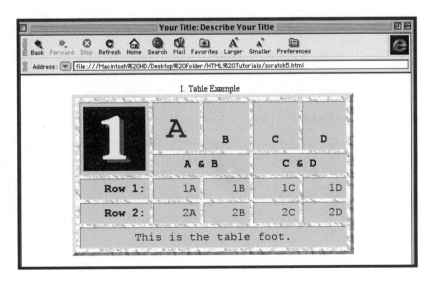

Figure C-28

TBODY style properties will be applied to all of the cells in a table, even though THEAD, TFOOT, and TBODY are absent.

You can also include the style sheet codes in a linked style sheet. Just save the codes (from THEAD to TFOOT) as a text file, table.css, for instance; then replace the STYLE tag with this:

```
<LINK rel=stylesheet HREF="table.css" TYPE="text/css">
```

You should realize, however, that Netscape Navigator 4.0+ has a bug that causes it not to recognize a linked style sheet that is not in the same folder as the HTML that is linked to it.

Actually, this is easier than using the FONT tag to assign font colors within a table, which you have to set within *every* cell where you want it to take effect. The latter is a bit laborious, in other words, if all you want to do is reset the font size and color for all the cells.

Inserting the THEAD, TBODY, and TFOOT Tags

To have one or more rows in your table show up with the properties defined in the style sheet, just bracket them in the THEAD, TBODY, or TFOOT tags. In the following example, apply the THEAD, TBODY, and TFOOT tags to your table, and add an additional row for the table foot. (As shown in Figure C-29, the latest version of Internet Explorer applies the properties defined in the style sheet to the different sections of the table.)

```
<TABLE BACKGROUND="backgrnd.gif" ALIGN="center"
BORDER="6" CELLSPACING="6" CELLPADDING="6" WIDTH="75%">

<CAPTION>I. Table Example</CAPTION>

<THEAD>

<TR VALIGN="bottom"><TH ROWSPAN="2" WIDTH="20%"><IMG
SRC="one.gif"></TH><TH WIDTH="20%"><FONT SIZE="7"
COLOR="blue">A</FONT></TH><TH WIDTH="20%">B</TH><TH
WIDTH="20%">C</TH><TH WIDTH="20%">D</TH></TR>

<TR><TH COLSPAN="2">A & B</TH><TH COLSPAN="2">C &
D</TH></TR>

</THEAD>
```

```
<TBODY>

<TR ALIGN="right"><TH ALIGN="right">Row 1:</TH><TD>1A
</TD><TD>1B</TD><TD>1C</TD><TD>1D</TD></TR>

<TR ALIGN="right"><TH ALIGN="right">Row 2:</TH><TD>2A
</TD><TD>2B</TD><TD>2C</TD><TD>2D</TD></TR>

</TBODY>

<TFOOT>

<TR><TD COLSPAN="5" ALIGN="center">This is the table
foot.</TD></TR>

</TFOOT>

</TABLE>
```

Getting Almost the Same Results in Navigator

You can get very nearly the same results in Netscape Navigator 4.0+. The only real difference is that you can't have a background image assigned in the TABLE tag if you want to use styles to assign background colors to individual cells. If you want to get the same results here in both Internet Explorer 4.0+ and Netscape Navigator 4.0+, you have to exclude the

Figure C-29

You can define styles that will render the head, body, and foot of your table in the format you prefer, although you'll only be able to see the styles in Internet Explorer 4.0+.

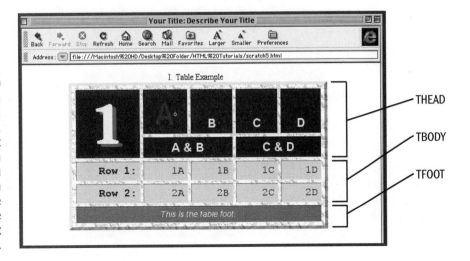

background image (which only displays between the table cells in Internet Explorer anyway). Setting your table up to display the same results (or virtually the same results) in both browsers involves adding CLASS attributes to the tags you want to format, which serve as "hooks"; off these, you can hang whatever style characteristics you want to assign (see Figure C-30).

NOTE Because percentage values are used to set the font sizes in the style sheet, you'll need to delete TBODY, THEAD, and TFOOT in the style sheet (I've struck through what you need to delete). If pixel values were used to set the font sizes, these deletions wouldn't be necessary. (I've also struck through the background image codes that need to be deleted.)

```
<HTML>

<HEAD>

<TITLE>Your Title: Describe Your Title</TITLE>

<STYLE TYPE="test/css">

<!--

TBODY TD.body, TH.body {font-family: monospace; font-
style: bold; font-size: 125%; color: navy; background-
color: aqua}
```

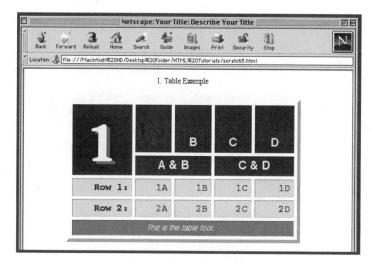

Figure C-30

You can get virtually the same results in Navigator by using CLASS attributes

```
THEAD TH.head {font-family: sans-serif; font-style:
bold; font-size: 150%; color: yellow; background-color:
maroon}

TFOOT TD.foot {font-family: sans-serif; font-style:
italic; color: white; background-color: #ff6600}

-->

</STYLE>

</HEAD>

<BODY>

<TABLE BACKGROUND="backgrnd.gif" ALIGN="center"
BORDER="6" CELLSPACING="6" CELLPADDING="6" WIDTH="75%">

<CAPTION>I. Table Example</CAPTION>

<THEAD>

<TR VALIGN="bottom"><TH CLASS="head" ROWSPAN="2"
WIDTH="20%"><IMG SRC="one.gif"></TH><TH CLASS="head"
WIDTH="20%"><FONT SIZE="7" COLOR="blue">A</FONT></TH>
<TH CLASS="head" WIDTH="20%">B</TH><TH CLASS="head"
WIDTH="20%">C</TH><TH CLASS="head" WIDTH="20%">D</TH>
</TR>

<TR><TH CLASS="head" COLSPAN="2">A & B</TH><TH CLASS=
"head" COLSPAN="2">C & D</TH></TR>

</THEAD>

<TBODY>

<TR ALIGN="right"><TH CLASS="body" ALIGN="right">Row
1:</TH><TD CLASS="body">1A</TD><TD CLASS="body">1B</TD>
<TD CLASS="body">1C</TD><TD CLASS="body">1D</TD></TR>

<TR ALIGN="right"><TH CLASS="body" ALIGN="right">Row
2:</TH><TD CLASS="body">2A</TD><TD CLASS="body">2B
</TD><TD CLASS="body">2C</TD><TD CLASS="body">2D</TD>
</TR>

</TBODY>

<TFOOT>
```

```
<TR><TD CLASS="foot" COLSPAN="5" ALIGN="center">This is
the table foot.</TD></TR>

</TFOOT>

</TABLE>
```

The COLGROUP and COL Tags

There are two other table tags specified by HTML 4.0 that allow you to define column groups, the COLGROUP tag and the COL tag. These tags are supported only by Internet Explorer 5.0, which is available only for the Windows 95/98 platform. When Internet Explorer 5.0 for the Macintosh becomes available it should also support these tags. Here's an example of using the COLGROUP and COL tags (see Figure C-31).

```
<HTML>

<HEAD>

<TITLE>Your Title: Describe Your Title</TITLE>

<STYLE type="text/css">

<!--

THEAD {font-family: sans-serif; font-style: bold; font-
size: 130%; color: aqua; background-color: maroon}
```

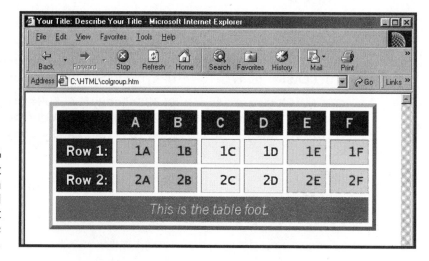

Figure C-31

You can also format column groups in tables, but you'll need Internet Explorer 5.0 for the Macintosh to see it.

```
TFOOT {font-family: sans-serif; font-style: italic;
color: white; background-color: #FF6600}

COL {font-family: monospace; font-style: bold; font-
size: 130%; color: blue; background-color: yellow}

COL.rowhead {font-family: sans-serif; font-style: bold;
font-size: 130%; color: yellow; background-color: blue}

COL.1 {font-family: monospace; font-style: bold; color:
blue; background-color: lime}

COL.2 {font-family: monospace; font-style: bold; color:
blue; background-color: yellow}

COL.3 {font-family: monospace; font-style: bold; color:
blue; background-color: aqua}


-->

</STYLE>

</HEAD>

<BODY>

<P>

<TABLE ALIGN="center" BORDER="6" CELLSPACING="6"
CELLPADDING="6" WIDTH="90%">

<COLGROUP>

 <COL CLASS="rowhead" WIDTH="20%">

 <COL SPAN="2" CLASS="1">

 <COL SPAN="2" CLASS="2">

 <COL SPAN="2" CLASS="3">

</COLGROUP>

<THEAD>

<TR><TH></TH><TH>A</TH><TH>B</TH><TH>C</TH><TH>D</TH>
<TH>E</TH><TH>F</TH></TR>

</THEAD>

<TR ALIGN="right"><TH>Row 1:</TH><TD>1A</TD><TD>1B</TD>
<TD>1C</TD><TD>1D</TD><TD>1E</TD><TD>1F</TD></TR>
```

```
<TR ALIGN="right"><TH ALIGN="right">Row 2:</TH><TD>2A
</TD><TD>2B</TD><TD>2C</TD><TD>2D</TD> <TD>2E</
TD><TD>2F</TD></TR>

<TFOOT>

<TR CLASS="foot"><TD COLSPAN="7" ALIGN="center">This is
the table foot.</TD></TR>

</TFOOT>

</TABLE>

</P>

</BODY>

</HTML>
```

The COLGROUP tag takes the following attributes: SPAN, WIDTH, ALIGN, VALIGN, CHAR, and CHAROFF, with the COL tag supporting the same attributes (with the exception of the SPAN attribute). The SPAN attribute specifies the number of columns in a particular column group (SPAN="4", for instance). The WIDTH attribute specifies the width of the individual columns within the group, as either a pixel or a percentage value. The ALIGN attribute specifies the horizontal alignment (center, right, and left) of cell contents within the column group, while the VALIGN attribute specifies the vertical alignment (top, bottom, and middle). The CHAR attribute aligns cell contents on a particular character (such as a decimal point)—not even Internet Explorer 5.0 supports this. Additionally, you can use the ID and CLASS global attributes (the CLASS attribute is used in the previous example to link a style with a "class" of tag elements).

The FRAME and RULES Attributes

There are two other table attributes specified by HTML 4.0, the FRAME and RULES attributes. The FRAME attribute is used in the TABLE tag to draw a frame around a table. This attribute differs from the BORDER attribute, in that it draws lines only around the table, but not between the cells. The RULES attribute draws lines between rows, columns, or row and column groups. Right now, the only browser that supports these attributes is Internet Explorer 4.0+. The values that can be used with the FRAME attribute are void, above, below, hsides, vsides, lhs, rhs, box, and border. The values that can be used with the RULES attribute are none, groups, rows, cols, and all.

Using Microsoft Table Attributes

Internet Explorer supports three additional attributes that can be used in the TABLE tag. BORDERCOLOR, BORDERCOLORDARK, and BORDERCOLORLIGHT are used to specify different colors for the different parts of the border, using either color names or RGB hex color codes. These attributes have not yet been included in HTML 3.2 or 4.0, and will not be displayed in any version of Netscape Navigator. Because these attributes are not part of standard HTML, you may want to avoid using them, but go ahead and experiment with them to see what they'll do.

Putting It Up On the Web

Once you've created your first Web page, you're going to want to put it up on the Web for all to see. That is often a cause of some trepidation for beginning Web publishers, but there really is no need for any anxiety; in most cases, transferring pages onto a Web server is a snap.

Finding a Web Host

Before you can put a Web page up on the Web, you need to find a server to host your page. The options available to you are many and varied. Getting free Web space may serve your purposes, or you may find that you need to purchase commercial services.

Getting Free Web Space

If you are a student, your school may provide free Web space you can use to publish your own Web pages. Many ISPs now offer relatively generous allotments of free Web space; if you're primarily concerned with putting up a personal page, this can be a great way to go, since it won't cost you any more than what you're already paying. If your dial-up provider doesn't provide very much free Web space, and you don't want to switch, there are quite a few companies that provide free Web space in return for being able to include either an advertising banner at the top of your page, or a window with advertising that pops up when surfers access your page. To find out more, go to my Web Hosts Lists page at **www.callihan.com/webhosts/**.

FIND IT ON ▶
THE WEB

In case you're an AOL customer, here are some resources on setting up an AOL Web site that you'll find especially useful. First, go to the keyword "My Place" in AOL; for help in using My Place to publish your files, select Frequently Asked Questions. You can get additional information on how to use My Place at these Web sites:

- ✿ "AOL: Uploading your web page" at
  www.patmcclendon.com/aol.html

- ✿ "Web Site Design by AWEBPAGE.COM" at
  www.awebpage.com/upload.html

- ✿ "How Do I?" at
  http://members.aol.com/ftpmaster/faqs.htm

Finding a Commercial Web Host

If you want to create a commercial Web page, hope to generate a considerable amount of traffic, think you'll need more space, or want to have access to a fuller range of features and services, you might want to consider finding a Web host that focuses on providing raw Web space. The cost for this can be quite reasonable, averaging from about $35 to $50 for setup, and $20 to $30 a month to rent the space.

Apart from a setup fee, your Web host provider shouldn't charge you anything extra for registering and maintaining a domain name for you. The cost of registering your own domain name is $70 for the first two years, and then $35 per year thereafter. You'll be billed separately by Network Solutions, Inc., for these fees. If you want to find out whether the domain name you want is available, go to **www.networksolutions.com** and use their search form (the form says "Register a Web Address," but you can just search to see if a domain name is available, without having to register it). Once you find that a domain name you want is available, just let your Web host know what it is when you sign up for your account (they'll handle getting it registered and maintaining it on their server). The main things to look for in a Web host are:

- Lots of space. 20 MB or more of space is common. 40 MB or more is better.

- A big traffic allowance. Don't settle for less than 2 GB per month. More is better. (One provider, NetGate.net, provides a traffic allowance of 200 MB a day.)

- Any special features you may need to have, either free or at a reasonable cost. These might include extra e-mail accounts, virtual FTP, autoresponders, and so on.

- An upgrade path. This might include accounts that provide for access to a secure server, so that you can take credit card orders. If you think that this may be in your future, make sure in advance that your provider's charges will be reasonable after you upgrade. You may also want to see if they have any Web applications available that can help you create an online store—one provider, pair Networks (**www.pair.com**), can implement a shopping cart application for your site for only $14.95 a month.

What You Need to Know

Your Web space provider should provide you with all of the information you need to be able to connect to your Web space folder. Generally, this information is the same, whether you'll be using an FTP program or PageMill to transfer your files. Here's a quick rundown on the information that you'll need to know to connect to your folder on your Web server:

○ **Host name.** This is the name of the server where your folder is located. It'll look something like this: serv3.yourhost.net. If you have a domain name, you may also be able to access your folder using your domain name.

○ **User ID.** You should have a unique username that identifies you to your server. If you have received your Web space from a local ISP or a commercial online service, this will very likely be the same as the user name you use to log on. In most cases, your User ID is case-sensitive, so you'll need to type it exactly as it is written.

○ **Password.** You need to have a password so that only you, and no one else, can access your Web pages on your server. Your password is also usually case-sensitive, so you'll need to type it exactly as it is written.

You may in some cases also need to provide the path to your folder on your server, but that is increasingly rare. The vast majority of Web hosts will automatically switch you to your root folder on your server.

FTP Programs for Transferring and Maintaining Web Pages

FIND IT ON ▶ THE WEB

There are several FTP programs available for the Macintosh that can be used to upload your Web pages to your folder on a Web server, or to maintain your Web site (create and delete folders, copy, move, or rename files, and so on). Here are some you might want to try:

○ Fetch at **www.dartmouth.edu/pages/softdev/fetch.html**

○ Anarchie Pro at **www.stairways.com/anarchie/**

○ Transmit at **www.panic.com/**

○ NetFinder at **www.ozemail.com.au/~pli/netfinder/**

FIND IT ON ▶ THE CD

You can find all of these FTP programs on this book's CD-ROM. Just open the Browsers and FTP section in Prima Tech's interface to install any of these programs.

NOTE

If you're creating your Web pages using Adobe PageMill, you should use PageMill to transfer them and the other files in your Web site to your server, and not an FTP program. If you're using PageMill to create your Web pages, skip ahead to "Using PageMill to Transfer Your Pages."

Using Fetch to Transfer Your Pages

Fetch is one of the most popular FTP programs available for the Macintosh. Fetch will work with just about Macintosh. The minimum requirement is a Mac Plus running System 6.1 or later.

NOTE

The steps required to connect to your Web server folder should be very similar for other FTP programs.

FIND IT ON ▶
THE CD

In most cases, you should be able to use Fetch to connect to your Web space folder. On this book's CD-ROM, it's located in the Browsers and FTP list. When you run Fetch, you'll see a New Connection dialog window prompting you for the host name, user ID, and password for your Web space account (see Figure D-1).

Just type the host name, user ID, and password your Web host provided (see the "What You Need to Know" section above). In the Directory box, type any

Figure D-1

Fetch opens with the New Connection dialog window.

New Connection...
Enter host name, userid, and password (or choose from the shortcut menu):
Host:	ftp.dartmouth.edu
User ID:	
Password:	
Directory:	pub
Shortcuts: ▼	Cancel	OK

further path required to access the root folder of your Web site—my Web space root folder has two folders, ftp and www, which are used to contain FTP and Web page files, respectively. (If you're not sure what to type in the Directory box, just leave it blank.) Once you've filled out the New Connection dialog window, just click OK to connect to your Web site (see Figure D-2).

If this doesn't work, you may need to check Fetch's configuration settings; just select Customize and Preferences from the menu bar. If your computer is logging onto the Internet from behind a firewall, you'll probably need to fill in the Firewall tab section of the Preferences dialog window. Check with your system administrator to find out the information you need to fill in, if this is required. If necessary, check with your Web space provider for any additional information you may need to properly configure Fetch to access your Web server folder.

Often a little preparation can go a long way. Before trying to transfer your pages up onto your Web server, do the following:

- Thoroughly test out your pages on your local computer, making sure that all your links work, all your images show up, and so on. If need be, connect to the Internet to check out any links to sites on the Web.

- Other than for the folder you're using to hold your Web pages (My Pages, for instance), make sure that there are no spaces in any of the file or folder names for your site.

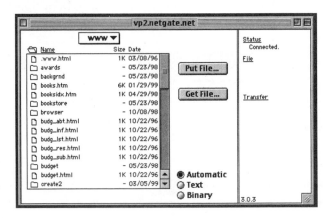

Figure D-2

Fetch has opened a www folder on a Web site.

✿ Make sure that any file names (or folder names, if you're already using relative URLs) in URLs for hypertext links or inline images exactly match the actual file names (or folder names). Unix servers are case-sensitive and would see MyPage.html and mypage.html as two different files. (A good way to avoid this problem is to always name any files or folders in your site in all lowercase, and then always refer to them in all lowercase in your local URLs.)

Transferring Your Files

To transfer a file from your local computer to a folder on your Web site using Fetch, just do the following:

1. In Fetch's file window, double-click on and open the folder into which you want to transfer your file.

2. Click the Put File button to select the file you want to transfer. Open the folder on your computer that contains your Web pages, and double-click the file you want to transfer.

3. Select the format of the file you're transferring. If you're transferring an HTML file, select Text as the format. If you're transferring an image file (whether inline or background) or other binary file format (such as a program file, a SIT file, and so on), select Raw Data as the format. Click OK. (See Figure D-3.)

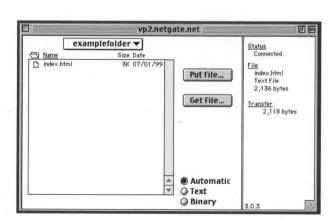

Figure D-3

A file, index.html, has been transferred to the examplefolder folder on a Web site.

■■

TIP You may have noticed the Shortcuts menu in Fetch's New Connection dialog window. To add your site to the list, after connecting to your Web server folder, choose New Shortcut from the Customize menu. If you want to have Fetch remember your password, just type your password in the Password box. (Fetch will save your password on your hard drive in an unencrypted form, so if you're concerned about security for your site, you may want to leave this blank and just retype your password each time you connect to your site.) To save your shortcut (or bookmark), just click OK.

If you want the New Connection dialog window to default to your Web site, after connecting to your Web server folder, choose Preferences from the Customize window. Choose your server's name from the Default shortcut pop-up menu. Click OK.

■■

Creating New Web Folders

Just starting out, you should stick to keeping all of your Web page files in the same folder on your server—either in the root folder for your site or in the folder designated to contain your Web page files (a www folder). Before too long, you'll probably outgrow this approach and want to create a Web site using multiple folders. To add a new folder to your Web site using Fetch, just do the following:

1. In Fetch's file window, open the folder where you want to create the new folder.

2. Choose Create New Directory from the Directories menu on the menu bar. Type the name of your new directory, and click OK.

Finding Out More About Using Fetch

There's a lot more you can do using Fetch, including accessing anonymous FTP sites, downloading files ("getting" files), deleting files, and renaming files. For information on using these and other features, check out Fetch's Help file, which includes a quick guide and a tutorial, as well as a full reference for using Fetch. For a nice online tutorial on using Fetch, check

FIND IT ON ▶
THE WEB
out **http://macassistant.com/tutor/fetch/fetch.html**.

Using PageMill to Transfer Your Pages

If you've created your Web pages using Adobe PageMill, you should use it to transfer them onto your Web server. As with using an FTP program, you will need to get some information from your Web space provider: your server's host name, your user name, and your password, so you can enter these items when you fill out PageMill's upload settings.

Filling Out PageMill's Upload Settings

1. Choose Show Settings from the Site menu on PageMill's menu bar.

2. Click your site's name (if your local site is already open in PageMill, it'll be highlighted) and click Edit (see Figure D-4).

3. Fill out the Host Name, User Name, and Password boxes.

4. If you want to automatically switch to another folder in your Web site (other than your root folder), type the folder (or folder path) in the Remote Folder box. For instance, typing **www** would automatically upload your files to a www folder in your Web site's root folder. Typing **www/pages/** would automatically upload files to a www/ pages/ folder in your Web site's root folder.

5. Click OK and Close.

Uploading Your PageMill Pages

1. Open your local site in PageMill.

2. Choose Upload from the Site menu on the menu bar. (If you're not already connected, your Remote Status dialer will connect you to the Internet.) All the files in your PageMill site will be transferred to your root folder (or to whichever folder you designated in the Remote Folder box) on your Web server.

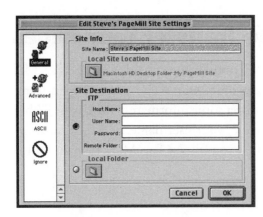

Figure D-4

PageMill lets you specify your site settings.

Transferring Individual Files

Sometimes you'll just want to do a quickie transfer of a single file (a Web page or other object, such as an image file). In this case, just do the following:

1. To upload an individual page or frameset, open the Web page or frameset in PageMill.

2. To upload an object (such as an image), open the page in which the object located and select the object you want to upload. You can also just open an image you want to upload in an image window—just open the image from the list of files contained in your site.

3. Choose Upload from the File menu, and then choose the type of item (Object, Page, or Frameset) you're uploading—this will already be highlighted for you (with the others grayed out, depending on which type of file you've opened in PageMill).

HTML– Past and Future

To understand where HTML is going, you have to have some idea of where it's been. The following is a brief rundown on what has lead up to the current state of affairs, and what is likely to happen in the future.

Basic HTML: HTML 1.0 and HTML 2.0

HTML 1.0 and 2.0 were the two earliest versions of HTML. In this book, the Basic HTML Tutorial (Saturday Morning) focuses exclusively on these versions of HTML. HTML is in many ways like the layers of an onion, with the earlier versions still surviving as the inner layers of later versions. Some of the features that date back to these first versions of HTML include inline images, bullet and numbered lists, definition lists (glossaries), and input forms.

Ad Hoc HTML: Netscape and Microsoft Extensions

Both Netscape and Microsoft developed their own special extensions to HTML for use in their browsers. These can be used in any Web document, but they translate into special formatting only when a user views the Web page in the particular browser for which they were created (unless the other browser's manufacturer provides support for the extensions, too).

Most of the extensions to HTML that Netscape pioneered have been incorporated into either HTML 3.2 or 4.0. The only purely "Microsoft extension" to be included in HTML 4.0 is the FACE attribute for the FONT tag, although Microsoft supported a number of proposed HTML 4.0 elements in its Internet Explorer 3.0 browser prior to the release of HTML 4.0. Some extensions, both old and new, such as Microsoft's MARQUEE tag and Netscape's BLINK tag, can only be displayed in one or the other of these browsers. Unless everybody in your target audience uses the same browser, you should avoid using HTML that will only work in one browser. Preferably, you want your HTML to work in *all* browsers.

Probably the most noteworthy of Netscape's recent innovations is frames (using the FRAMESET and FRAME tags). The use of frames is rapidly proliferating on the Web, compelling other Web browsers to follow suit and incorporate the display of frames in their repertoire. Frames have since been incorporated into HTML 4.0, despite a certain amount of controversy. Although some people hate them, others swear by them. As usual on the Web, what Web publishers use is what matters, and on that score the vote is in: a qualified thumbs up. The primary objections to frames are two fold: a "formal" objection that they violate the spirit of SGML (of which HTML is supposed to be a subset) and a "functional" objection that they make it difficult to link into a subpage within a frameset (meaning that a bookmark would return you not to the subpage where you were at, but only to the initial "front" page defined in the frameset).

◄ ◄

A page using frames is defined using the FRAMESET tag, so a collection of Web pages defined by a FRAMESET tag is often referred to as a *frameset*. Every Web page that uses frames starts from an initial frameset, although further framesets may be nested inside of the initial frameset. For a couple of HTML templates that can assist you in setting up framed Web sites, see the HTML Templates folder in the Book Examples folder on the CD-ROM.

◄ ◄

Microsoft has introduced a number of extensions to HTML that have remained unique to its Web browser, Internet Explorer. These include the capability to automatically play background sounds using the BGSOUND tag (you can add background sounds to Navigator, but only by using an entirely different method). Microsoft has introduced scrollable background images (when you scroll down through the text, the background image remains fixed). This same effect can be done using Cascading Style Sheets. Microsoft's addition of the FACE attribute to the FONT tag has since been supported in Navigator 4.0 and has been included in HTML 4.0.

A Failed Initiative: HTML 3.0

HTML 3.0 was proposed as the next standard for HTML following HTML 2.0. However, the ambitiousness of HTML 3.0 ultimately proved its downfall—coming to an agreement on how to implement it simply was impossible. Ultimately, the W3C abandoned HTML 3.0 in favor of a much more modest proposal, HTML 3.2.

A number of HTML 3.0 features found support in Web browsers—the most notable of which is tables. Other proposed HTML 3.0 elements that gained the favor of Web browsers to one degree or another include superscripts and subscripts, font size changing (with the BIG and SMALL tags), and underlining. Many tags and attributes that were first proposed as part of HTML 3.0 have since been incorporated into HTML 3.2 and HTML 4.0.

Current HTML: HTML 3.2 and HTML 4.0

The two latest "official" versions of HTML are HTML 3.2 and HTML 4.0. HTML 3.2 was released in January of 1997, and HTML 4.0 was released in December of 1997.

HTML 3.2

Here are some of the primary features included in the HTML 3.2 standard:

- Tables
- Applets (for Java and JavaScript)
- Background images
- Background, text, and link colors
- Font sizes and colors
- Flowing of text around images
- Image borders
- Height and width attributes for images
- Alignment (left, center, or right) of paragraphs, headings, and horizontal rules (the CENTER tag)
- Superscripts and subscripts (the SUP and SUB tags)
- Strikethroughs (the STRIKE tag)
- Document divisions (the DIV tag)
- Client-side image maps (the MAP tag)
- Provisions for style sheets (the STYLE tag), left otherwise undefined

A large part of the HTML 3.2 specification is a rubber stamping of what originally were Netscape's unofficial and *ad hoc* extensions to HTML. The rest of the HTML 3.2 specification covers features of HTML 3.0 that had already gained wide acceptance and implementation (tables) in Web browsers. HTML 3.2 really offered little that hadn't already been widely implemented.

HTML 3.2 should be fully supported by all current graphical Web browsers. Support for many of the new HTML 4.0 features among current graphical browsers is much more spotty. If you want to be conservative and make sure that your pages will display the way you want them to in all current graphical browsers, you should stick to using tags and attributes included in HTML 3.2, with the possible exception of the FRAMESET and FRAME tags, new HTML 4.0 tags that have already gained wide support among current browsers. To check out the official specification for HTML 3.2, see **www.w3.org/TR/REC-html32.html**.

FIND IT ON ▶
THE WEB

HTML 4.0

HTML 4.0 is the officially recommended specification for HTML. Like HTML 3.2, HTML 4.0 is a mix of both the old and the new. Included in it are elements that were previously either Netscape or Microsoft extensions (frames and font face changes), as well as a number of entirely new elements and capabilities. Here are some of the primary features included in HTML 4.0:

- Frames, including inline frames

- Cascading Style Sheets, level 1 (CSS1)

- New form elements, including the BUTTON element, which allows the creation of graphical form buttons

- New table elements, including the ability to apply formatting to column and row groups

- New text-markup elements, including the INS (insert), DEL (delete), Q (quote), S (strikeout), and SPAN elements

- Microsoft's FACE attribute, which allows you to specify font faces that can be used when displaying text marked by the FONT element

- New universal attributes (ID and CLASS) that can be used to apply styles to individual instances of tag elements, as well as additional "intrinsic event" attribute handles that can trigger the activation of scripts from events such as passing the mouse over an element, clicking an element, and so on

Full browser support for HTML 4.0 has yet to become a reality. Full agreement on how Cascading Style Sheets should be displayed has yet to be achieved—the same style sheet may have radically different results depending on whether it's displayed in Navigator or Internet Explorer. Also, a number of the new tags in HTML 4.0 have yet to be supported by either major browser. Before using a particular HTML element, you should at least check to see if it's supported yet by current Web browsers.

Here are some of the current initiatives afoot to expand and extend HTML:

- The recommendation for Cascading Style Sheets, level 2 (CSS2) was released in May, 1998. CSS2 style sheets allow you to specify fonts on the Web that can be downloaded with a Web page, create rectangular regions containing other elements that can overlap and be positioned anywhere on a Web page, and define multiple style sheets for a single Web page that can be used by different media types (such as speech synthesizers, Braille printers, handheld devices, and so on).

- The Dynamic Object Model (DOM) is the keystone for the full implementation and development of Dynamic HTML, allowing the dynamic addressing of any "objects" in a Web page via scripts or programs. It allows much more interactivity (that is, the dynamic updating and accessing of Web page content in response to user actions). Netscape and Microsoft support different versions of the DOM and Dynamic HTML, but they have agreed to standardize on the same DOM in their next generation of browsers.

- Mathematical Markup Language (MathML) provides complex formatting capabilities for equations and formulas.

You covered the some of the relevant new HTML 4.0 features in the Intermediate HTML Tutorial (Saturday Afternoon) and in Appendix C, "Creating Tables." Frames are another new HTML 4.0 feature, although they have long been supported by both major Web browsers—while I don't specifically cover creating frames in this book, you can find a couple frames templates for creating two-frame and three-frame Web sites among the HTML Templates included on the CD-ROM—just open the index page for the template to see instructions on how to use it.

FIND IT ON ▶
THE WEB To find out more about HTML 4.0, you can check out the HTML 4.0 specification at **www.w3.org/TR/REC-html40/**. For other links to where you can find out more about HTML, including links to tutorials, guides, quick references, and style guides, see my Web Links site at **www.callihan. com/weblinks/**.

XML and XHTML

FIND IT ON ▶
THE WEB HTML 4.0 is the last version of HTML. Future development of standards for the display of Web-based documents will be focused on XML (Extensible Markup Language) and XHTML (Extensible HyperText Markup Language). XML is not strictly a markup language, as much as it is a "meta-language" that allows for the further development of other markup languages (MathML, for instance). HTML 4.0 is just one more markup language residing under the overall umbrella of XML. Conceivably, any interested group could create its own markup language, publish an SGML-conforming DTD (Document Type Definition) on the Web, and then have it instantly recognized by any XML-compatible Web browser. This would allow academic groups to create their own markup language for displaying academic and scientific papers and articles, including footnotes, citations, bibliographies, figure captions, and so on. To find out more about XML, see **www.w3.org/XML/**.

XHTML 1.0 is intended as a version of HTML that has been brought entirely into conformance with XML (and thus with SGML), as opposed to the "Wild West" variant that has finally evolved into HTML 4.0. I don't think that individual Web publishers need to be overly concerned with creating Web documents that strictly conform to XHTML. The W3C (World Wide Web Consortium), the organization responsible for HTML and Web development, has committed itself to maintaining the character of HTML as a "language that the ordinary person can use" and its accessibility to individuals who "still find value in writing their own HTML from scratch." Such language is unlikely to be used to describe XHTML. Thus, the future of HTML is quite secure.

With millions and millions of documents currently residing on the Web that have been written as HTML 1.0, 2.0, 3.2, and 4.0 documents, there is little possibility that Web browsers will ever drop support for HTML. The capabilities of HTML 4.0, through the development of Cascading Style Sheets (CSS1 and CSS2) and the Dynamic Object Model (DOM), will continue to evolve and change. These developments alone will ensure that the capabilities of HTML will continue to evolve for many years to come. It is unlikely that there will be any new HTML tags or attributes added any time soon, which may not be such a bad thing.

The real advantage of XML and XHTML is realized when it comes to producing documents that can be displayed across multiple media and for variable audiences, something that straight HTML is not very adept at doing. You might want to produce a single document to be printed out in hard copy form, displayed on the Web to be browsed, or interpolated so someone who is visually impaired could read it using a Braille browser.

FIND IT ON ▶
THE WEB

There are a number of changes to long standing HTML practice that are required to create documents conforming to XHTML. Most Web publishers will be resistant to recoding HTML documents that have already been created and published to the Web, simply to be in conformance to XHTML. XHTML has no real impact on how those documents are displayed in current or future Web browsers. To find out more about XHTML, see **www.w3.org/TR/xhtml1/**.

What's on the CD-ROM

The CD that accompanies this book contains shareware that will help you to create your first Web page, providing tools and utilities to make your efforts more efficient. To make the CD more user friendly and take up less of your disk space, no installation is required; the only files transferred to your hard disk are the ones you choose to copy or install.

 **CAUTION**
This CD has been designed to run under Mac OS 7.1 or later. Neither the CD itself nor most of the programs on the CD will run under earlier versions of the Mac OS.

Since there is no install routine, running the Prima Tech CD Interface Program is a breeze. Simply insert the CD in your drive, navigate to the folder CYFWPIAWMac, and double-click on the icon labeled *Click Here to Start*.

The Prima License

The first window you will see is the Prima License Agreement. Take a moment to read the agreement, and click the "I Accept" button to accept the license and proceed to the user interface. (If you do not agree with the license, click the "I Do Not Accept" button to close the user interface and end the session.)

The Prima User Interface

Prima's user interface is designed to make viewing and using the CD contents quick and easy. The opening screen contains two panels, with two buttons in the lower-left corner. The left panel contains a listing of the categories and programs on the disc; to see a list of programs for a category, click on that category in the panel. The two buttons in the lower-left corner allow you to jump to Prima Tech's Web site (you must have an Internet connection and browser to do this) or to trigger detailed help on how to use the Prima Tech CD Interface Program. The right panel displays a description page for the entry you selected in the left panel. After you select a program from the list in the left panel, the three buttons in the right panel make it possible to send an e-mail to the publisher of the software, jump to that publisher's Web site, and install the program.

As with any window, you can resize the user interface. To do so, position the mouse over the lower-right corner, hold down the mouse button, and drag the corner to a new position. To close and exit the user interface, choose Exit from the File menu.

Using the Left Panel

The left panel of the Prima user interface is an expandable list that contains the categories of software and the programs in each category. To view the description of an entry in the left panel, simply click on the entry. For example, to view the information about the HTML Utility "Color Finder," click on the category "HTML Utilities" (and the list of programs in this category will expand automatically), then click on "Color Finder".

Using the Right Panel

The right panel displays a page that describes the entry you chose in the left panel. You will see such details as what functionality an installable program provides. In addition to a general description, the page provides the following:

Web Site: Many program providers have a Web site. If one is available, the description page provides the Web address. To navigate to the Web site using your browser, simply click on the "Browse the Website" button. (Of course, you must be connected to the Internet and have a working Web browser for this to work.)

E-mail Address: Many program providers are reachable via e-mail. If available, the description page provides the e-mail address. To use the e-mail address, click on the "Send an E-mail" button to open your e-mail program (to send e-mail, you must be connected to the Internet).

Easy Install: Each of the programs is provided with an automatic installer. This installer performs all the necessary changes to your hard drive to get the new program installed and ready to run, or in the case of a program that doesn't need any special installation, it simply decompresses the program and places all its elements in a folder on your hard drive (after you specify the name of the folder).

Custom Help Menu

The Custom Help menu provides you with some help in using the Prima Tech CD Interface Program. The entries in this menu are:

About Prima Tech CD Interface. Displays the "About" dialog, which tells you how to contact Prima Tech.

Read License Agreement. This entry enables you to re-read the license agreement.

Help on "Create Your First Web Page." Use this menu item to display the contents of the Help file provided with the Prima Tech CD Interface Program. This help file provides detailed instructions on using the user interface, as well as searching for information on a particular program.

Accessing the Book Examples

All of the book examples and other files contributed by the author are included in the Book Examples folder on the CD-ROM. These include:

○ **HTML Tutorials**—This folder includes all of the example files that are used in the book's HTML tutorials. To use this folder, just drag and drop it from the CD-ROM to your Desktop. See the Saturday Morning session, "The Basic HTML Tutorial," for further directions.

○ **Web Page Examples**—This folder includes three Web page examples that are used in the Sunday morning and afternoon work sessions. To use this folder, just drag and drop it from the CD-ROM to your Desktop. See the Sunday Morning session, "Planning Your First Web Page," for further directions.

○ **HTML Templates**—This folder includes a set of HTML templates created by the author that the reader can customize for their own purposes. Included are templates for creating an online calendar, two-frame and three-frame Web sites, your own genealogy Web site, an online newsletter, and an online résumé. Also included are a set of generic Web page templates that can be used as a basis for creating many different kinds of Web sites. To use a template, just drag and drop its folder from the CD-ROM to where you want to use it on your hard drive or the Desktop. For further directions, see the readme text files that are included in the HTML Templates folder and in each of the template folders.

The Software

This section contains a brief description of the shareware and evaluation software you will find on the CD.

NOTE ·

The software included with this publication is provided for your evaluation. If you try this software and find it useful, you must register the software as discussed in its documentation. Prima Publishing has not paid the registration fee for any shareware included on the disc.

· ·

A Smaller GIF. A Smaller GIF compresses animated GIFs so they download faster, without changing their appearance at all. The program also provides full viewer functionalities: you can randomly access frames, or you can play (forward and backward) frame-by-frame, at normal speed, or at a faster pace.

Anarchie Pro. Anarchie Pro is a fast, efficient FTP client that is useful for downloading batches of files together. It can download, extract, sort, and list the links contained in a Web page, or enable you to maintain your Web or FTP site from a local folder.

BBEdit Lite. BBEdit Lite is a less powerful, but still extremely flexible, free version of the popular BBEdit text editor. BBEdit is highly extensible. Version 4.1 includes many improvements and refinements to the user interface, and a number of performance enhancements and bug fixes are also included.

Cascade Light. Cascade Light is the freeware version of Cascade, an editor that makes it easy to design the presentation style of your Web site. It is a comprehensive cascading style sheet (CSS) editor that gives you complete control over presentation style without requiring detailed knowledge of CSS technical specifications.

Clip art A large collection of web-compatible clip art is included on the CD. You can either use the clip art directly from the CD (it is all in the "ClipArt" folder) or you can drag the ClipArt folder to your hard drive. Several of the utilities included on the CD can open and view the Web clip art.

Color Picker Pro. Color Picker Pro aids in finding color hex values for use with HTML production. More than just an RGB-to-hex converter, it can pull colors out of windows, icons, and desktop backgrounds.

ColorFinder. ColorFinder enables you to easily pick a color to use in an HTML page. It has the ability to pick a color from the desktop, which lets you quickly grab colors from other people's Web pages, icons, other windows, or the menu bar.

CompuPic. CPIC/CompuPic is a feature-rich multimedia viewer and file manager for digital photos, clip art, sound, and video files. The program, which offers true multitasking, lets the user quickly and easily view, catalog, edit, convert, capture, scan, print, and play image, video, and sound files.

DropStuff. DropStuff lets you easily create StuffIt archives (regular .sit or self-extracting .sea) simply by dragging and dropping files onto the DropStuff icon. With its companion, StuffIt Expander, you can expand and decode virtually any type of compressed or encoded file from both Windows and Mac users.

Electrifier Pro. Electrifier Pro is a tool for creating fast-downloading, interactive Web multimedia. It lets you create Web multimedia using every kind of content conceivable—vector and bitmap animation, digitized audio, synthesized music (MIDI), video, 3D, VR, and more than 150 special effects, such as fades, transitions, fire, and ripples.

Fetch. With this FTP client for the Macintosh, commands that would normally be set by complex UNIX commands can easily be set by the user. You even have the ability to set permissions to directories and files. Drag-and-drop downloading is supported on Macs that have this feature. Version 3.0.3 is a feature revision that now includes the ability to resume interrupted downloads; it also corrects a problem where files were not viewed properly from within the application.

FrameWork. FrameWork is a PPC-native, WYSIWYG HTML editor that allows you to easily create Netscape-style frames by clicking and dragging; it's also compatible with some of the newer frame syntax in Internet Explorer. Features include creating, deleting, or resizing with a click of the mouse; saving templates for later use; and exporting HTML source code.

GraphicConverter. GraphicConverter is an all-purpose image editing program that opens and saves images in just about any graphics format. The program includes high-end editing tools for graphic manipulation, as well as providing the ability to use Photoshop-compatible plug-ins.

HTML Colors. HTML Colors is the quick and easy way to make color-coordinated text, backgrounds and links. It lets you choose the colors you want from the color wheel and gives you a preview of the color combinations, and then all you do is paste the code into your page.

HTML Grinder. HTML Grinder is designed to be used with your current HTML editor rather than replace it. HTML Grinder comes with numerous features, such as search and replace, that make coding easier than with a standard editor.

HTML Rename. HTML Rename! ensures that files and Web pages will work on any operating system. This cross-platform utility augments your HTML editor by generating universally compatible file names and fixing URL links. Using HTML Rename! before you transfer files (for example, uploading a Web site to a UNIX server) saves you the need to repair mangled file names, broken links, and extra or missing carriage returns in text files.

HTML Vocabulary. HTML Vocabulary is a reference for almost every HTML tag available, including forms, frames, tables, special characters, and maps.

HTML Web Weaver Lite. HTML Web Weaver Lite is a scaled-down version of the popular commercial title for creating Web pages. Designed to accommodate the diverse work styles of users, it lets you write your document and then edit in your tags via a select-and-tag method.

ImageViewer. ImageViewer lets you import and view common graphics formats, including GIF, PICT, and JPEG files. ImageViewer also allows you to perform simple editing tasks, such as cropping and rotating.

ItsAGIF. ItsAGIF converts PICT (Mac) or BMP/WMF (Windows) files into colorful GIFs, which can contain as many colors as desired (without any 256-color restriction).

MacZip. MacZip is a free tool that includes both zipping (for compression) and unzipping (for extraction) capabilities. It can extract or compress files for a variety of systems. This port supports Apple events, so you can install it in your Web browser as a helper app.

MapMaker. MapMaker is a full-featured Macintosh image map editor, with support for client-side image maps, as well as the traditional server-side ones. You can easily open a JPEG, GIF, or PICT, and create a map by just drawing the objects on the image, which you can zoom within the range of 25-500%.

Mapper. Mapper is an easy-to-use image mapper that lets you just open your image, place the objects, and then save either server-side or client-side image maps. JavaScript comments are supported.

NCSA Mosaic. NCSA Mosaic is a Web browser that allows you to easily access networked information with the click of a mouse button. Mosaic accesses data via protocols such as HTTP, Gopher, FTP, and NNTP (Usenet News) natively, and other data services such as Archie, WAIS, and Veronica through gateways.

NetFinder. NetFinder is an FTP browser that's simple enough for new users to understand, yet powerful enough for advanced users. NetFinder can automatically resume interrupted downloads.

Scribbling Works. A small notepad application for the Mac. Use this for writing notes, making links and hyperlinks between notes, creating automatic links, sorting notes by topics, and setting markers for notes.

SiteEater. SiteEater is a cross-platform tool for off-line browsing, site mirroring, and file retrieval. SiteEater includes project management features, can continue interrupted downloads, and is able to work with your proxy server.

SpellTools. This software is capable of checking spelling in nearly any document, and it can read text aloud so that you can listen to what you have written. SpellTools also offers macros that allow you to quickly complete certain tasks, such as converting text to all-uppercase characters.

StuffIt Expander. This utility will decompress just about any file. It can call helper applications to process file formats that have not yet been built in.

StuffIt Lite. StuffIt Lite is a shareware compression utility. Maintained for users of earlier Mac systems (pre-Mac OS System 7), it is also accelerated for the Power Macintosh. It creates archives that can be expanded by any version of StuffIt, but only opens and expands archives created with versions of StuffIt prior to 5.0. (You need to register it following the 15-day evaluation period to get added benefits, free technical support and updates, enhanced features, and special pricing on other Aladdin products.)

Style Master. Style Master gives you control over the whole process of creating, editing, applying, and tweaking your CSS style sheets.

Theseus. Theseus is a link validator that can save you the embarrassment of publishing pages with broken links.

Transmit. This FTP client performs basic FTP operations. It also has the ability to resume downloads if they're interrupted, a Mac OS 8 look and feel, and full drag-and-drop capability.

VSE Animation Maker. VSE Animation Maker is a shareware tool that has many features for creating animations for Web sites. It is compatible with nearly all multimedia authoring tools and with nearly all Web browsers.

VSE HTML Turbo. VSE HTML Turbo is an HTML optimizer that makes your Web pages twice as fast, displaying your Web pages as quickly as possible, and enabling Web surfers to receive your pages quicker.

Glossary

absolute URL—A complete path, or address, of a file on the Internet (such as http:/www.someserver. com/somedir/somepage.html). Also called a complete URL. See also *relative URL*.

adaptive palette—A color palette for an image that has been reduced to only the colors present in the image. Also referred to as a *customized palette* or an *optimized palette*.

alternative text—Text describing an image that is included in an IMG (Image) tag using the ALT attribute and that functions as an aid to surfers who have turned graphics off or are using a Braille or speech browser.

anchor—In Adobe PageMill, refers to a *target anchor* (the "landing spot" for a hypertext link to a location in the same or another HTML file).

anti-aliasing—The blending of colors to smooth out the "jaggies" in fonts.

applet—A client-side program, usually Java or ActiveX, that is downloaded from the Internet and executed in a Web browser.

ASCII—American Standard Code for Information Interchange. Defines a standard minimum character set for computer text and data. ASCII files are sometimes called *DOS text* files or *plain text* files.

bandwidth—The transmission capacity of a network, but also the amount of capacity being consumed by a connection. A Web page containing many graphics will consume more bandwidth than one containing only text.

binary file—A non-text file, such as an image or program file.

BinHex—The standard method on the Macintosh of converting a *binary file* into *ASCII* (text) so it can be transferred as an e-mail attachment.

bookmarks—A means, in Netscape Navigator, for "bookmarking" the URLs of favorite Web sites so they can easily be returned to. Bookmarks are saved by Navigator in an HTML file (bookmarks.html). A similar feature in Microsoft Internet Explorer is called *favorites* (but these are saved as separate files rather than in a single file).

Cascading Style Sheets—A means for defining styles, using the STYLE tag, in order to control the display of HTML elements. A style sheet can reside either inside the HTML file, or in a separate file that's downloaded along with the HTML file. Current versions are Cascading Style Sheets, Level 1 (CSS1), and Cascading Style Sheets, Level 2 (CSS2).

CGI—Common Gateway Interface. An interface to a gateway through which a Web server can run programs and scripts on a host computer.

client—A computer on a network that makes a request to a server.

customized palette—See *adaptive palette*.

definition list—A glossary list in HTML that's created using the DL (definition list) element.

dithering—To create a new color by interspersing pixels of multiple colors so that the human eye "mixes" them and perceives the intended color. This is a technique used by browsers to display colors that are not included in the default color palette of systems that can only display 256 colors.

domain category—A major grouping of domain names (such as .com, .org, .net, .edu, .mil, and .gov), as well as many national domain categories (.us, .uk, .ca, and so on).

domain name—An alphanumeric alternative to an IP address. Both are registered with InterNIC (Internet Network Information Center).

download—To transfer files from a server to a client. See also *upload*.

Dynamic HTML—Various means of providing dynamic Web content to respond interactively to user actions. Interactive responses may include producing on-the-fly Web pages, starting and stopping animations, and so on.

end tag—The end of a non-empty HTML element (...</P>, for example). See *start tag*.

extension—A non-standard extension to HTML, implemented by a particular browser (as in *Netscape extension* or *Microsoft extension*), that may or may not be displayable in other browsers.

favorites—A feature in Microsoft Internet Explorer that is similar to Netscape Navigator's bookmarks feature, allowing you to save a list of your favorite sites.

fragment identifier—A string at the end of a URL preceded by a "#" character, used to identify a target anchor name. Allows a hypertext link to jump to a specific location in another or the same Web page.

frames—An extension to HTML, pioneered by Netscape, incorporated into HTML 4.0. Allows HTML documents to be presented inside multiple frames in a browser window.

FTP—File Transfer Protocol. The protocol used for downloading or uploading both ASCII and binary files on the Internet.

GIF—Graphic Interchange Format. A graphics format developed by CompuServe that has become one of the standard image formats for displaying graphics on the World Wide Web. A GIF can include up to 256 colors, transparency, interlacing, and multiple frames (GIF animation). See also *JPEG*.

GIF animation—A GIF image file containing multiple images, usually viewable only in a Web browser.

Gopher—A menu-driven system, predating the World Wide Web, for sharing files over the Internet.

HTML—HyperText Markup Language. A markup language for preparing documents for display on the World Wide Web. The current standard version is HTML 4.0 (previous versions were HTML 1.0, HTML 2.0, and HTML 3.2).

HTML editor—A software program that edits HTML files, usually with the aid of pull-down menus, toolbars, and wizards.

HTML element—May be a standalone tag (such as <HR>) or everything between a start tag (such as <P>) and an end tag (such as </P>).

HTML tag—May be a standalone tag (such as <HR>) or an HTML start tag or end tag.

HTTP—HyperText Transfer Protocol. The protocol used to exchange Web pages and other documents across the Internet. A Web server may also be called an *HTTP server*, in contrast to an FTP (File Transfer Protocol) server.

hypermedia—The interlinking of multiple media (text, images, sound, animation, and video).

hypertext—A means of providing for non-sequential linking of information.

hypertext link—A means, using the A (anchor) element in HTML, for jumping from a location in an HTML document to another Web page or object file on the Web, to a location in another Web page, or to a location in the same Web page. Also called a *hyperlink or hot link*.

image link—An inline image inserted inside a hypertext link, usually displayed with a blue border to show that it's an active link.

image map—An image displayed in a Web browser that has hidden "hot spots" that can be clicked to link to their designated URLs. Older browsers only supported server-side image maps (image maps executed from a server), but newer browsers also support client-side image maps (image maps executed from the desktop, or *client*).

in-context link—A hypertext link inserted within a paragraph or other text, rather than in a separate list or menu of links.

inline image—An image (GIF, JPG, or PNG) that's displayed *inline* ("in a line") on a Web page.

Internet—A set of protocols for transmitting and exchanging data among networks.

IP address—Internet Protocol Address. A unique number, such as 185.35.117.0, that is assigned to a server on the Internet.

IPP—Internet Presence Provider, also often called a *Web host* or *Web space provider*. A company that rents out Web space.

ISP—Internet Service Provider, also often called an *access provider*. A company that provides dial-up access to the Internet.

Java—A computer language developed by Sun Microsystems for the delivery of cross-platform, client-side *applets* over the Internet.

JavaScript—A scripting language developed by Netscape for the execution by a browser of client-side scripts embedded in a Web page. A close variant, JScript, has been developed by Microsoft.

JPEG—Joint Photographic Expert Group. JPEG and GIF are the most common graphics formats for the display of images on the Web. Images can be created from a palette of up to 16.7 million colors. However, JPEG images (unlike GIF images) cannot be transparent, interlaced, or animated. These are often referred to as *JPG format images*, because the file extension for JPEG images under DOS/Windows is ".JPG." See also *GIF*.

keyword—A word used in an Internet or Web search. It is a good idea to include keywords you think others might search for in your Web page's title, level-one heading, introductory paragraph, and alternative text. You can also use the META tag to include a list of keywords in your Web page; this tag will be read by many search engines.

link—A *hypertext link.*

link list—A list of hypertext links, sometimes also called a *hot list.*

link text—The text displayed in a hypertext link, usually in blue and underlined.

MathML—Mathematical Markup Language. The proposed standard for displaying equations and mathematical symbols on the Web.

MPEG—Moving Pictures Expert Group. A means of compressing video and audio files.

Netscape palette—A color palette composed of the 216 colors utilized by Netscape Navigator to display images on a computer displaying 256 colors. Also called a *safety palette.*

offline browsing—Browsing HTML files on a local hard drive, without connecting to the Internet.

optimized palette—See *adaptive palette.*

ordered list—A numbered list in HTML.

plug-in—An application that provides a Web browser with the ability to display or play additional types of media, such as streaming audio or video.

PNG—Portable Network Graphics. The newest standard graphics format for the display of images on the Web. Supports up to 48-bit true color (JPEG supports up to 24-bit true color), as well as transparency and interlacing. So far, PNG is supported only by the latest browsers.

POP3 server—Post Office Protocol, Version 3. An "incoming mail" server (e-mail is received from a POP3 mail server). See also *SMTP Server.*

QuickTime—A method developed by Apple Computer for delivering video, animation, and audio files.

refresh—To reload a Web page in Internet Explorer, by clicking the Refresh button. The equivalent action in Netscape Navigator is performed by clicking the Reload button. In both browsers, Control-R refreshes or reloads a Web page.

relative URL—A Web address stated in relation to the current (or linking) page (as in `<IMG SRC="images/mypic.jpg">` or `<A HREF="../frames/myframe.html">`). Internal links within a Web site should always use relative links. This technique allows the linked files to be uploaded onto a server or moved to another location, without the links having to be changed.

search engine—A Web site that has compiled a searchable index of sites on the Web, such as AltaVista or Lycos.

server—A computer on a network that responds to requests from clients. See also *client.*

SGML—Standard Generalized Markup Language. The parent markup language of HTML.

SMIL—Synchronized Multimedia Integration Language. (Pronounced "smile.") An HTML-like language for describing multimedia presentations, composed of streaming media (audio/video), images, text, and other media. SMIL, like HTML, can be composed in a text editor.

SMTP server—Simple Mail Transfer Protocol. An "outgoing mail" server (e-mail is sent to an SMTP mail server). See also *POP3 Server.*

start tag—The start of a non-empty HTML element (`<P>...`, for instance).

style sheet—A set of descriptions of how elements in a Web page should be displayed by a browser that can display styles. See *Cascading Style Sheets.*

TCP/IP—Transmission Control Protocol/Internet Protocol. The standard protocol for transmissions across the Internet.

target anchor—A hypertext anchor that defines the "landing spot" for a link.

unordered list—A "bulleted" list in HTML.

upload—To transfer files from a client to a server.

URL—Uniform Resource Locator. An address on the Web.

Web browser—A software program that browses HTML and other files on the World Wide Web.

Web master—System operator for a server on the World Wide Web.

World Wide Web—A "wide-area hypermedia information retrieval initiative aiming to give universal access to a large universe of documents," according to Tim Berners-Lee, inventor of the World Wide Web. Also, "the universal space of all network-accessible information" (a more recent definition, also from Tim Berners-Lee).

XHTML—Extensible HyperText Markup Language. A reformulation of HTML as conforming to *XML*.

XML—Extensible Markup Language. Slated as the next-generation markup language for the display of documents and data on the Web. XML is properly thought of as an SGML-compliant superset for HTML, and not as HTML's replacement. It will facilitate the development of specialized markup languages, as well as multi-modal publishing (Web, print, Braille, and so on) from a single document.

XSL—Extensible Stylesheet Language. The specification for style sheets for XML documents.

Index

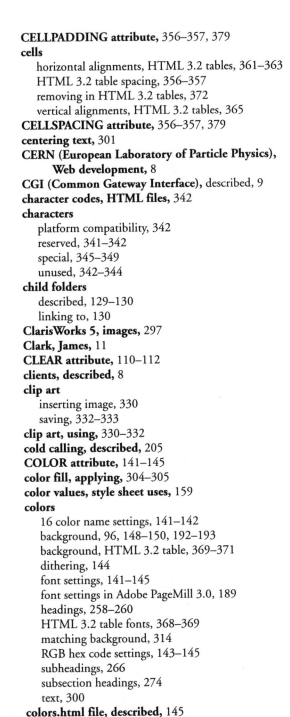

X

Y

Z

License Agreement/
Notice of Limited Warranty